SAFETY FIRST
NO SMOKING
RAMP MAX LOAD 150t
145m
RAMP MAX AXLE LOAD
55t/4 WHEELS
50m
HARD HAT AREA

RO-RO HANDBOOK

RO-RO HANDBOOK

A PRACTICAL GUIDE TO ROLL-ON ROLL-OFF CARGO SHIPS

CAPT. DELYAN
MIHAYLOV TODOROV

Schiffer Publishing Ltd
4880 Lower Valley Road • Atglen, PA 19310

Dedication

I would like to thank my wife, Petia, and both my daughters for being so patient to me during all this time; to all my Masters I had the privilege to work with and who taught me a lot; to all my deck officers who, even without realizing, brought my attention to many subjects in a light differing from mine. This book is for all of them!

Library of Congress Control Number: 2016939430

Cover design by Molly Shields

Interior design by Matthew Goodman
Type set in Minion Pro, Din & Square721

ISBN: 978-0-7643-5123-5
Printed in China

CONTENTS

ACKNOWLEDGMENTS

I have written this book from my point of view as a chief officer and, then, as a master, but without the considerable amount of help from many individuals and companies this book would have never been as it is now.

In addition, I would like to express my thanks to the following companies and institutions for permitting references to their publications and for the advice they have given me:

Stamco SM—for references to their safety management system and allowing me to take a myriad of pictures while serving on board their ships

Walter Vervloesem—for his enormous assistance and for agreeing to review the draft manuscript of the book

Capt. Peter Green— for agreeing to review the draft manuscript of the book

Pete Schiffer—for agreeing to publish the book

IMO—for references to their numerous publications

CargoTec—for references to their catalogs for cargo handling equipment

MOL Lines—for references to their operation manuals for car carriers

NYK Lines—for references to their operation manuals for car carriers

HOEGH AUTOLINERS—for references to their operation manuals for car carriers

IACS—for references to some of their regulations

Jaap Heinsius, marketing director of “Load-Lock”—for allowing me to refer to their catalogs for lashing

Span Set—for references to their catalogs for lashing

Internet—some pictures have been used from the Internet. I have been unable to obtain their sources and I do hope that any organizations and / or individuals whose images I have used will appreciate this difficulty.

PREFACE

The idea for this book emerged in my mind when I was promoted to Chief Officer. I realized that there was no guide or handbook that a newly appointed senior officer could use to assist with the variety of problems and quandaries that can be faced during the daily routine on board Roll-on/Roll-off (Ro-Ro) ships and car carriers. There were books for tankers, for gas carriers, for bulk carriers, etc., but nothing had been written for Ro-Ro ships, at least to my knowledge. Because of their origins, the various manuals that were available were very simplistic and, in my opinion, did not give detailed explanations of many of the things encountered on board Ro-Ro ships.

This book is the result of more than four years of research into Ro-Ro shipping. During that time, I have read and consulted many publications, articles, and manuals, and have gathered much important information from many masters, deck officers, superintendents, port captains, stevedores, technicians, and others involved with Ro-Ro shipping. Added to my personal experience, these were the basis for my writing.

I tried to write this book in a way that would be most helpful. I have divided the content into thirteen chapters covering all the aspects of Ro-Ro shipping, including cargo, cargo-handling equipment, ship handling, maintenance, and more. The chapters are not in any particular order; the topics are meant to be read and consulted when needed.

For many readers the content of some chapters probably will be overly scientific and in excess of what they need to know. In every case, I have tried to explain the subjects as simply as I could so every reader gets a basic understanding, but still give a thorough explanation of a given matter, as I believe this is indispensable if one is to be a real professional. Other chapters are focused on the legal issues involved in shipping. Today's deck officer should be knowledgeable of the many laws regarding Ro-Ro ships, so I have tried to include these. If a reader does not like to torment himself with formulas, graphics, or legal stuff, he or she can just turn the page.

I hope this book will be very helpful to the senior and junior deck officers on board Ro-Ro ships and especially car carriers. I spent more than twelve years on board car carriers, starting as a deck cadet and reaching the position of master. During that time, my daily tasks and routines confronted me with one problem after another. I often thought that it would be very helpful to have some reference book available that covered almost everything regarding Ro-Ro ships. But there was no such book.

I have named this book the *Ro-Ro Handbook* because one can find the answer to almost any question concerning these ships. If you need to know how to resolve the unpleasant situation of damage to cargo, you can refer to the relevant chapter of the book. If you face difficulties with specific cargo, maintenance of cargo handling equipment, fire prevention, or stability, you can easily refer to the respective chapters in this book. As I was writing this book, my goal was that, for every question concerning the Ro-Ro ships, the ship's personnel involved could find the relevant and correct answer here. In other words, I wanted to produce a book that would be considered as a reference work for the Ro-Ro industry.

This book, then, is an attempt to collect, into a single volume, all the specialized knowledge that senior and junior officers on Ro-Ro ships need to possess for the safe and efficient operation of these ships. More than that, I think this book will be an important resource for ship operators, managers, superintendents, and surveyors involved in inspections of Ro-Ro ships.

CHAPTER 1

DEVELOPMENT OF RO-RO SHIPS

Construction and Machinery

This chapter is about the construction of Ro-Ro ships. Ro-Ro (Roll-on/Roll-off) ships are designed to carry wheeled and tracked vehicles. Their peculiarities, such as the lack of internal bulkheads and the presence the openings in the hull, make them very susceptible to quick capsizing if the ship is bilged. In addition to this, the large surface area exposed to the wind makes them very vulnerable to its influence, which presents a lot of difficulties, especially during berthing and unberthing. In the recent years, the international trade of cars/vehicles has been developing rapidly. This has entailed the building of a great number of specialized Ro-Ro cargo ships called car carriers.

Of course, the transportation of vehicles and passengers between various ports has existed for many years, utilizing ferries. The ferry is a combination of Ro-Ro ship and a passenger ship designed to carry passengers along with their vehicles.

Ro-Ro passenger ships are included in the category of passenger ships and therefore must comply with the requirements of passenger ships along with the additional requirements for Ro-Ro ships. Ro-Ro cargo ships must comply with the requirements for conventional ships and additional requirements for Ro-Ro ships.

Peculiarities of Ro-Ro Ships

The main peculiarities of the Ro-Ro ships are:

- **Low freeboard and a respectively larger area exposed to the wind compared with the other types of ships**
- **Large openings in the hull.** The doors on these openings are watertight and weathertight, and must guarantee the integrity of the ship. Watertight means that the doors need to be designed to be capable of preventing the passage of water in any direction under the head of water likely to occur in both intact and damaged conditions. Weathertight means that in any sea conditions water will not penetrate into the ship. These openings are weak spots and during years of service they can become twisted or damaged. When they are damaged the ship's seaworthiness is jeopardized.

- **Ramps:** The necessity of ramps for loading/discharging makes these ships relatively expensive to build. The presence of such ramps requires the crew to be trained in their operation and basic maintenance.
- **Lack of internal bulkheads.** In order to facilitate cargo operations on board Ro-Ro ships, there are no internal bulkheads. The lack of such bulkheads presents serious risks for Ro-Ro ships because, if the ship's hull is breached, there are no barriers to prevent the ingress of the water. Irrespective of the fact that car carriers are fitted with watertight collision subdivisions, the huge car decks make it possible for water to enter very rapidly and for fire to spread quickly as well. Typical Ro-Ro ships, being fitted with a main deck, lower hold, and garage deck only, have no watertight doors which, makes them more vulnerable to quick capsizing in case of water ingress.
- **Securing of the cargo.** In all shipping, cargo units must be secured properly before the ship leaves the berth. This is a challenge on board the biggest car carriers, where more than 8,000 units can be carried. Indisputably, it will take some time to secure all units, especially if they are heavy, which require more specific and stringent lashing/securing arrangements.
- **Stability:** Due to the specific nature of the cargo they transport, Ro-Ro ships are more vulnerable to cargo shifting. A sudden cargo shift would cause an unpredictable list and could even breach the hull of the ship. This would create a sudden ingress of water that could have disastrous consequences for the ship. Normally the center of gravity of Ro-Ro ships is low, which means they have a comparatively high GM—metacentric height. In normal loading conditions, Ro-Ro ships are stiff ships; this results in a rolling period of a few seconds, which results in high loads on the lashing of the cargo. Some Ro-Ro ships, especially older ones, are equipped with bow visors, a design that allows the bow to articulate up and down to give access to the cargo ramp and storage deck. These constitute a serious stability problem.

Types of Ro-Ro Ships

The modern roll-on/roll-off ship can be traced back more than one hundred years to the dawn of the steam locomotives. At the beginning, these ships were specially designed to carry trains across rivers that were too wide for bridges. The train simply rolled straight onto the ship, which sailed across the river to a rail berth on the opposite shore, where the train rolled off again. In the late 1940s and early 1950s, this same roll-on/roll-off principle was applied to merchant ships. As the name of the principle implies the vehicles can drive straight on to a ship and off at a discharging port within minutes upon berthing of the ship. In the 1960s, the volume of vehicle transportation by ship began to increase to such an extent that a special ship type was developed for this purpose. At first, mainly passenger cars and vans were transported on these ships (PCC: Pure Car Carrier type), about 2, 000–4, 000 at a time. The ships returned empty. In the past few years, a multipurpose ship type (PCTC-Pure Car & Truck Carrier, with a payload of 4, 000–8, 000 passenger cars) has been developed that has about 20% of the available deck area designed to receive heavier wheeled or general cargo.

The present Ro-Ro fleet can be divided into two main categories:

- Ro-Ro passenger ships
- Ro-Ro cargo ships

Classification of Ro-Ro Passenger Ships

Ro-Ro ferry ships are designed to carry vehicles and less than twelve passengers. Cargo is loaded through a stern ramp, which is generally on level to the main deck, with internal ramps to the lower hold and upper deck. The upper deck is generally uncovered for most of its length.

Ro-Ro passenger ferry ships are designed to carry more than twelve passengers. The decks are large and the passenger facilities are limited. The vessel is called a **Ro-Pax** ferry. The peculiarity of this type of Ro-Ro ship is the presence of a lower hold, a main deck, and an upper deck (garage deck) for Ro-Ro cargo. The upper deck is partly covered. Most Ro-Pax ships have stern and bow ramps to accelerate the process of loading and discharging the cargo.

Pax Car ferries have adequate passenger facilities and are suitable for longer routes. The peculiarity of these ships is their full-length superstructure to accommodate passenger cabins and public spaces. Hoistable platforms are installed on the Ro-Ro decks to increase the deck area for private cars.

Cruise ferries have cabin space for all passengers. They operate on overnight routes. The Ro-Ro decks are small and the passenger cars occupy a large portion of the Ro-Ro space.

Classification of Ro-Ro Cargo Ships

Ro-Ro ships designed to carry freight vehicles and containers: These Ro-Ro cargo ships designed to carry vehicles without passengers (the number of passengers is not more than twelve), including containers, trucks, general cargo, cars, and vans on hoistable decks

PCTC, pure car and truck carrier

Ro-Ro ships designed to carry vehicles, freight vehicles, and containers. Car carriers are included in this group. They can be divided into:

- **Pure car carriers (PCC):** designed for transportation of cars only
- **Pure car and truck carriers (PCTC):** designed for transportation of cars and other heavy units
- **Large car and truck carriers (LCTC):** designed to accommodate more than 8,000 units

Post-Panamax car carriers: The length of the vessels has remained around 200 meters, but the vessel's width has increased to about 35.5 to 36.5 meters, giving greater flexibility in choosing a one- or two-pillar arrangement and the engine room arrangement, all of which adds more flexibility, greater variety, and larger capacity in the cargo. The new main dimension ratio also gives the potential of significantly increased hull efficiency with improved fuel economy.

Con-Ro ship in Antwerp

Con-Ro ships designed to carry vehicles as well as containers: Some of these ships are modified container ships, but others are specially designed with a weather cargo deck to allow carriage of containers. This design allows for flexibility of operation by incorporating container and other wheeled cargo handling capability. These vessels carry containers on and under the deck forward, and have a stern ramp with tween decks for the carriage of roll-on/roll-off cargo in the aft underdeck area. The Ro-Ro cargo may consist of over-sized pieces, such as construction equipment like bulldozers and excavators, which are driven onto the vessel via the ramp. Containers can also be stowed on the Ro-Ro decks, but are brought aboard on a chassis and removed by forklifts or by cranes. If space and equipment is available the container can be left on its chassis during transport.

Other Multipurpose Ships

Other multipurpose ships can be used pretty successfully for transportation of vehicles at sea, but these ships are beyond the scope of this book.

Container ship loaded with trucks on top of the containers. The stowage of the trucks can be problematic in case of boisterous weather.

Sto-Ro (Stowable Ro-Ro): Unlike the Ro-Ro, no cargo remains on wheels, but is directly loaded onto the vessel's decks. The stowage is similar to an open Load-on/Load-off (Lo-Lo) vessel, but the cargo is brought on board either over a stern/bow quarter ramp or through a side port door. Vessel operations can turn to this concept of cargo handling as a means of combining the undoubted handling advantages of the Ro-Ro (improved turnaround times) with the efficiency of a Lo-Lo (increased utilization of a ship's cubic capacity).

Float-On/Float-Off: A heavy deck semi-submersible vessel designed to permit oversized, indivisible cargo to be floated into position for deck stowage. The reverse procedure is used at the destination port, where the load is floated from the submerged deck, which is ballasted down for the outturn. The vessel travels with its deck and load above the water.

Trot-On/Trot-Off: A version of Ro-Ro in which vessel trailer decks are transformed into modern cattle pens capable of accommodating in excess of 2,000 animals. New installations include the provision of fresh water through evaporation or reverse osmosis, increased tankage "barns" for 1,600 cubic meters of hay or straw, and an air-circulation plant.

Ro-Lo: Another hybrid vessel type with ramps serving vehicle decks, but with other cargo decks accessible only by crane.

Ferry: A ferry is any vessel used to transport passengers between places that are no more than 300 miles apart.

Wagon carrier: Wagon carriers are primarily designed to carry wagons. For this purpose, they have one cargo/wagon elevator, which is electro-hydraulic driven, and with a safe working load (SWL) that varies between 170 and 200 metric tons (tonnes). To allow free movement of the wagons inside the ship and to facilitate loading and offloading, there are two pairs of rails made of square bars welded to the decks. These rails are provided on the weather deck as well as on the lower decks. In order to stow the wagons from the center to both sides of the ship, sets of switchgears are fitted. Wagon handling units (pushers) are used for wagon stowage.

Construction of Ro-Ro Ships

Ro-Ro ships can be categorized into two main types:

- Passenger Ro-Ro vessels
- Non-passenger Ro-Ro vessels

These can be either mono-hull ships or catamarans, but there are few catamarans and these are predominantly high speed vessels.

Mono-hull ships can carry cars and trucks as well as passengers, including truck drivers. These ships have a deep double-bottom, where the inner bottom is the bulkhead deck. The inner bottom, first, and sometimes second decks are designed as vehicle decks and the third deck is generally the passenger/public space deck. Car carriers are generally of mono-hull type.

Conventional mono-hull Ro-Ro ships have speeds from 18 knots up to about 28 knots and are subject to SOLAS conventional ship regulations. The faster Ro-Ro passenger ships have speeds up to 40 knots and consequently are subject to the *IMO High Speed Craft Code*. These Ro-Ro ships are not permitted to operate at maximum service speed more than four hours from a place of refuge, and are not allowed to have passenger and crew sleeping berths.

Catamaran Ro-Ro vessels are high-speed vessels. They consist of two narrow twin hulls connected by a transverse structure. These hulls are used to reduce wave-making resistance. The transverse structure provides the space for passengers and vehicles. The lowest deck of the structure is the vehicle deck, the second deck contains passenger public rooms, and the top decks are for crew and navigation bridge. These ships have a low displacement-to-length ratio and very high speeds reaching up to 50 knots. Catamaran ships are subject to the *IMO High Speed Craft Code*. They do not have passenger or crew sleeping berths, and passengers are seated in the public room. Catamaran Ro-Ro vessels are limited to operate at maximum service speed when they are within four hours of a place of refuge. The catamaran vessels designed for cargo can operate at maximum speed up to eight hours from a place of refuge. Catamaran Ro-Ro vessels are generally made of aluminum to attain a light structural weight. The twin hulls are longitudinally framed and the transverse structure between the hulls is transversely framed, because the maximum stresses can be found in this area.

The **SWATH (Small Waterplane Area Twin Hull)** is another twin-hull construction, with a high proportion of twin-hull buoyancy below the waterline and a narrow twin-hull beam at the waterline. Propulsion of these ships requires a prime mover in each pod or a propeller on each.

The main flow of vehicles is from Asia to Europe, from Asia to Australia, from Europe to the Americas, and vice versa. The deep sea Ro-Ro sector consists of car carriers with a dwt (dead weight tonnage) above 20,000 and CEU (car equivalent unit) capacity reaching up to 8,000 units. The coastal sector consists of smaller vessels operating on ferry/liner type services on short-haul routes such as the Baltic, Mediterranean, US Gulf, and Japan.

Purpose-built vehicle carriers have multiple decks (4–13), high speed, roll-on/roll-off discharging and loading facilities, and internal decks and ramps carefully designed to reduce damage and speed up loading and discharging. The Roll-On/Roll-Off (Ro-Ro) shipping system involves the direct driving-on and driving-off the cargo. The Ro-Ro method enables shippers to load cargo on chassis and trailers at the plant or warehouse site, transport the vehicles to embarkation points, and have them loaded directly onto the vessel. By rolling cargo on board these vessels and rolling it off at its destination, shippers can reduce the number of times their cargo is handled.

The inherent disadvantage of Ro-Ro is the waste of cargo carrying capacity due to undercarriage. When the heavy-load decks are loaded with heavy cargo, the cargo carrying capacity of the remaining light decks is decreased significantly. The free space between heavy-load decks is considerably more than that of the normal car decks.

Car carriers usually have ten to thirteen cargo decks, and two or three of these are mainly reserved for transportation of heavier cargo. On the heavy-load decks, or on some parts thereof, containers may also be placed . The containers are placed in stacks of one to two layers on the decks, but four layers is normal on new Con-Ro ships.

To facilitate loading and unloading, space is required for drive lanes, as well as openings in transverse bulkheads, sides, and decks. The ship has to be equipped with a stern ramp, sometimes with bow visor, and usually with one to two side ramps. The cargo decks must have openings and be equipped with ramps, some of which are fixed and some hinged or hoistable. In some cases, there are also a few lift platforms for handling cargo between two decks. There are generally several pillar rows in the fore-and-aft direction on the decks, which reduces the hull weight but creates restrictions as to the positioning of vehicles and cargo. The vehicles are normally driven into the ship using their own engine power, though they might be towed. Because of exhaust gases emitted by the cargo during the loading and discharging processes, the ventilation system of the ship must be exceptionally efficient. A large number of ventilation ducts also split the deck areas.

The vehicles themselves are homogeneous, light transport goods, with stowage factor being on an average four to five times higher when compared with container and general cargo. In a pure car carrier, the weight of car cargo represents about forty to fifty percent of the dead weight of the ship, while in PCTC-type ships it is only about twenty to twenty-five percent of the dead weight.

A considerable quantity of ballast water has to be transported to ensure the stability of the ship in the most unfavorable conditions, the amount thereof exceeding the weight of the vehicle cargo. As a result, more engine power is needed and more fuel is consumed; the Shipping Company does not gain anything from transporting "dead water ballast."

The crew accommodation is on the uppermost deck, and so are the life-boat stations. The ship design in the cargo spaces is based on a steel plate deck being reinforced with stiffening girders. The total thickness of such a construction may be from 200 to more than 450 mm, and the plate thicknesses of fixed light-weight car decks are 5 to 6 mm at the minimum, exceeding considerably the local-strength thickness required for the cargo. In a plate field of any deck there are lower beams in each frame space and high frame girders at sparser intervals. On the edges of deck openings and drive ramps there are high, strong stiffening beams.

Ships for the transportation of new passenger cars have been designed with multiple decks and internal ramps permitting the stowing of cars. The maneuvering of these comparatively light cars is much easier than the maneuvering of heavy vehicles or container transporting trucks, so it is acceptable that a car performs sharp turns inside the ship. With heavy loads that must be avoided.

To facilitate firm fastening of wheeled cargo, the fixed structures of a ship have to be appropriately constructed; separate fastening and securing equipment, and plenty of manual labor aboard are also needed.

The strengthened decks of Ro-Ro ships are dimensioned for heavy wheeled cargo, whereby the local strength of the decks is on an average eight to twenty times higher than that required by a load of passenger cars and vans. There are two or three strengthened decks on new vessels. It should be noted that the revenue from high and heavy cargo (as stowed on strengthened decks) is around three times more than that from new cars for the same area of deck space.

On Ro-Ro vessels, vehicles, semi-trailers in particular, rolltrailers, and cassettes are secured in the fore-and-aft direction by using different chains, webbings, and wires to fasten each cargo unit to the deck of the vessel. The lashing is done by hand, which is rather expensive and time-consuming.

When using lashings, the adequate number used for securing and their proper distribution must be calculated. The forces that are caused by the movement of the vessel are greatest in the transverse direction, which means that transverse securing is very important when cargo units are lashed to the vessel. In addition to chains, webbings, etc., a trestle or a trailer horse is used for securing semi-trailers, the wheelless end of the semi-trailer being supported by means of the trestle during the time of transport on the vessel. Semi-trailers are conventionally provided with their own landing legs, which can support the wheelless end ashore. These legs, however, are not capable of supporting the combined load of the semi-trailer and its cargo during the accelerations encountered on a sea voyage, so a trestle or equivalent support is needed to support the trailer. The trestle is usually made of steel and is manually placed under the wheelless end of the semi-trailer.

The shape of conventional Ro-Ro ships, car carriers in particular, makes them very susceptible to wind pressure, which causes leeway, that is, the sideways drift of a vessel.

Construction of Car Carriers

Car carriers have a distinctive form, akin to a box. This is because they have a number of car decks located one over the other and connected by internal ramps or slopes. On some older ships the connection between the separate car decks was eventuated by lifts. Today this practice has been forsaken due to many shortcomings of the lifts, though car carriers fitted with such lifts are still to be found. While such lifts are commonly used on Ro-Ro ships for trailers, they are not so useful or profitable on large car carriers.

On car carriers most of the car decks are fixed, but two or three decks are liftable in order to allow the loading of high and heavy units. There are three main positions for the movable car decks: normal, medium (one step), and high. The height of the deck can reach up to 5.2 meters (the height of "Tonsberg," the largest car carrier ever built, reached 7.1 meters). The decks can be safely secured in these positions by means of supports or hooks.

Decks on car carriers and ferries can be divided in the following categories:

- **Vehicle (car) deck:** This is a deck designed for parking vehicles that constitute the cargo on board. The vehicle deck can either be a closed Ro-Ro space, open Ro-Ro space, or a special category space or weather deck (SOLAS).
- **Ro-Ro cargo space**: A space not normally subdivided in any way and extending to either a substantial length or the entire length of the ship, in which goods in rail or road cars, vehicles (including road or rail tankers), trailers, containers, pallets, demountable tanks, or similar stowage units and receptacles are loaded and unloaded, normally in a horizontal direction.
- **Open Ro-Ro space:** Ro-Ro cargo space either open at both ends or open at one end and provided with adequate natural ventilation that is effective over its entire length through permanent openings in the side plating or deckhead.
- **Closed Ro-Ro space:** Ro-Ro cargo space that is neither open Ro-Ro space nor the weather deck.
- **Special category space:** An enclosed vehicle space, above or below the bulkhead deck, that is intended for the carriage of motor vehicles with fuel in their tanks for their own propulsion, into and from which such vehicles can be driven, and to which passengers have access. These spaces can be accommodated on more than one deck provided that the total overall clear height of the vehicles does not exceed 10 meters.
- **Weather deck:** A deck that is completely exposed to the weather from above and from at least two sides. This deck is also known as a garage deck. The garage deck can be used for the loading of trailers on board Ro-Ro ships. On the largest car carriers, the weather deck also can be used for loading of comparatively light cargoes.

Specially designed machines, called deck lifters, can lift or lower the decks on board car carriers The lifting capacity of deck lifters is usually about 25 tonnes SWL (safe working load). The movable decks consist of several panels that can be heaved up or lowered down independently, allowing different stowage depending on the rotation of the ship. (See chapter 7: Cargo Handling Equipment, Liftable Decks for further information.)

The hull of car carriers consists of a short, parallel body with flares forward and aft. This will cause some problems when berthing/unberthing, especially when there is construction or equipment on the pier. Loading or discharging of vehicles is performed through ramps with SWL up to 300 tonnes. Most deep-sea car carriers are fitted with quarter ramps and side ramps. The slope of the quarter ramps can be adjusted by means of so-called "buttress" cylinders to adapt to the height of the quay and tidal conditions. The opening of the hull where the ramps are being fitted defines the so-called "vehicle envelope." Actually it represents the maximum space through which a vehicle can safely pass. This vehicle envelope is not of a fixed size but can vary depending on the slope of the ramp, trim, and other conditions. The ramps, normally one stern (or quarter) ramp and one side ramp (though a variety of ships exist with different numbers of ramps) are fitted to the hull by means of hinges. While the stern ramp is fixed to the hull and its height is not adjustable, the side ramp can be lifted by wires and positioned in way of a higher deck. This was prompted by the fact that very often the car carriers visit ports that are not suitable for operations via the stern ramp, so the side ramp is the only option. Whether adapting to the tidal range or the obstacle posed by the height of the quay, the need for adjusting the ramp has to be considered by the shipbuilders.

Many small feeder car carriers have stern ramps and Ro-Ro trailer ships have a straight stern ramp.

The Ro-Ro ships trading in Europe are fitted with bow visors. Unfortunately, several very serious accidents have been caused by open bow visors, which has resulted in the use of such ramps being reduced.

Design of Ro-Ro Ships

Dimensions

The dimensions of Ro-Ro ships vary significantly due to the large differences in the service speed. The breadth depends on the number of lanes selected for Ro-Ro decks. There are Ro-Ro ships with up to eight cargo lanes, which corresponds to a breadth of 28 meters. However, car carriers have a standard breadth of 32 meters, which allows them to transit safely the Panama Canal. The breadth of car carriers is independent of the number of cargo lanes, as is the case on Ro-Ro ships.

The length of the most Ro-Ro cargo ships is about 200 meters, but the length of the most modern car carriers can reach even 265 meters, thus significantly increasing the cargo capacity.

The draft of Ro-Ro ships is small compared to the other ships. The depth to the main deck indicates the freeboard. If complying with the Stockholm agreement, the minimum freeboard is about 10% of the breadth.

Hull Form

The design of the hull form represents a very important part of the design of a Ro-Ro ship. The standard design of the hull is the so-called "displacement-type" and is used for speeds corresponding to a Froude number below 0.35. The speed and length selected for typical Ro-Ro ships give Froude numbers between 0.25 and 0.35.

The block coefficient used is between 0.4 and 0.7 with its maximum between 0.5 and 0.6.

Car carriers have very specific hull form, box-shaped with a short parallel body. This type of hull acts to increase the cargo capacity. They have huge flares fore and aft, which constitute a danger of overhanging the berth during mooring operations.

The ferries can have different hull forms depending on the type of the vehicles, the number of passengers, and the routes they travel, as well as their speed and depth requirements. Ferries, being a variation of Ro-Ro ship, can be of the double-ended, hovercraft, hydrofoil, pontoon, cable, or foot ferry types. These ferries are briefly discussed below, but are beyond the scope of this book.

Double-ended ferry

- **Double-ended ferries** operate between two terminals without the need to turn around. Therefore they have an interchangeable bow and stern.
- **Hydrofoil ferries** operate in the English Channel and other locations and carry only passengers. There are two main types of foil systems used: surface piercing foils and completely submerged foils. They are affected by weather conditions and if the craft comes off the foil it is very difficult to get it up again. Hydrofoil ferries require strengthening of the forward part of the ship. This is because the impact of the ferries with the water could be severe if it comes off the foils. These ferries are being replaced by the catamaran ferries, which can carry vehicles as well.
- **Hovercraft ferries** were developed mainly to carry cars. They are affected by the weather conditions, however, and are being replaced by catamarans.

There are also some less popular types of ferries, including pontoon ferries, turntable ferries, foot ferries, and cable ferries.

- **Pontoon ferries** are used mainly on lakes and rivers. One or more vehicles are loaded on the pontoon with ramps on either end.
- **Turntable ferries** have a vehicle platform that can be turned, allowing vehicles to load from the "side." When loading, the platform is turned sideways to allow vehicles to load. Then the platform is turned back, in line with the vessel, to make the journey across the water.
- **Foot ferries** are designed to carry foot passengers and, often, cyclists over rivers. These are either self-propelled craft or cable ferries.
- **Cable ferries** are used for very short distances. They are propelled and steered by a system of chains or cables. Some cable ferries, called reaction ferries, use the perpendicular power of the current as a power.

Bridge Location

The bridge of many Ro-Ro ships is on the forward part of the superstructure about 17% to 20% back from the bow. This fulfills the requirement of SOLAS Ch. V, Reg. 22 for navigation bridge visibility. The location of the bridge more or less coincides with the location of the pivot point when the ship is moving ahead. For this reason Ro-Ro ships and car carriers have very good maneuverability and a very good rate of turn. With the superstructure being located in the forward part, the center of the windage area is shifted towards the forward part as well, which has a great impact on the maneuvering characteristics of this type of ship.

There are Ro-Ro ships with bridges located well aft, in which case their maneuvering characteristics depend entirely on the windage area.

Mooring Stations

Mooring stations on board newer Ro-Ro ships are totally protected against the environment. This protects the personnel working on the mooring stations, but can cause some difficulties during maneuvering. Mooring winches should be tested before arrival at the loading or discharging port. They should be maintained as per the adopted Planned Maintenance Schedule:

MBL of bitts properly labeled

- If they are electric, the control stand should be properly covered to avoid becoming wet.
- All windlasses, winches, fairleads, and rollers should be properly greased through greasing nipples and they should rotate without any difficulties. It is good practice to properly mark them with their minimum-breaking load (see photo).
- All brake linings should be checked and adjusted if necessary.
- The level of lubricating oil should be checked and refilled if necessary.
- The anchoring system—gypsy, windlasses, chains, and anchors—should be checked and maintained

Deck Equipment

The provision cranes, Suez boat crane, and gangways are parts of the deck equipment that are not included in cargo handling equipment. It is vital that all these cranes and gangways be maintained as per the adopted Planned Maintenance Schedule.

- Their SWL (safe working load) should be clearly marked.
- All wires should be greased and all greasing points should be lubricated.
- Limit switches are fitted on such cranes. Their purpose is prevent the crane from going too high or too low, or slewing too far to either side. These switches should be periodically inspected to ensure they are operational.
- Special attention should be paid to the mooring boat crane when approaching the Suez Canal.

The draft standards for the construction of the gangways should be approved. Gangways will be subject to survey, during which they will be inspected for proper operation and the condition of the winches. Existing standards for the gangways are cited in ISO 5488:1979 "Shipbuilding—accommodation ladders," and ISO 7061:1993 "Shipbuilding—aluminum shore gangways." The MSC 1/Circ. 1331 stipulates guidelines for construction, installation, maintenance, and inspection/survey of means of embarkation and disembarkation. Since January 1, 2010, gangways and accommodation ladders are required to be load-tested every five years. This should normally be carried out at the first scheduled dry-dock after that date.

Ballast System

Indisputably, the ballast system is one of the most important systems on board ships. It guarantees the appropriate stability, trim, bending moments, and shear forces when the ballast is properly distributed. The officer in charge of ballast operations should be familiar with the ballast system, especially the capacity and type of ballast pumps, location of piping, sounding pipes, etc.

The ballast exchange is regulated by the IMO's international Ballast Water Management Convention, and the existing IMO Res. 868 (20), "Guidelines for the Control and Management of Ship's Ballast Water to Minimize the Transfer of Harmful Aquatic Organisms and Pathogens." Apart from this internationally adopted legislation, there are many local regulations concerning ballast water exchange. The Master and Chief Officer should be aware of them in order to avoid any problems resulting from the rules. The regulations of US, Canada, and Australia are among the most rigorous in the world.

The ballast system on Ro-Ro ships consists of several pairs of double-bottom tanks, usually four or five pairs, as well as fore-peak and after-peak tanks. Each tank may have its own ballast line or all the tanks on each side may be connected by only one pipe. The first arrangement, each tank having its own line, is the most common on new car carriers.

The pipes inside the tanks of newer ships are made of GRP (glass reinforced plastic) in order to avoid corrosion due to the salty water. In the ballast tank the pipe ends up in so-called "bell mouth" (see illustration), which is an enlargement of the pipe in the lowest part of the tank, a few centimeters above the tank base.

Bell mouth inside ballast tank of PCTC

The pumps used for ballast operations are of the centrifugal type. There are two sea chests, one on the side and one on the bottom, for water suction. In ice conditions, it is necessary to perform ballast operations through the bottom sea chest to avoid blockage of piping and damage of the ballast pump. The strainers of the sea chest are subject to the Planned Schedule Maintenance.

Each tank is provided with air pipes, which will allow the air to flow out of the tank. The design of the air pipes does not allow the water to come inside the tanks, but will allow the ballast water to flow out. These pipes are subject to maintenance as per the Planned Maintenance Schedule. Moreover, they are subject to inspection during the Load Line Survey. Therefore, special attention should be given to the non-return arrangement, which in most cases consists of a float. This arrangement should move freely and should be adjusted correctly.

The ballast system can be operated either manually or from a centralized console. In the latter system, the quantity of water in each ballast tank will be measured remotely and displayed on the monitor in the ship's office, engine room, or bridge. These figures should not be trusted blindly; very often they are inaccurate and do not take into consideration the trim of the ship. In both types of ballast system, each tank is equipped with so-called "sounding pipes." Through these a manual sounding can be taken and used to calibrate tables so the Chief Officer can calculate the quantity of water inside each ballast tank. The appropriate correction for trim, if any, should be taken into account. As a rule, the sounding pipes are in the after part of the tank, where the soundings can be made most precisely.

These sounding pipes are subject to maintenance as well. It is vital that these pipes are not blocked by deposits or ice debris.

Due to the very dynamic cargo operations based on the roll-on/roll-off principle, Ro-Ro ships can list very heavily for a short period of time. Recently a Con-Ro capsized in port for that reason. It is essential that Ro-Ro ships are equipped with a so-called "anti-heeling" system, which constitutes part of the ballast system and contains a pair of tanks that have the righting lever. The pipes of the anti-heeling system have a bigger diameter compared to the other tanks, which allows for a higher flow and quick response in case the list reaches threshold values, which usually do not exceed 1°. Generally, one or two pairs of tanks can be utilized as anti-heeling tanks.

Ballast tanks should be inspected at least two times per year. It should be borne in mind that ballast tanks are enclosed spaces, so all preventive measures for entering enclosed spaces should be strictly adhered to (see: IMO Res. A. 1050 [27], "Revised recommendations for entering enclosed spaces aboard ships," and IACS Recommendation 72, "Confined Space Safe Practice"). Each ballast tank should have at least two access openings and these should be opened well in advance of the planned inspection. The appropriate ventilation procedure should be performed and the oxygen concentration checked. Most companies have special procedures for entering into ballast tanks as a part of their SMS and they must be adhered to. In all cases, a "Permit to Work" should be issued before entering a ballast tank.

Some countries require pre-arrival information for ballast water on board to be submitted well in advance. Non-compliance with this requirement could lead to a detention of the ship and severe penalties. Normally, the information for the ballast is being sent as a standard form as stipulated in Appendix I of IMO Res. 868 (20). However, the Master should be aware of any local forms or regulations concerning notification of ballast water. (The Ship's Agent may provide the necessary information)

Stabilizing Systems

Considering the hull form of Ro-Ro ships and especially car carriers, they are very susceptible to rolling and pitching in heavy weather. In order to avoid large roll angles (as the rolling represents the highest risk for cargo and passengers), Ro-Ro ships are fitted with stabilizing systems. There are different types:

- **Bilge keels** are the simplest stabilizing system with the smallest damping effect. Having no moving parts, this system is considered as the safest one. The bilge keels are mounted on each side of the ship's hull in order not to increase the draft. The roll opposing force at the bilge keel is proportional to the bilge keel width and roll velocity. That is why the larger the bilge keel, the larger will be the roll-damping effect. In addition, the damping force will not be limited by the roll angle. One disadvantage of bilge keels is that they increase resistance. Another shortcoming is that the wider the bilge keel is, the larger stresses it will have to support. These bilge keels are located in places where they do not interfere with flow lines to the propeller in calm waters. The bilge keels give a roll damping effect of about 5–10%.
- **Fin stabilizers** consist of a pair of fins projecting from a ship's side. They can create a considerable roll moment when tilted at full speed ahead. These stabilizers are designed as balanced foil sections, therefore they need a relatively small torque to move the fins to angles capable of offsetting wave moments. These stabilizers require a control system to tilt the fins in the shortest possible span of time, and also large tilting motors. When fins are being selected it is very important that the ship's operating conditions are taken into account. This will allow the designers to determine the fin's physical size and tilt-drive characteristics. The fin moment is proportional to the square of the ship's speed. When the ship's speed is low or zero, the fins completely lose their stabilizing effect. The fin stabilizers can achieve a roll damping effect of over 90% and reduce the roll angle to about 3°, but only when the ship is running at full speed.
- **Uncontrolled passive tank system** has a stabilizing effect independent of the ship's speed. The system consists of a rectangular tank extending from side to side, sometimes with a built-in damping device. The tank is filled with liquid (sea water, fresh water, fuel oil) and the liquid level is adjusted to suit various rolling conditions. When the ship starts to roll the fluid inside the tank will be set in motion. The damping device in the tank is designed to give the moving fluid a phase displacement of 90° compared with the ship. The moving fluid has a stabilizing effect due to positive distribution of the fluid in the tank from one side, and the kinetic energy of the fluid moving from one side of the ship to the other. This system does not work properly in following seas.
- **Controlled passive tanks** ensure that the transfer of water always occurs at the end of the roll. These tanks are usually U-shaped and the water flow is controlled by a system of valves and pressure sensors. The flow of water across the tank remains passive, but the processor unit and valve operation require power supply and therefore it does not work in blackout situations (unless properly backed up with emergency supply).

Class of Ro-Ro Ships

The classification of Ro-Ro ships is based on certain presumptions depending on the operation of the vessel. Nowadays it is not uncommon for Ro-Ro ships and car carriers to visit ports that are ice-bound in winter conditions. Therefore they should be additionally classed for sailing in ice conditions.

Different classification societies have their own class. For example DNV can give the following classification to car carriers:

1A1 ICE-1A CAR CARRIER MCDK PWDK E0 NAUT-OC CLEAN TMON

1A1: The main character of the class, it indicates that the ferry (in our case a car carrier) can carry vehicles on enclosed decks only.

Ice-1A: Ice class, allowing the ship to sail in first year unbroken ice with thickness up to 0.8 m. Different classification organizations can apply their own ice classes, but they are based mainly on either the Baltic Ice Rules or the Arctic Ice Rules; this particular example is based on Baltic Ice Rules. The assigned ice class depends on the reinforcement of the hull.

MCDK: Indicates that the ship is equipped with movable car decks.

PWDK: Indicates that the decks are strengthened for wheel loading

E0: Indicates unattended machinery space. If the machinery operations are being supervised from a centralized control station, this symbol will be substituted by ECO.

NAUT-OC: Indicates that the bridge design and workstation arrangement correspond with safety requirements

CLEAN: Indicates that the ship complies with only basic requirements for controlling operational emissions and discharges. If the ship complies with additional requirements for controlling operational emissions and discharges, she will be assigned CLEAN DESIGN. Moreover, this notation specifies design requirements for protection against accidents and for limiting their consequences.

TMON: Indicates that the ship is fitted with tail shaft condition monitoring arrangement.

More details regarding class notations can be found in class documents.

Machinery of Ro-Ro Ships

Ro-Ro ships require good maneuverability and high speed. Very often they visit ports with restricted draft. All these requirements impose the necessity for Ro-Ro ships to be equipped with twin-screw propulsion with a CP propeller and twin rudders. While such propulsion is justified on board Ro-Ro ferries it is not the case on board car carriers.

Many Ro-Ro ships are fitted with bow and stern thrusters to assist them during maneuvering. Podded propulsion is also very suitable for ferries.

Car carriers are fitted with one screw propulsion and one rudder. This design is prompted by the fact that the car carriers are traveling long distances and, compared to the common Ro-Ro ships, are not often in ports.

Becker-type rudders, when fitted, will improve the maneuverability to a great extent. On the newer generation car carriers, the rudder can be rotated up to 60° on both sides.

The introduction of new safety requirements, such as SOLAS Regulation 2, "Casualty threshold, safe return to port and safe areas" adopted on Resolution MSC 216 (82), Annex 3, which came into force in July 2010, puts an extra burden on the shoulders of designers of Ro-Ro passenger ships. The idea behind this rule is to ensure that a passenger ship (including Ro-Ro passenger ships) can safely make port with any single compartment put out of action due to fire or water ingress. Without question, this rule will affect the design of Ro-Pax vessels by precluding the concentration of all the main machinery into one room.

Propulsion on Ro-Ro Ships

Apart from the conventional fuel propulsion, Ro-Pax ferries are generally equipped with medium-speed diesel engines. The advantage here is that these engines are compact and low weight and still can operate on heavy fuel oil. Diesel electric propulsion using podded propulsion has been used as well.

More Ro-Ro vessels are being built with liquid natural gas (LNG) propulsion. In addition, some car carriers are partially driven by solar power. This is achieved by photo-voltaic panels mounted on the weather deck. An example is the car carrier *Auriga Leader*, owned by NYK. The *Auriga Leader*'s solar power capabilities produce an anticipated 0.05% of the ship's propulsion power and 1% of its electrical usage. This will contribute to lowering the ship's fuel usage by approximately thirteen metric tons (tonnes) and its CO_2 output by forty metric tons.

Many modern Ro-Ro passenger ships have multi-engine installations that directly drive the main propulsion shafts. A typical arrangement is two engines connected to a propulsion shaft via a gearbox. This allows the operators to choose the amount of power used for propulsion.

Slow steaming (about 16–17 knots) is normal on car carriers and most Ro-Ro ships today. The car carrier speed requirement on new vessels is also reducing.

The so-called "EEDI," Energy Efficiency Design Index, should also be considered when discussing the propulsion of Ro-Ro ships. It was proposed by IMO with the principal aim being to gauge the ship's CO_2. Behind this EEDI is a simple formula that estimates CO_2 output per tonne-mile of cargo carried. This index is better suited for conventionally powered and propelled ships than for more sophisticated Ro-Ro ships. In *The Energy Efficiency Design Index (EEDI) for Ro-Ro Vessels.* Stefan Kruger, Technishe Universitat Hamburg, Hamburg, Germany, shows that, for Ro-Ro ships, this index (in its present form) is not favorable, as it imposes severe speed limits. Ro-Ro ships can fulfill the requirements for EEDI only at physically impossible negative wave resistance.

CHAPTER 2

PORTS AND TERMINALS

Ro-Ro ships are usually handled at specially designed terminals. These terminals should be properly fendered and located in close proximity to the stowage areas of the cars/vehicles. Unfortunately, this is not always the case. Very often the car carriers visit ports that are not properly arranged, and perhaps even could be considered "not safe." The Master should be very vigilant when visiting such ports and should do his best to avoid any damage either to the ship or the berth.

This chapter provides detailed information about the relationship between the ship and the port. Special attention is paid to the stay of the ship in the port and clauses in the Charter Party (C/P) regarding safe ports/berths. Last but not least, we will have a look at the auto terminals, their development and their efficiency.

Information Exchange Between the Ship and the Port

The Master has the responsibility to inform the Agent and port officials in the port of loading or discharging well in advance. The information required to be sent normally includes the following:

- ETA
- Cargo for discharging—numbers of cars and metric tons (tonnes)
- Transit cargo, if any
- Draft on arrival
- Air draft
- Other info, if required

From their side, the Charterers or their representatives are obliged to inform the Master about any peculiarities of the port in question such as limited depths, requirements for under keel clearance (UKC), details for the port, etc.

Due to the rapid expansion of the auto market today, it is not uncommon for huge car carriers to visit almost unknown ports, which are neither equipped nor designed to receive this type of ship.

Essential Information for the Ship about the Berth

Maximum Safe Draft in Berth

It is of vital importance that the ship stays afloat when in port. This means that there must be sufficient under keel clearance (UKC) at all times, taking into account the swell, surge, and tidal range. The Master must get this information well in advance of docking. Normally, the information can be obtained from the publications, but this is not always reliable due to changes in the bottom causing the depth to be reduced or depth surveys may be out of date or inaccurate. It is good practice for the Master to take into account the depths mentioned by the Agent or shore representative, but the best practice is to ask the Pilot about the depth; he is the one with the latest information about the port and its peculiarities.

In all cases the prudent Master should always allow a greater margin of safety, especially when visiting unfamiliar ports without sufficient information about the depth. Needless to say, the echo sounder should always be used, although the depth it reports must be treated with caution since echo sounders are liable to suffer from a variety of errors in cases of very low under keel clearance. It also must be remembered that there are berths where the depth at one end is greater than at the other. Because of this, it is necessary to know the maximum depth of water that can be guaranteed at each end of the berth.

Protection of the Berth

Because Ro-Ro ships and car carriers are very susceptible to the influence of the wind, it is very important for the berth to be protected to the maximum effect against any meteorological condition. It is not uncommon for car carriers to visit ports well away from the major hubs. The swell in such ports, especially those on the Pacific Coasts of North and South America, is very dangerous for several reasons:

- As the swells cause the ship to rise and fall, the ramps are exposed to the risk of damage. In such cases, it is advisable that additional ropes are made fast and that rubber mats be put underneath the flaps of the ramps in order to avoid the friction between the flaps and the pier. At most of the berths, the pier is rough and the danger for causing a structural damage to the ramps is real. At all times the duty officer must keep an eye on the tension of the wires and, if necessary, give them some slack.
- The ship will tend to move in fore-and-aft direction. This will increase the possibility of parting the mooring ropes. For car carriers this is very dangerous, because the wind can cause the ship to move away from the berth. With the ramp down on the pier, this can be dangerous for the ship. In one particular case, a car carrier was safely berthed in US port. Both ramps were lowered when gusts of very strong winds suddenly started blowing off the berth. The forward ropes parted and the ship swung with her stern ramp lying on the pier and side ramp in the water. In such cases, the crew should be alert and ready to pick up all ramps simultaneously in order to avoid such occurrences. The duty officer should check the ropes regularly.

Air Draft

When deciding if the ship can pass safely under a bridge or overhead power cable in a light condition, the air draft of the ship is very important. It is sometimes listed in the ship's particulars. The air draft must also be considered when gantry cranes are present on the pier. There are several cases in which car carriers hit the cranes when berthing or unmooring. Due to their high freeboard (actually it is not a free board but an area exposed to the wind), the danger of touching a bridge with ship's mast must be taken into account.

It is wrong to calculate the air draft as:

Air draft = height of the mast – deepest draft

The correct air draft must be calculated at the longitudinal position of the mast:

From the scheme below we could derive the following equation:

$$\frac{\text{IAD}}{\text{Trim}} = \frac{\text{Xmast}}{\text{LBP}} \rightarrow \text{IAD} = \frac{\text{Trim x Xmast}}{\text{LBP}}$$

Where:

IAD = air draft, meters

Xmast = horizontal distance of the highest mast from the aft most part of the vessel (it could be the forward most part, depending of the system of the vessel's measurement), meters

LBP = length of the vessel between perpendiculars, meters

Trim = the difference between draft forward and draft aft, meters

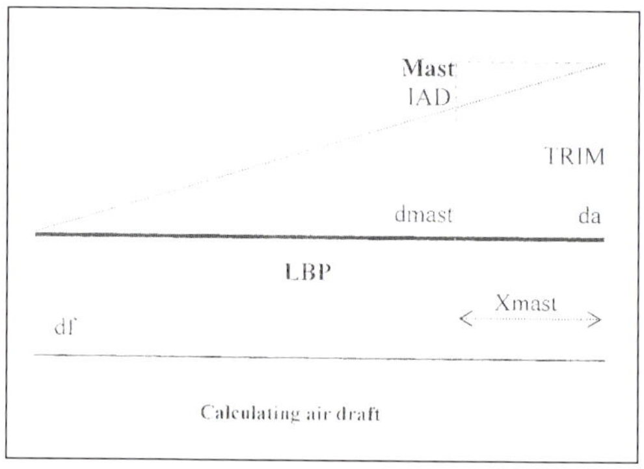

Calculating air draft

On the newer ships the antennas and some masts are foldable in order to decrease the air draft and to ensure safe passage under bridges. On car carriers with foldable masts, the highest point of the ship when the mast is down will be the upper part of the funnel, and the longitudinal distance of the funnel, not the mast, should be used in the above formula.

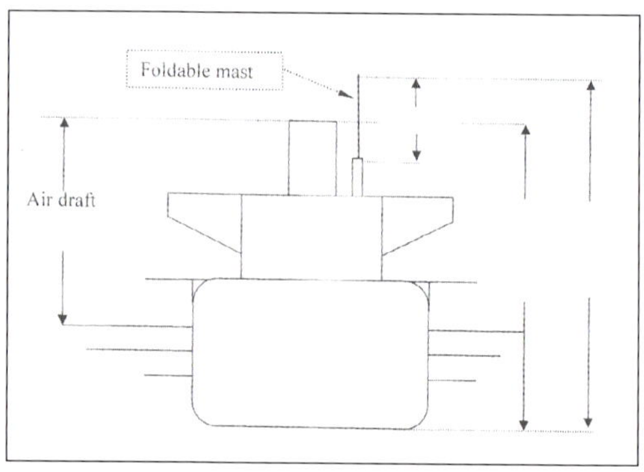

Adjusting for a foldable mast when calculating air draft

Special attention should be paid on the Charter Party (C/P) clauses: if C/P contains the clause "below bridges" it means that the ship is to be kept at the appropriate draft in order to ensure that she will have sufficient clearance above its highest point to pass safely below bridges. As a rule, the responsibility of ensuring safe passage of a car carrier under the bridge lies with the Owner.

Positions of Structures on Quay

Very often car carriers are berthed with their stern first. This often leads to the stern overhanging the berth until the vessel has been brought into alignment and moored. For this reason, the Master must be sure that any traveling, loading, or discharging gantries and structures have been moved well clear of the position where the bow of the ship is to be moored. Normally the largest car carriers, even when equipped with bow thrusters, are assisted by two tugs to moor the ship parallel to the berth. The approach speed should be controlled and kept to a minimum in order to avoid a speedy approach to the berth.

The clearance between the ramp and gantry crane was only one meter. The positioning of the ship was exacerbated due to the fact that the crane was not operational.

Locks

Entering locks should be done with the utmost attention because damage to the lock could lead to exorbitant claims against the Ship Owner.

Fenders

Almost all berths in the major car terminals are suitably equipped with fenders. A problem may arise when a large ship is to be berthed on a smaller berth.

In some ports, however, there are no fenders at all, which may cause structural damage either to the ship or the berth. If this is the case, the Master should lodge a Letter of Protest against the port.

The "YOKOHAMA" fender type is frequently seen in major hubs and provides good protection for the ship. These may cause problems when lowering the ramps, as ramps are designed to operate when the ship is at most to 1.5 to 2 meters off the berth. Yokohama fenders are normally less than 2 meters in diameter.

In all cases, the Master must discuss the fendering system with the Pilot before berthing.

Yokohama fender and berth with Yokohama fenders

Bollards, Slips, or other Construction on Pier

At berths specially designed for car carriers, the distance between the bollards is about 20–25 meters in order to allow normal, safe lowering of the ramps. Normally there are no obstacles at such berths and the ramp position is clearly marked. Some berths, however, are equipped with railways, hydrants, etc., that can obstruct the lowering of the ramp or even make it impossible.

The time for cargo operations is usually fixed and any delay in cargo operations may constitute clear grounds for claims against the ship. That is why preliminary information about the berth must be obtained from the Agent. In some congested ports, it is not uncommon that an inappropriate berth is assigned to the ship. In that case, the Master must lodge a Letter of Protest and refer to the clause for "Safe port/berth" in the Charter Party (C/P). Additionally, if the berth is not appropriate and causes the ramp to be very steep (with a high slope), it may be impossible to load high and heavy units such as trailers, mafis, and others.

In some private berths, it is a requirement to protect the berth by all means. As a rule, the strength of Ro-Ro berths is calculated in such way that they will not be damaged by the load exercised by the ramp (and the cargo) when lowered down.

Plywood under the flap will protect the ramp as well as the pier.

Very often the port authorities may attempt to charge the ship for damage that happened long before its arrival. Therefore, it is recommended to take pictures of any damage to the berth or structure as contemporaneous evidence against any claim that can be filed at a later date.

If the ramp has rollers, it is necessary to put steel plates underneath it. In ports where the risk of gusting exists, additional storm bollards must be fitted. Their purpose is to mitigate the effect of the wind on the car carrier. The storm bollards are strengthened (SWL up to 100 metric tons) and are placed farther apart than normal bollards.

The information that the Master needs about the berth and the intended loading or discharging operations may be given to him in writing in an e-mail, telex, or fax. Information received verbally from the Pilot, Agent, or other officials is essential, but verbal advice is best when supported by written information.

Normally it is obligation of the Charterer to ensure a safe port and berth. The traditional and most popular, widely used time charter in the car carrier trade is "NYPE 93" (New York Produce Exchange). Clause 12 "Berths" states that: "The vessel shall be loaded and discharged in any safe dock or at any safe berth or safe place that Charterers or their agents may direct, provided that the vessel can safely enter, lie, and depart always afloat at any time of tide."[1]

If the C/P states that the ship must be "always afloat," it is assumed that UKC (under keel clearance) will be enough for the whole stay of the ship in the port. If, however, it states "not always but safe aground" in the C/P, it means that the ports are affected by strong tides and they have soft bottom—mud, sand, etc. This means that the ship could touch the ground during ebb tide, but this is not very common for car carriers or Ro-Ro ships.

Having received the orders from the Charterers, the Master must advise the Owners about the condition of the berth. If the port in question is not considered safe the Owners may reject it.

The Master must pay special attention when visiting unknown ports. Damage caused by the vessel to any harbor, dock, pier, quay, jetty, or anything that is fixed or movable can give rise to large claims. In many countries, Owners will be held responsible for any accidental damage, even though the vessel and the crew were in no way at fault. Damage to the port's infrastructure appears to be considered as similar to collisions. The American word for contact between the ship and fixed or floating object is allision. Under paragraph 4.3 of IMO Res. 849, "Code for the Investigation of

Marine Casualties and Incidents," it would be considered a "Serious Casualty" unless it also resulted in loss of life or severe pollution, when it would be considered a "Very Serious Casualty."

Considering the vulnerability of car carriers to the wind, especially if the port is narrow or involves difficult maneuvering, the Master must be very careful. If he is in doubt about the good outcome of the maneuver he is conducting, he has the right to postpone it (Ref: ISM code Reg. 5.2). However, if damage occurs when a vessel is entering a port, the Master should report the incident as soon as possible to the Owners. If possible, the Master should also contact the local P&I Club correspondent and request them to attend and assist. If damage occurs while the vessel is leaving the port, the Master should resist any temptation to ignore the incident, hoping that the damage will be overlooked. Owners should be notified as soon as possible in order that inquiries may be made to ascertain the extent of the damage.

When entering a port where the berth is unsuitable, the Master and the crew, in all cases, must collect evidence in order to argue any claim filed against the ship.

Terminals

Introduction

Car terminals are usually concentrated in areas with good access to road and railway infrastructure facilities. Car terminals that are close to major roads and railways have a considerable competitive advantage.

The scheme of cargo transportation by Ro-Ro ships or car carriers means that a cargo transport unit (CTU) has to complete numerous formalities at the terminal prior to embarkation, i.e., entering the terminal, customs procedures, and storage at the storage site pending loading on board. Storage site capacity and its location at the terminal are important issues for efficient operations. Cargo arrives at various times, and that which arrives early has to wait. While it is not possible to avoid exposure to the weather, these CTUs need to be parked in a safe area that has proper security and protection.

Terminal for high and heavy vehicles

Typical car terminal

In order to achieve optimization of the Ro-Ro ship's processing time several factors have to be considered:

- Close cooperation between the terminal and shipping operator is mandatory
- To ensure proper terminal operation and efficient ship processing, a certain number of CTUs should be available on the berth and ready for embarkation. When the vessel arrives, it should not be necessary for her to wait for the cargo operations to commence.
- All terminal facilities, like gateways, customs and border control, storage sites, and their arrangement, must be duly coordinated

Types of Berths

The ports visited by Ro-Ro ships are usually properly equipped. Car carriers do not require special facilities, as they can berth on both sides depending on the location of the ramps. Ro-Ro passenger ships are berthed alongside terminals fitted with evacuation boarding and disembarking systems for passengers and so-called "link" spans for loading or discharging the vehicles, which consist of a ramp designed to alter in height and slope depending on the height of the tide. Ro-Ro cargo ships are berthed alongside special terminals that are equipped with link spans. The type of the link span depends on the type of Ro-Ro ship being handled:

- **Mechanically lifted link span:** This link span is mounted to a frame suspended by piles. The link span is raised and lowered by lifting equipment, such as hydraulic cylinders, wire ropes, or a rack-and-pinion, in order to accommodate the variations of tides and the vessel's threshold. The height of the link span automatically responds to the vessel's movements. This type is one of the most common types of link span.
- **Floating link span:** This link span is connected to a pontoon with a hinged connection. The pontoon moves up and down with the variations of the tide, consequently changing the slope of the ramp. The slope can vary within a range of working angles, thus allowing a secure way of loading or discharging vehicles. The floating link spans can be divided into the following types:
  - Straight-ramp type
  - Quarter-ramp type
  - Single-access type
  - Double-access type
  - Submerged type

Floating link span

- **Floater link span (integral tank)**: In this type of link span, unlike the previous one, the ramp has a fixed connection to the pontoon. As the tide rises and falls, the pontoon, ramp, and ship will move together, maintaining the slope of the ramp and allowing cargo operations to continue uninterrupted.
- **Combined link span (floating-hydraulic link span)**: This is the most complicated type of link span. A hydraulically operated ramp is attached to the floating pontoon and adjusts the pontoon's height to the vessel's threshold. Hydraulic cylinders are located under the movable ramp.
- **Adjustable shore ramp:** These adjustable ramps can be used for trailers and vehicles, but also for loading and discharging wagons
- **Railway link span.** This span has rails and serves as an access between the vessel and the berth for railway cars.

The design and construction of link spans are dealt with by the BS (British Standard) 6349-8:2007 "Maritime structures. Code of practice for the design of Ro-Ro ramps, linkspans and walkways. A guide to procurement, operation and maintenance," as well as "Lloyd's Register (2008), Rules & Regulations for the Classification of Linkspans 2008."

BS 6349-8:2007 gives some guidance on loading with link spans. It should be kept in mind that the link spans are less reliable than static structures.

CHAPTER 3

HOLD VENTILATION

Ventilation on board car carriers constitutes an integral part of the "due diligence" exercised by the Carriers regarding the cargo being shipped. In fact, if ventilation is not working properly during loading, the ship will be considered unseaworthy.

Accumulation of gases and moisture inside car decks should be avoided. To accomplish this, car carriers are fitted with a number of powerful ventilation fans, which are subject to SOLAS regulations. They are a vital part of the cargo equipment and should be inspected at regular intervals as stipulated in Planned Maintenance Schedule. The responsible crew should be very well aware of the main principles on which proper ventilation is based.

Hold ventilation is not only for exhausting gasoline vapors, but also for controlling the hold condition in general. These include the following:

- Avoiding moisturizing of cargo holds and consequent damage to the cargo
- Exhaust gasoline vapors coming out of the cars when the ship is in port
- Cooling the tank top to prevent damage to the car tires

Compared with other cargoes, wheeled cargo is not particularly susceptible to deterioration due to water condensation. Ro-Ro cargoes are non-hygroscopic; they do not have a moisture content. However, some machinery transported by Ro-Ro vessels is supported by wooden dunnage, which is hygroscopic.

There are cases, however, where vehicles transported by sea have suffered from rusty spots, which gave rise to huge claims against the Carrier. In order to avoid such occurrences and to protect the Owner's interests, the Master must be very well aware of the principles of ventilation and apply them when the ship is at sea or in port. In this chapter, the ventilation principles and their application on Ro-Ro ships will be discussed.

How Can Moisture on the Cargo Be Avoided?

When a ship comes from the tropics, her hold is filled with warm and moist air. If the ship suddenly enters cold water or cold weather, the metal surfaces of the hold will cool off rapidly because the steel is a good heat conductor. As soon as these surfaces become colder than the dew point of the air in the hold, moisture will condense on them. This moisture will collect on the beams and underside of the deck plates, and will drip down on the cargo. The same principle applies for goods stowed inside a container or box that is loaded on truck, trailer, or mafi, but in that case the moisture will condense on the walls of the box or container.

As stipulated in "IMO/ILO Guidelines for Packing Cargo in freight Containers or Vehicles," the main factors leading to condensation inside surfaces of containers are:

- Sources of moisture inside the container that, depending on ambient temperature conditions, will affect the moisture content of the atmosphere in the container
- Difference between the temperature of the atmosphere within the container and the surface temperature of either the cargo or the inner surfaces of the container itself
- Changes in the temperature of the outer surface of the container which affect the two factors above

Definitions

Dew point is the temperature at which air saturated with moisture at the prevailing atmospheric pressure will start to shed moisture by condensation. Dew point can be obtained by tables or by formula. Indisputably the formulas will give more precise results, but using them will be time consuming. Using tables will save calculating time and the result will only differ slightly from the result obtained by formula. For practical application this difference can be ignored. The dew point depends on the absolute humidity of the air. There is a procedure for obtaining dew point posted in *Brown's Nautical Almanac* (Brown, Son, & Ferguson Ltd., Glasgow: 2015).

Temperature reserve of air (Q°_{AIR}) is the difference between the temperature of the air used for ventilation and its dew point (DP)

Minimal temperature reserve of air ($Q^\circ_{AIR\ MIN}$) is the minimal temperature reserve of the air preventing sweating during an abrupt decrease of its temperature. A $Q^\circ_{AIR\ MIN}$ of 3° C is recommended.

Actual temperature reserve of the cargo (Q°_{CARGO}) is the difference between the temperature of the cargo (T°_{CARGO}) and DP of the air inside the hold around the cargo.

These definitions must be familiar to the officer in charge of the ventilation as well as the Master. Their complete knowledge of them will pave the way to successful ventilation of cargo holds, thus preventing any claims that may arise due to cargo damage resulting from inappropriate ventilation.

Principles for Ventilating Cargo Holds:

During Winter

In winter, the temperature of the water is always higher than the temperature of the air. In order to prevent condensation in the cargo, the DP of the hold air (DP_{HOLD}) must be less than the temperature of the cargo minus the value of its Q°_{CARGO}:

$$DP_{HOLD} < T^\circ_{CARGO} - Q^\circ_{CARGO}$$

Ventilation of the cargo holds is not recommended if the following condition exists:

$$DP_{HOLD} > T^\circ_{CARGO} - Q^\circ_{CARGO}$$

During Summer

In summer, the temperature of the water is always less than the temperature of the air. It is preferable not to ventilate the cargo holds. Preventing condensation could be done only by equalizing the temperature of the cargo with the temperature of the air outside, but would create condensation problems of its own.

On passage from warmer area to colder area: Cars loaded in warmer areas will have higher temperatures. When sailing to a colder area, the temperature of the outside air and water will decrease, while the temperature of the cargo will remain comparatively high and the dew point of the air inside the hold will be higher than the temperature of the sides of the hold. Consequently the moisture will condense on the colder metal surfaces. There is a risk of the condensation trickling down onto the covers of the cars or onto valuable cargo being transported on a mafi, trailer, etc. If humid air is ventilated, the moisture on the metal surface will be reduced, but the cargo will sweat. Nevertheless, it is always recommended to ventilate cargo holds on passages from warmer to colder areas.

On passage from colder to warmer area: Cargo loaded in colder areas will have a low temperature. When sailing to a warmer area, the temperature of the surrounding air and water will increase gradually, while the temperature of the cargo will remain comparatively low and the dew point of the air inside the hold will be less than the temperatures of the sides of the holds. Consequently the moisture will condense on the covers of the vehicles. If it is decided to ventilate the holds with surrounding air, which is hotter than the air inside the cargo hold, the process of sweating the cargo will increase. Therefore, it is strongly recommended not to ventilate the cargo holds on passages from colder to warmer areas. Air should be recirculated inside the cargo holds.

Recommendations for Ventilating Cargo Holds

- On passage from warmer to colder areas, ventilation is a must. The ventilation must be arranged in such a way that at least one air change per hour is provided for each hold compartment.
- One or more hold fans must run as "EXHAUST" and a suitable number of ventilators must be opened as air intakes (to run as "SUPPLY").
- On passage from a colder to a warmer area, it is necessary to recirculate the air inside the cargo holds.
- If the humidity of the outside air is less than that of the air inside the hold, the compartment must be ventilated using outside air.

It must be kept in mind that the surface temperature of the cargo is only increasing slowly and if the ship enters warmer areas the saturated air outside could lead to condensation on the colder cargo.

- **Criterion of Dew Point:** Ventilation must be conducted when dew point of the air used for ventilation is higher than dew point of the air inside the hold being ventilated with this air.
- **Criterion of Three Degrees:** The hold must be ventilated when the dry bulb temperature of the air used for ventilation is three degrees less than the temperature of the cargo. The temperature of the cargo is assumed to be equal to the temperature of the air in the loading port. This criterion is applicable for hygroscopic cargoes, and here it is cited for clarification and reference only.

- When ship encounters rough sea, i.e., wind force exceeding BF 7 (>28 knots [13.9 m/s]) and/or wave heights exceeding 5 meters, ventilation is prohibited.
- To avoid moisturizing the cargo, ventilation is prohibited when it is raining.
- It is recommended that ventilation be avoided during nighttime for safety's sake. If nobody is supervising the ventilation, it could moisturize the cargo in case of rain. In addition, in case of some malfunction of a ventilation fan, it would not be discovered at once and could lead to damage to the fan or cargo.
- Prior to starting the ventilation, it is necessary to inform the duty engineer to ensure sufficient power is available.

Ventilation to Avoid Build-up of Gasoline Vapors in Cargo Holds

The most important function of ventilation in the cargo holds of Ro-Ro ships is to avoid and exhaust gasoline vapors that may accumulate inside them. As stipulated in SOLAS CH. II-2, Reg. 20 3.1.1:

- The ventilation system on board Ro-Ro ships, including car carriers, must be able to perform six air changes per hour. For Ro-Ro passenger ships, the ventilation system must be able to perform ten air changes per hour.
- In case of fire, there must be arrangements to permit rapid shutdown and effective closure of the ventilation system from outside the compartment in question.
- As an additional precaution against the accumulation of fumes during loading or discharging, cargo doors could be kept open, provided there is adequate freeboard in way of these openings.
- If the stevedores find the ventilation system to be in bad condition, they may refuse to work on board such vessels.

The following recommendations should be taken into account before entering the loading port:

- Make sure that the hold ventilation system is in good order. Defective parts should be repaired or replaced and the system should always be operational.
- Before starting the loading or discharging operation, make sure that the ventilation system is working well, with all the dampers in correct open positions.
- During the loading or discharging operations, the ventilation system should be checked carefully to ensure it is always running and in good condition.

When in doubt about the oxygen content, the atmosphere must be monitored inside the cargo hold in question, testing it to ensure that the air is 21% oxygen with a carbon monoxide content below 50 ppm.

It is advisable to request that the stevedores stop their engines as soon as practicable after embarking and do not start them up prior to disembarking. SOLAS CH. II, Reg. 20, 3.1.2.2 requires ventilation to run continuously when vehicles are on board. On some occasions, however, this is impracticable, especially in case of boisterous weather. In this case, the ventilation should be run for a limited period of time to avoid the accumulation of gas pockets in the car decks. The presence of toxic gases should be checked daily when cargo is on board and results should be recorded respectively.

Ro-Ro vessels should have proper, portable instruments for detecting combustible gas.

In the table below are permissible densities of toxic gas components and their effect on the human body.

Component	Permissible Exposure Limit	Effect on human body	Source
CO	OSHA PEL: 50 ppm / 8-hr shift	Headache, nausea, dizziness	US Dept. of Labor, "Occupational Health Guideline for Carbon Monoxide"
	NIOSH PEL: 35 ppm f/ 10-hr shift	Weakness, unconsciousness	
	WHO PEL: 9 ppm / 8-hr shift	Death	WHO
SO_2	NIOSH PEL: 0.5 ppm / 10-hr shift	Irritation, coughing	US Dept of Labor, "Occupational Health Guideline for Sulfur Dioxide"
	OSHA PEL: 5 ppm / 8-hr shift		
CO_2	OSHA PEL: 5000 ppm / 8-hr shift	Headache, sweating	US Dept of Labour, "Occupational Health Guideline for Carbon Dioxide"
	NIOSH PEL: up to 10000 ppm / 10-hr shift	Mental depression	

From the tables, it is clear that the content of CO inside the holds must not exceed 50 ppm. For this purpose appropriate measurements should be taken continuously and proper ventilation should be carried out. A record book of the concentrations of gases inside car decks should be kept as part of the ship's SMS.

Technical Specifications of the Ventilation System

Ventilation fans used on board Ro-Ro ships, including car carriers for car deck ventilation, are of the marine axial-flow, explosion-proof type. They are designed for displacement of air contaminated with vapors or dust particles that are classified as dangerous. The fans can be used as exhaust or supply.

The working parameters of fans must be observed and followed. Normally these are defined by performance curves, which are available on board and must be taken into account. Allowable tolerances of the working parameters of fans (airflow, pressure, power consumption, and efficiency) are in accordance with specific standards. There is a restriction for the temperature of the air in which the fans can operate safely: normally it is about 45°C. Dust contents are limited to a maximum of 0.30 g/m^3.

Each fan consists of the following components: housing, air guide, impeller, and electric motor. The housing is a steel pipe terminated on the lower end with a drilled flange; it is welded and coated with marine paints. The inside of the fan housing, in way of the impeller, is lined with a 2 mm thick brass sheet. The air inlet is usually conically shaped and fitted with a wire net for protection, with free spacing 50 mm; it is attached with screws. The air guide is made of welded and painted sheet metal. The purpose of the air guide is to strengthen the air stream, but it is also a supporting bracket for the electric motor/impeller set.

The impeller is made of a sea water-resistant aluminum alloy. The blades are screwed to the hub and stabilize the impeller statically and dynamically. Electric motors can vary, but they must be suitable for 50 or 60 Hz installation and be totally enclosed so they are protected from the hostile marine environment. Generally the motors are the three-phase, inductive type, squirrel-caged, and placed in a flameproof enclosure.

The sizes and diameters of fans vary depending on the compartment they are serving. Each fan must be properly marked. An example for such marking is shown below:

AXIAL FLOW FAN * * * 710/380 – 45°C

This marking indicates the following:

- The fan is **axial-flow**
- * * * indicates where the model of the fan would be
- **710** indicates the nominal diameter of the fan
- **380** indicates the impeller hub diameter
- **45°C** indicates the maximum temperature of conveyed air, which must not be exceeded

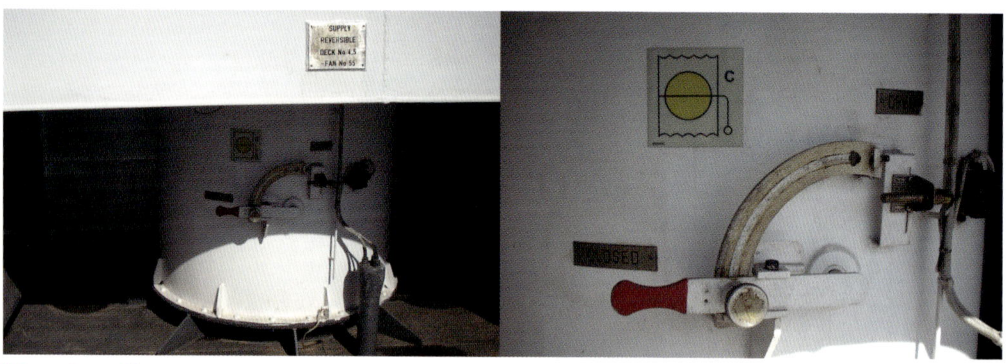

"Open" and "closed" positions for ventilators and a typical vent housing

Ventilation Procedures

Starting Hold Ventilation

Before starting hold ventilation, the following actions should be carried out:

- Confirmation that all ventilation dampers are open.
- Confirmation from the engine department that all two or three generators are simultaneously running.
- Reset the flaps of the fans before starting ventilation.
- Switch on the source supply.
- Confirm that fans are started and running completely by determining that the indicator lights on the starting panel are illuminated.

During Operation

During operation the fans do not require continuous inspection, but their operation should be occasionally observed.

- In case of any unpredictable vibrations, impeller grazing, low insulation alarm on the control panel, or loud operational sounds from the bearings, the fan must be stopped and defects remedied.
- Maintenance of the ventilation system should follow the manufacturer's instructions and Planned Maintenance Schedule adopted on board. Before any cleaning or repair of the impeller, the fan should be turned off and the main switch disconnected.
- The electrical components of the fan should be protected against the harmful action of lubricating agents, moisture, or chemicals. The condition of the electric installation is to be checked at least once a month.
- Periodic inspections should be performed at intervals specified in the manufacturer's instructions, but usually at least twice a year. The inspection should include, but should not be limited to:
  - *Cleaning and visual checking of impeller and air guides*
  - *Checking and tightening of screwed connections of fan and impeller, as well as connections between air guide and motor*
  - *Checking of fan grounding. It is not permitted to use an ungrounded fan.*

Ventilation for Cooling the Lowest Car Deck (Tank Top)

In areas where the temperature is extremely high or when the fuel in the tanks beneath it is heated, the lowest car deck, or tank top, can be excessively warm when cargo is to be loaded. This is potentially dangerous for the tires of the cars and, if the temperature of the tank top is very high, there is the risk of damage (mostly melting) to tires. The Chief Officer and Master must always be alert to the danger and take appropriate measures to prevent it. Various types of digital thermometers are normally supplied to check the temperature of the tank top.

Needless to say, the temperature of the tank top must be reduced to acceptable values before loading. If this is not done by the responsible officer, the stevedores may refuse to commence cargo operations. If the stevedores overlook this fact (actually it is not their duty to take care of this) and load the cargo regardless, the Carrier will be responsible for any damage that may occur. Because it is the carrier's responsibility to make sure that the cargo holds are suitably fit at the beginning of cargo operations, in both cases the ship will be held responsible, either for delaying cargo operations or for damaging the tires. (In the Hague-Visby Rules, Art. III Rule 1, the Carrier is obliged to ensure suitably fit cargo holds.)

When ventilation is to be used for cooling off the tank top, it must be started well in advance of the commencement of cargo operations. If ventilation to cool down the tank top has to be carried out during the voyage, it is indispensable that ventilation be started at once, after having considered other factors, such as moisture, humidity, rough weather, etc., that could adversely affect the cargo. The temperature of the tank top should be regularly checked and records should be kept on board in the "Car Decks Temperature Checklist."

Ventilation Logbook

Because their cargo is, by its nature, not vulnerable to damage due to moisture, it is not common for Ro-Ro ships to have a ventilation logbook on board; ventilation is not often carried out. Considering the above discussion, however, which requires ventilation of the cargo holds, the prudent Chief Officer will always have such a logbook properly kept. In addition, some Charterers and Cargo Owners will require such a logbook to be duly kept on board. The ventilation logbook must include the following information:

During loading:

- Air temperature.
- Air relative humidity.
- Air dew point.
- Sea water temperature.

During voyage:

- Cargo temperature in different holds. The wet bulb temperature and the dry bulb temperature must be taken and used to obtain the dew point (DP). Taking into account that it is impracticable to measure the temperature of the cars when loaded, it can be assumed that cars will have the temperature of the port of loading.
- Hold temperature and outside temperature.
- Ventilation conditions and ventilation conducted during the voyage.

Below is a typical example of a ventilation logbook. However, if the Owner or SMS stipulate another form, that form must be used.

	TIME	Tdry	Twet	Dew Point
Hold1				
Hold2				
Hold3				
Hold4				

Problems that May Arise During Ventilation

Adequate ventilation for the cargo holds is a must. However, there are several issues that must be taken into account when using the ventilation system on board:

- Excessive grease on movable parts on the dampers can contribute to cargo damage when blown into the car decks. To avoid such damage, the lubricating plan for vent flaps should be strictly followed. This is the only way to avoid accumulation of excessive quantities of grease and at the same time keep the dampers properly greased.
- The ventilation ducts must be maintained as per the ship's Planned Maintenance Schedule. This will avoid the formation of rusty spots inside the duct and damage to the cargo caused by rust being blown into the car decks. Special attention should be paid on board older ships, where rust formation inside the ducts could be significant.
- When cargo is on board, any deck work consisting of de-scaling, grinding, etc., being performed near the ventilation ducts should be postponed. Otherwise the dusty and rusty cloud created by such maintenance could be sucked into the hold by the ventilation and cause damage to the cargo. If, however, such deck work must be carried out, some precautions must be taken, including stopping ventilation fans near the area in question and closing the dampers tightly. Upon completion of deck work, the responsible officer must make sure that no rusty powder has been left near the ventilator in question.
- Ventilation during heavy weather or rain must be avoided in order to avoid any water damage to the cargo.
- Whenever ventilation of the cargo holds is required, the basic principles for ventilation as discussed above must be strictly followed and applied.

This is what happens if the appropriate maintenance is not carried out. During the voyage, damage to the cargo due to carelessness of the crew will be clear grounds for severe cargo claims.

Although wheeled cargo is less vulnerable to moisture damage, there are other reasons for which proper ventilation of cargo holds is required. Ventilation on board car carriers or Ro-Ro ships that are sailing on long voyages and passing different climatic zones is important. For short-trade ships and voyages, some deviation in applying the basic ventilation principles can be accepted. It must always be borne in mind, however, that any damage to the cargo resulting from inappropriate ventilation of the cargo holds or total lack of such ventilation will be the Carrier's responsibility.

CHAPTER 4

LOADING & DISCHARGING CARGO

The Carrier is obliged under the Hague-Visby Rules to exercise due diligence regarding the cargo during the voyage. This means that the Carrier should perform regular inspection of the cargo and carry out proper ventilation, if necessary. However, the Cargo Owner is obliged to deliver the cargo suitable for sea transportation. In this respect, the Master should make sure that the cargo is fit for sea transportation before it is loaded on board. Practically, this is not possible because very often the Master only sees the cargo just before loading. But there is a vital role the Master can play: as the cargo is being loaded, he must make sure that the cargo is not damaged, and if it is, he should reject the damaged cargo. If the cargo is suitable for sea transportation, it should be properly secured before the ship leaves the berth.

Cargo operations on Ro-Ro ships are performed on the roll-on/roll-off principle, i.e., the cargo is driven on and driven off the ship. The Ro-Ro method enables shippers to load cargo on a chassis or trailer at the plant or warehouse site, transport the vehicles to embarkation points, and have them loaded directly onto the vessel. By rolling cargo on board these vessels and rolling it off at its destination, shippers can reduce the number of times their cargo is handled.

The inherent disadvantage of Ro-Ro is the waste of cargo carrying capacity due to undercarriage. As was mentioned in chapter 1, these ships are designed to carry not only light passenger cars, but also high and heavy units, which have different heights. Therefore there are generally two or three car decks that are strengthened in order to allow loading heavier cargo on board. In order to allow the loading of tall cargo, the decks above the strengthened ones are retractable. They are called "deck panels" or "movable decks." The number of movable decks is the same as the strengthened decks.

Cargo on Ro-Ro ships includes more than wheeled units. Very often it includes containers, different pallets, heavy units, etc. In this respect, it would be correct to analyze the peculiarities of these cargoes and the requirements for their stowage, lashings, and transportation. Cargo and cargo operations present several issues to be considered:

- **Loading plan:** When preparing the loading plan, also known as Stowage Plan, the responsible officer must take into account the number of vehicles to be loaded, their stowage (including their weight and dimensions), the reduction of the handling time, and the prevention of damage and injury to vehicles, ship, and personnel. The preparations for cargo operations include the following:
  - *Preparation of loading plan*
  - *Execution of loading plan*
  - *Deviation of loading plan*

- **Lashing materials:** Lashing materials that will be used for securing the cargo are important for the safe and effective transportation of vehicles at sea. Taking into account the size of present car carriers and, especially, their height, it is necessary to examine the stress on vehicles due to anticipated vibrations and to provide adequate lashing that will prevent vehicles from moving. The cargo itself will tend either to slide or tip over, depending on its size and shape, the position of the center of gravity, and the coefficient of friction between the cargo and the deck. There are many types of lashing equipment and many different dunnage materials. It is the obligation of the responsible officer to choose the appropriate material in order to secure the vehicles properly and to increase the friction between the cargo and deck. Detailed analysis of lashing equipment used on board Ro-Ro vessels can be found in chapter 5.
- **Types of cargo—cars, high and heavy units, etc.:** As was pointed out earlier, Ro-Ro ships transport not only cars, but also containers, pallets, and other types of commodities. It is important that the responsible officer receives preliminary information about the cargo to be loaded. Based on this information, he can calculate the required deck strength for particularly high and heavy cargoes and estimate the necessity of lifting the movable decks. The proper distribution of cargo inside the cargo holds will ensure sufficient stability and facilitate cargo operations. Different cargoes require different lashings and different methods of loading and stowage, so the Master must insist on receiving information about the cargo at the proper time. Charterers almost always send the required information well in advance. One problem that might arise is the actual weight of the cargo in question. Sometimes the information contained in the Cargo Manifests differs from the actual weight of the cargo. If this is the case, some structural damage can be expected due to overloading of the decks, especially if the cargo consists of heavy units. Another problem is the effect of the cargo on the ship's stability. As a rule, the heavier cargoes must be loaded in lower decks, taking into consideration the deck strength.

Safety Measures During Loading and Transportation of Vehicles at Sea

Taking into consideration the type of cargo being loaded or discharged, a number of safety precautions must be taken well beforehand. Most of these precautions are listed in the Company's procedures and the respective Charterer's guidelines. It is a must that the crew is made familiar with these requirements and strictly applies them.

Loading Plan

In order to perform the safe and efficient transportation of vehicles at sea, a detailed loading plan should be prepared on the basis of an adequate preliminary survey of the ship structure and equipment, the particulars of the vehicle, the port conditions, the rotation of the voyage, and other factors.

- **Preliminary survey:** The size of vehicles to be loaded varies greatly, ranging from compact passenger cars to large heavy units with lengths of 16–17 meters. Weights can vary from lightweight cars of 0.6 metric ton to heavy ones exceeding 60 metric tons. Additionally, the vehicles can be self-propelled or not. The purpose of a preliminary survey is to clarify whether or not the vehicles can be loaded and to determine the total number of vehicles that can be loaded. When performing a preliminary survey the following items must be taken into account:

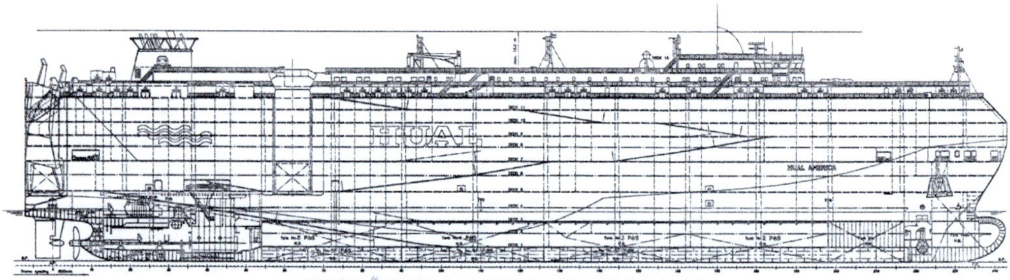

DECK AREAS AND CARS SUMMARY

Deck No	Fixed/ liftable	Location	Height ab. B.P.	Free height	Uniform load	Axle load	Deck area	Standard Cars	LCM from A.P.	TCM from C.L.	VCM1 above B.P.	VCM2 above B.P.	VCM3 above B.P.
		Fr. – Fr	m	m	t/m2	t/wheels	m2	Units	m	m	m	m	m
12	fixed	5 – 231	32.74	1.850	0.180	1.2/2	4360.1	505	95.79	+0.21	33.31	33.51	33.68
11	fixed	-7 – 237	30.27	2.000	0.180	1.2/2	5685.7	704	94.42	+0.02	30.84	31.04	31.28
10	fixed	-7 – 239	27.70	2.200	0.250	1.5/2	5742.2	708	94.64	-0.03	28.27	28.47	28.81
9	fixed	-7 – 242	25.01	2.300	0.300	2.7/2	5765.5	714	95.09	-0.03	25.58	25.78	26.17
8	liftable	-7 – 242	22.88	1.700	0.165	1.2/2	5748.4	709	94.20	-0.01	23.45	-	-
7	fixed	11 – 223	19.98	2.50/4.20	0.500	8.0/2	5022.2	625	92.80	+0.07	20.55	20.75	22.09
6	liftable	-7 – 224	17.22	2.200	0.200	1.5/2	5355.6	662	87.11	-0.05	17.79	17.99	-
5	fixed	-7 – 224	14.00	2.80/5.00	2.000	22.2/2	5095.1	632	84.94	-0.10	14.57	14.77	16.51
4	liftable	54 – 217	10.80	2.300	0.200	1.5/2	3460.3	422	103.36	-0.30	11.37	11.57	-
3	fixed	38 – 217	8.08	2.30/4.60	1.000	15.0/2	3475.6	423	98.02	+0.27	8.70	8.90	10.39
2	liftable	54 – 198	5.65	1.700	0.165	1.2/2	2604.8	314	99.23	-0.81	6.22	-	-
1	fixed	54 – 198	2.95	2.30/4.00	1.000	15.0/2	2294.7	273	89.70	-0.18	3.55	3.73	4.96
						TOTAL:	54610.2	6693	94.05	-0.04	20.73	-	-

NOTE:
VCM1 – vertical centre of mass for standard cars (0.130t/m2) = 0.56 m above deck
VCM2 – vertical centre of mass for pick-ups (0.168t/m2) = 0.76 m above deck
VCM3 – vertical centre of mass for homogeneous. load = 0.5*free height above deck

Deck areas and cars summary for car carriers

- **Nominal vehicle carrying capacity:** This is the largest number of standard-sized vehicles that the ship can load. This capacity is stated in the ship's documents and especially on Car Deck Plans. If the ship is designed to carry 5,000 units, it means that she can load 5,000 standard-size cars. The standard-size varies from ship to ship and can be found either in the drawings or in the Car Deck Plan. It must be kept in mind, however, that, because the actual size of the cars to be loaded differs from the standard, the total number of vehicles that can be loaded on any given voyage most probably will differ from the nominal vehicle capacity. Normally the number of vehicles that can be loaded is less than that stated in the Car Deck Plan.

- **Deck strength:** When building a new ship, the deck strength is determined based on the cargo intended to be carried. Considering this, we can say that the deck strength is sufficient for ordinary cargoes. If, however, the cargo consists of some high and heavy units, attention must be paid to the deck strength. From strength figures and safety factors, such as an allowance for corrosion, the deck strength is calculated and is given as the maximum permissible load (MPL). MPL is given in metric tons (tonnes) per square meter (t/m^2) for each car deck. The figures will remain the same throughout the lifetime of the ship, as long as no structural changes are made. MPL is given for each car deck and can be found in the ship's Car Capacity Plan, in the ship's Trim and Stability Booklet, and in the Cargo Securing Manual.

SUMMARY TABLE OF LOADING CONDITIONS

Cond. No.	SPECIFICATION	Sto res	Stores +DWT const.	Cargo	Water Ballast	DWT	Displa-cement	Draughts d at LCF	dA Aft	dM Mid.	dF Fore	Trim t	VCM' cor-rected	VCMmax acc. IMO	GM' cor-rected	SWBM
		%	t	t	t	t	t	m	m	m	m	m	m	m	m	kNm
00	Light Ship	-	0	0	0	0	16869	5.57	7.76	5.34	2.96	4.80	17.370	-	2.569	1544260
01	Water ballast condition	100	4000	0	7352	11353	28222	8.11	8.97	7.96	6.95	2.03	12.254	15.501	5.010	1592157
02	Water ballast condition	10	860	0	6986	7846	24715	7.33	8.03	7.26	6.50	2.05	13.527	15.344	3.827	1777319
03	Docking condition	10	860	0	5067	5927	22795	6.88	6.96	6.88	6.81	0.15	14.324	15.227	2.844	1814261
04	Homog. Load 0.240 t/m2	100	4000	7881	4042	15923	32792	9.00	9.13	8.98	8.83	0.30	15.381	15.636	1.195	1642549
05	Design Draught d= 9.00 m	10	860	7881	7182	15923	32792	9.00	9.16	8.98	8.79	0.37	15.639	15.639	0.954	1989685
06	Homog. Load 0.600 t/m2	100	4000	13601	3581	21182	38051	10.00	10.00	10.00	9.99	0.01	15.557	15.737	0.779	1431773
07	Scantling Draught d= 10.00 m	10	860	13601	6721	21182	38051	10.00	10.08	9.99	9.89	0.19	15.750	15.755	0.604	1719782
08	Homog. Load 0.778 t/m2	100	4000	10964	959	15923	32792	9.01	9.83	8.85	7.87	1.96	14.594	15.668	2.322	1382226
09	Design Draught d= 9.00 m	10	860	10964	2997	14821	31690	8.78	8.78	8.78	8.78	0.00	15.021	15.564	1.508	1861494
10	Homog. Load 1.600 t/m2	100	4000	16434	748	21182	38051	10.00	10.64	9.88	9.12	1.52	14.627	15.873	1.845	1269486
11	Scantling Draught d= 10.00 m	10	860	16434	2335	19628	36497	9.71	9.71	9.71	9.71	0.00	15.216	15.787	1.180	1770544
12	Standard Car Load	100	4000	7099	3364	14464	31333	8.71	8.72	8.71	8.70	0.03	15.199	15.581	1.345	1887849
13	0.130 t/m2	10	860	7099	5584	14543	30412	8.53	8.53	8.53	8.53	0.00	15.547	15.547	1.018	1947321
14	1-tonne Car Load	100	4000	7645	3314	14959	31828	8.81	8.81	8.81	8.81	0.00	15.297	15.600	1.229	1879701
15	0.140 t/m2	10	860	7645	5771	14276	31145	8.68	8.68	8.67	8.67	0.00	15.573	15.575	0.971	1946307
16	Mixed Car Load	100	4000	8857	3167	16024	32893	9.02	9.02	9.02	9.02	0.00	15.589	15.640	0.914	1848563
17	0.130 + 0.168 t/m2	10	860	8857	6408	16125	32994	9.04	9.04	9.04	9.04	0.00	15.651	15.643	0.860	1915778
18	Homog. Load 0.6 t/m2+Iceing	100	4000	13213	3655	21182	38051	10.00	10.00	10.00	10.00	0.00	15.418	15.736	0.918	1439218
19	Scantling Draught d= 10.00 m	10	860	13213	6796	21182	38051	10.00	10.06	9.99	9.92	0.13	15.728	15.749	0.621	1737442

Summary table of loading conditions

The vehicle weight is first transferred to the car deck and to the substructures. The weight is then transmitted to the main structure (web frames and deck girders in longitudinal direction; deck girders in athwart ship direction), and finally to the ship's hull pillars. The weight that is transferred to a car deck panel or substructure does not exceed the weight of the car that is sitting on it. However, the main structure must bear a far greater weight of all the cars that is transferred to it. For this reason it is necessary to make a difference between the local strength and overall strength. The strength to withstand the smaller weight is local strength and the strength to bear the larger weight is called overall strength.

Both the local and overall strength must be calculated. The local strength of the car deck must be checked first, and if it turns out that the local strength is not enough, the vehicles cannot be loaded. If the local strength is enough but the overall strength is not, less cargo can be loaded in order to meet the design strength.

The following definitions should be well known to all officers:

Calculation of maximum permissible cargo weight:

Maximum permissible cargo weight (t)= area of deck (m^2) x MPL (t/m^2)

The corollary formula can be used to determine the minimum area over which the weight of the car must be spread.

Calculation of minimum area of deck or tank-top:

Minimum area of deck (m^2)= cargo weight (t)/ MPL (t/m^2)

- **Axle load:** Axle load is clearly marked on each deck and especially on decks for high and heavy cargo. Axle load is the load, which affects the load of a car. It is given as for example:

  Axle load = 20.0 t / 2 wheels *or* **25.0 t / 4 wheels**

- **Uniform load:** Uniform load is a car deck's maximum permissible load per 1 square meter. It is used to decide whether a piece of cargo can be loaded on board by comparing it with its dimensions.

  When loading heavy cargo, even though the weight of the cargo is underweight based on axle load, the cargo cannot be loaded if it is above the allowable uniform load.

  The weight of the cargo to be loaded should meet the condition for both loads stated above. When the Master of the vessel is loading heavy cargo, he should pay attention to obtaining the details of the cargo through the local Agent in order to ensure that the vessel's safety is not compromised and to prevent hull damage.
- **Deck height:** The deck height is normally 1.65–1.70 meters for decks used to accommodate passenger cars (low profile vehicles), 1.80–2.20 meters for decks used to stow commercial vehicles (high profile vehicles), and 2.40–3.00 meters for decks used for large vehicles (can be raised to 4.80–5.00 meters with liftable decks in their maximum position). It must be kept in mind that there could be some discrepancy between the actual height of the deck and the height as stated in the ship's plans. When preparing the Stowage Plan, therefore, it is advisable that the actual height be measured in order to avoid any damage to the cargo. Moreover, the apparent vehicle height is larger at the top and bottom ends of the inner ramps, while the actual clearance is smaller, so that special attention is required to avoid striking the vehicle's top and back.
- **Rotation of the ship:** Rotation should be taken into account in order to perform efficient handling of cargo. Expected changes in the rotation and the possibility of routing changes should be considered in advance. As a rule, the vehicles loaded first are to be discharged last and vice versa.
- **Usage of respective ramp:** When preparing the Stowage Plan, the Chief Officer should consider which ramp will be used—side or stern. Depending on this information, he can distribute the cargo in such a way that will facilitate loading and discharging. In some ports, only the side ramp can be used. The information about which ramp can be used should be obtained well in advance (if the Chief Officer has already been in the port in question, he can refer to his own experience from the past visits).
- **Stability of the ship:** Stability of the ship is one of the most important issues to be considered when preparing the Stowage Plan. As a rule, the heavier cargoes must be loaded in the lower car decks and the lighter cargoes in the upper car decks.

  The issue is how stable the ship should be. If the ship is stiff (large GM—metacentric height), it will experience violent rolling due to the short rolling period, and the forces and acceleration generated will be large, which could lead to damage to the cars. If the ship is tender (small GM), there is a real danger for her safety, especially in boisterous weather and in very strong winds. Therefore a reasonable GM should be ensured. A guide for the upper limit of GM is given in the advanced calculation method in the Code of Safe Practice for Cargo Stowage and Securing (CSS Code), where a correction factor must be applied when the ship's breadth divided by GM is less than 13. A practical guide for the upper limit of the GM is the ship's breadth divided by 13; a number that is greater than the GM is reasonable.

Consider the basic formula:

$$T = C_B \times B/\sqrt{GM}$$

Where:

T = the roll period

C_B = the block coefficient: the ratio of the volume of displacement of the ship to that of a rectangular block having the same length, breadth, and draft. It can be obtained from the ship's hydrostatic data or using the formula:

$$C_B = \frac{\text{Displacement}}{L_{WL} \times B \times d}$$

Where:

L_{WL} = length at the waterline, measured in profile from the forward-most point of the waterline to the stern-most point

B = the breadth of the ship in meters

GM = the metacentric height

It is easy to obtain roll-period T (seconds) or GM. For comparatively large ships, such as car carriers, a period of 12–13 seconds is considered to be safe. For example, a car carrier of standard dimensions 200 meters and 32 meters, and C = 0.6, it is easy to calculate that GM will be 2.18 meters. Comparing with the CSS Code guidance for upper GM (in our case upper limit of GM should be 32 / 13 = 2.46 meters) it becomes clear that GM = 2.18 meters is reasonable for a ship of these dimensions.

Regarding the lower limit of GM, the appropriate regulations of International Code on Intact Stability must be strictly adhered to. It is very important to take into consideration the weather criteria as well as to consider the vulnerability of car carriers to the influence of the wind. In all cases, reference to the Ship Stability Booklet must be made. Recommended minimum GM stated in various booklets vary between 0.8 and 1.2 meters. In addition, some specific requirements (in most cases more stringent) for the minimum GM required by the Charterer must be abided. The stability matter will be broadly discussed.

- **Effective use of the cargo space:** The effective use of the cargo space is of utmost importance. Because of the availability of inner ramps the usable space of cargo holds is sometimes reduced. The presence of pillars and the curved ends of the car decks reduce the space additionally. This loss of cargo space is known as broken stowage and on car carriers it can reach to 7–10% of the deadweight of the ship. The number of vehicles loaded can be increased when various types of vehicles are loaded in combination and in conformity with loading standards. The total tonnage of vehicles can be increased when over-height vehicles are loaded in spaces designated for them.

Having considered all of the above the Pre-stowage Plan can be prepared. The plan shows the proposed location of the units on the appropriate car decks. Very often the Pre-stowage Plans just show the number of the units on each cargo deck and their respective tonnage. When the Pre-stowage Plan is prepared it should be sent to the Charterers and the Stevedoring Company in the loading port. Normally during the loading there is some deviation from the Pre-stowage Plan due to the impossibility of loading certain units as planned. It is not uncommon for some cargo to be cancelled and replaced by other cargo. Usually this happens when feeder car carriers are involved. In such a case, the stowage of the new units should be dealt with on the spot, having considered all items as described in preliminary survey. When all the cargo has been loaded, the final Stowage Plan must be completed. An example of such a final Stowage Plan is shown in chapter 12, p. **195**.

The final Stowage Plan is prepared by the Stevedoring Company, or, more precisely, by their tallymen department. The Chief Officer is also obliged to prepare such a plan and to send it to the discharging ports in order of the ship's port-call schedule.

It is a good practice for the duty officer to count the cars loaded in the respective holds during the loading. Doing so will help the Chief Officer prepare the final Stowage Plan and will allow him to cross-check the number of units being loaded with the tallyman records. Unfortunately, in some ports there are often discrepancies between the cargo units being declared as loaded and those actually loaded. This practice of counting the cars by ship's officers will avoid any discrepancies. If the discrepancy is detected on the spot, it will protect the ship against any claims that might arise later.

On the Stowage Plan (see chapter 12, p. 195), the cargo for different ports is normally marked in different colors. The cargo for different ports must be separated by separation tape in the respective holds or car decks in order to avoid over- or short-landing. The heights of the car decks must be clearly marked on the Stowage Plans. As mentioned earlier, these heights can be adjusted only when movable car decks are fitted. Both the port of loading (POL) and port of discharge (POD) should also be indicated on the plan. Normally the loading and discharging ports are given by their codes. The table including these codes is usually available on board. If this is not the case, however, the Charterer must be asked for clarification. It is very important to mark clearly all packages and small parcels, because if they are overlooked there could be a real chance of short- or over-landing them. When high and heavy cargoes are involved, the situation is a little bit different.

It is strongly recommended that each unit be separately indicated on the plan. This procedure is more time-consuming but it has several advantages:

- The disposition of the cargo and its dimensions can be taken directly from the Stowage Plan, if, of course, the Stowage Plan is properly scaled. It will not be necessary to scrutinize the Cargo Manifest in order to get some information about the dimensions of the units in question.
- It will avoid short- or over-landing of the cargo.
- It will be much easier to obtain information on the free space, if any, in the cargo areas at the completion of loading.

Execution of the Loading Plan

There are established standards for the loading system in the hold, the distance between the vehicles, and the work procedure needed for the efficient cargo handling, the economic use of cargo space, and the prevention of damage. Before commencement of loading, a meeting with the stevedores must be held and all these standards and loading practices must be discussed.

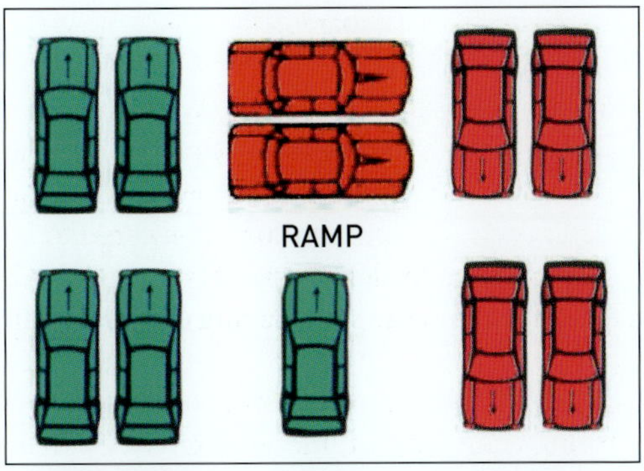

Clockwise system

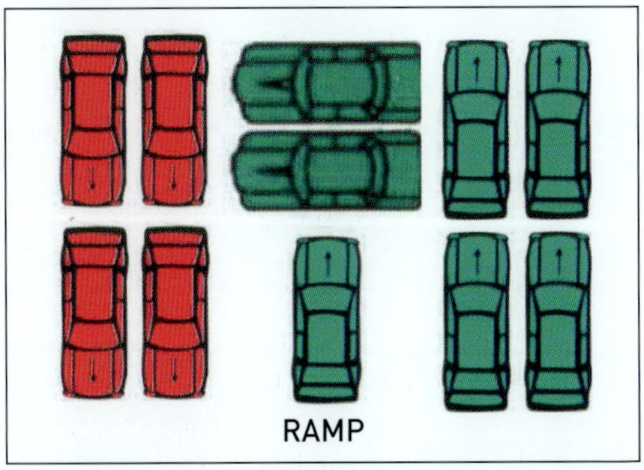

Counterclockwise system

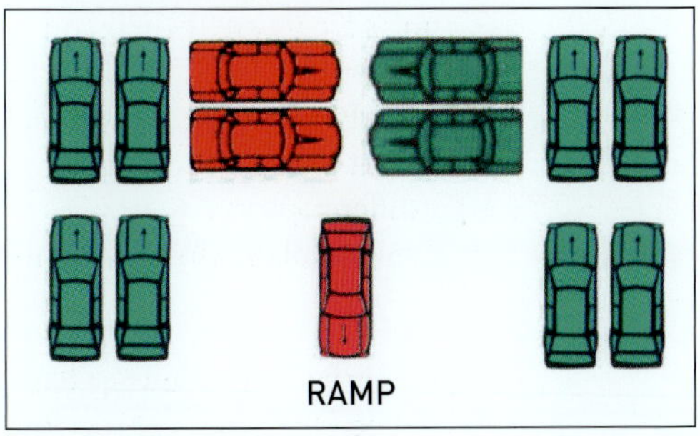

Head-out system

Vehicles can be run more easily with less damage when they are turned around the largest possible radius, when the driver can see obstructions from the driver's seat, and when the vehicle runs forward. There are three systems for loading of vehicles (cars) adopted worldwide, which will be discussed below. The strict adherence to one of them will guarantee safer cargo operations in loading and discharging ports, but it is not always possible to strictly adhere to one or another system. Depending on the hold arrangements, sometimes a combination of two of them, or even three, can facilitate the cargo operations significantly.

Clockwise system: This system is usually used for right-hand driven vehicles for export to UK, Australia, etc. When the cargo is being handled by this system the driver boards the vehicle from a passage on the driver's side and drives the vehicle forward clockwise so that the obstructions on the right side can be easily seen. By applying this system, the damage to the cargo can be reduced, as the efficiency of cargo handling operations will be increased.

Counterclockwise system: This system is used for left-hand driven vehicles for export to North America, Europe, etc. When the cargo is being handled by this system, the driver boards the vehicle from a passage on the driver's side and drives the vehicle forward so that the obstructions on the left side can easily be seen.

Head-out system: This system is used for vehicles for export to all places. All vehicles run forward directly towards the exit. This system is used in rather narrow spaces such as certain areas on the lower deck, where tight steering is required for discharging. It can be efficiently applied in spaces where it would be useless if the other systems were to be used.

Distance Between Vehicles

When the vehicles are being loaded and stowed, there must be some minimum distance between them. This is required for three main reasons:

- To avoid any contact between two neighboring vehicles in case of heavy rolling.
- To prevent the entering of vehicles during the sea passage.
- To allow lashing of already loaded vehicles and to allow lashing inspections during the voyage.

The different manufacturers of cars require different distances. During loading these distances should be observed by ship's crew. In case of any inconsistency, the Chief Officer must advise the stevedores.

At present the requirements are:

- Passage width: 40 cm minimum
- Longitudinal distance between the cars: 30 cm minimum

Transverse distance between the vehicles is another issue to be considered when preparing the Stowage Plan. Door-to-door or door-to-ship distance should be enough to avoid any contact between the cars when the ship encounters heavy rolling. At the same time, the transverse distance between the cars should be minimal to prevent the entering of cars by workers or ship's crew. Considering the above, the optimal distances door-to-door are estimated to be 10 cm minimum and door-to-ship distances are estimated to be 15 cm minimum. However, the specific requirements of any manufacturer concerning the distances should be respected.

During loading, some cars will be stowed close to the hold doors or hold emergency ladders. If this is the case, sufficient extra space is required in order to step in or out safely and to avoid any contact with the vehicles stowed in close proximity. The requirement for this extra space will vary, but generally the distance between the ladder or door and the car should be not less than 50 cm.

The distance between the vehicles and fire hoses must not be less than 50 cm. As required by SOLAS Ch. II-2, one water fog nozzle and one foam applicator must be located inside each car deck. The same 50 cm distance should be kept between the vehicles and water fog nozzles and between vehicles and foam applicators.

Another very important matter is the space around so-called "key" cars, which are the cars that will be discharged first from each hold or car deck. In order to facilitate discharging of that car, sufficient space around it must be left—50 cm minimum on driver's and passenger's sides.

The carriage of luxury cars requires more space around them.

All this information concerning the system for loading and the distance between the cars must be well discussed with the Stevedoring Company in order to facilitate the cargo operations in the loading port.

Loading the Vehicles

Preparation of Cargo Holds before Loading

Before commencement of loading operations, the ship's hold must be properly prepared. It is the responsibility of the Carrier under the Hague-Visby Rules Art. III Rule 1 to ensure suitably fit cargo holds. On car carriers, this means that the holds must be thoroughly cleaned to remove moisture, oil, salt, dust, etc. During the ballast voyage all holds must be checked for rusty areas and if found these areas must be cleaned and repainted in due time. All pillars inside the cargo holds must be properly protected with protectors and warning signs—reflective tiger stripe tape— must be positioned.

Clean and tidy holds

Pillars are protected against damage and marked with tiger-stripe tape

All lashings and chains not in use should be collected and arranged in the dedicated storage boxes. These boxes should be stowed in such a way that they do not obstruct cargo operations. They should be properly secured with chains, not lashings, because the lashings might break in heavy weather. The boxes should be stowed in one tier only, and should not be stacked two or three boxes high.

The sweeping of car decks is carried out by the so-called sweeping machine. These sweeping machines should be maintained as per manufacturer's instructions and should be properly secured when not in use.

The slip prevention on the ramps should also be inspected before loading the ship. Most of the ramps are coated with anti-slip paint, which is made by various manufacturers. This anti-slip paint contains small stones or sand. It is, therefore, very important for the ship's crew to ensure that all the small stones left from previous discharging are properly swept and removed. If some cars are scratched by such small stones during loading, it will give indisputably clear grounds for a claim against the ship.

Irrespective of the fact that this happens in the shipyard, the crew must ensure that all deck heights and deck numbers are properly stenciled where necessary. As mentioned earlier, the height clearance that is indicated could vary a little from the real one. The Chief Officer must be aware of the actual heights and bring this to the knowledge of the foreman.

In case of loading high and heavy cargoes, the liftable decks must be properly positioned well in advance in order to avoid any delays during cargo operations. However, it must be kept in mind that, depending on the rotation, this is not always possible. If there is cargo on the movable deck, this cargo must first be unloaded and then the deck lifted. If this is the case, the stevedores must be informed well in advance in order to avoid any consequent claims for idle time.

It is very important that safety ropes and cones properly indicate and protect any open ramps. There are many cases of cars falling from upper decks due to the lack of safety precautions. Needless to say, this unsafe practice is unacceptable and can lead to severe damage to the cargo and even to fatalities.

Lashing properly arranged

Correctly stowed lashings

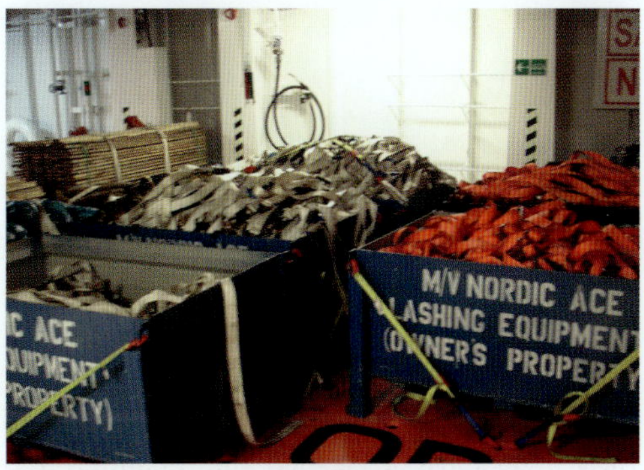

Incorrectly stowed lashings

Sweeping machine should be properly secured when not in use.

All lashing equipment must be properly arranged and ready for use.

During the ballast voyage, it is recommended that the lashings be inspected and the broken ones separated out. In all cases, the lashings must be inspected in accordance with the intervals stated in Cargo Securing Manual, and when such inspections are performed an appropriate entry in the manual must be made. Before commencement of loading, all fixed lashing terminals and securing devices must be inspected as well. If some are found defective or damaged they must be fixed or isolated from use until properly repaired. All lashings should be supplied with the appropriate certificates.

All pipelines and cable ducts should be checked for rust leakages. It is good practice to have rags and sawdust ready in each cargo hold for use in case of any oil leakage from cars. It is very important to take all precautionary measures in order to avoid having stevedores slip during cargo operations, because slip falls could result in exorbitant claims being filed against the ship. For the same reason, this also applies to damage to the cargo.

Fire extinguishing devices should be provided in accordance with the relevant regulations and "NO SMOKING" signs should be posted.

A safe passage must be established using safety railings and ropes when the ramp is lowered down. It is not uncommon for the stevedores to insist that the safe passage be dismantled in order to facilitate cargo operations. In no case should the ship's management agree with this; if they do, in case of any incident or accident, the ship will be considered guilty for not complying with safety regulations.

Safe passage on the ramps is of utmost importance.

Preparation for Cargo Handling

Preparing for cargo handling should start with a pre-operation meeting with the stevedores. During this meeting the loading method and accident prevention counter-measures should be discussed. The stevedores must be informed about the following:

- driving speed
- non-smoking policy adopted on board inside cargo holds
- peculiarities about the heights of the decks
- working load
- distances between the cars
- safety precautions when opening and closing inner ramps
- any other issues particular to the ship or cargo

As part of a safety management system adopted by the Company there must be a checklist that should be used for such meetings. This checklist must be duly ticked when the respective item has been discussed. As a confirmation that the stevedores have been informed about safety issues concerning the cargo operations the foreman must sign this checklist. It is imperative that this meeting is held before commencement of cargo operations; the Chief Officer should not allow commencement of cargo operations before the meeting had been held.

Ventilation inside the cargo holds in operation must be started and the fire detection system must be turned off.

Accepting Vehicles for Transportation

Before accepting vehicles on board the ship's management must ensure that the vehicles are suitable for transportation by sea.

We have been talking about "vehicles" without defining the term. In *Roll-on/Roll-off Ships—Stowage and Securing of Vehicles*, "Code of Practice," vehicle is defined as "vehicle with wheels or a track laying vehicle." In the same publication "freight vehicle" is defined as "a vehicle which is a goods vehicle, flat bed trailer, road train, articulated train, combination of freight vehicles, or a tank vehicle." This definition coincides with the definition for road vehicle in Res. A. 518(14), "Guidelines for securing arrangements for the transport of road vehicles on Ro-Ro ships," incorporated in the "Code of Safe Practice for Cargo Stowage and Securing,"which includes commercial vehicles, semi-trailers, road-trains, articulated road trains, and combination of vehicles as road vehicles. This resolution does not apply for buses.

"Tank vehicle" is defined as "a vehicle fitted with a tank, which is rigidly and permanently attached to the vehicle during all normal operations of loading, discharging and transport and is neither fitted nor discharged on board and is driven on board by its own wheels."

"Semi-trailer" is defined as a "trailer, which is designed to be coupled to a semi-trailer towing vehicle and to impose a substantial part of its total weight on the towing vehicle."

Saying that a vehicle is suitable for transportation by sea means that it has the appropriate securing devices and adequate strength to withstand the rigors of the voyage, and that the cargo on the vehicle (if any) will not shift during the voyage. In addition, there must be a proof that the vehicles have been examined and searched as per the requirements of ISPS Code, which requires that at least 3–10% in Level 1 have been searched by shore representatives before being loaded on board. The ship's management must be given this proof in writing either as a declaration or in another appropriate document.

The following requirements must be complied with when evaluating the fitness of the cargo for sea transportation:

- Normally passenger cars are considered fit for sea transportation if they are not totally destroyed or can be properly secured. If they cannot be properly secured, they are considered as unfit for sea transportation.
- The vehicles should be free of any defects that could affect their structural strength and must be provided with an effective braking system.
- If the car is damaged in such a way that there is severe leakage of oil and if this leakage could jeopardize the other cars in close proximity, the car(s) can be rejected for sea transportation.

Trailers and high and heavy cargoes are more dangerous for sea transportation and their suitability is more difficult to assess. In all cases, if there is cargo on the vehicle, it must be properly stowed and secured in such a way that it will not move during the voyage. If there is any machinery on flat bed trailers, it must be secured not only to the trailer but also to the deck. There must be a suitable number of suitable securing points on the cargo to allow this. If there are pallets, they must be properly secured to the trailer, but also to the deck. In addition, they must be properly chocked.

Occasionally so-called curtain-sided trailers are delivered for sea transportation. The cargo inside must be properly secured to the trailer (but not to the curtains) and properly chocked. It must be borne in mind that the curtains are not designed to secure the cargo but to protect it from adverse weather, like rain and snow.

When a semi-trailer is shipped without a truck-master or tractor unit, it must be supported on its front end by a trestle placed below the chassis close to the rear of the draw plate. This area of the chassis must be suitably re-enforced and clearly marked. If it is necessary to jack-up the chassis at the axles, these jacking-up points must be suitably strengthened.

Freight vehicles that are to be transported must be provided with documentation indicating their gross weight and any precautions that may need to be observed during sea transport

If dangerous goods are to be transported as a cargo on vehicle, they must be fully declared as required by SOLAS Chapter VII Reg. 4. The dangerous goods placards required for sea transport should be clearly visible on the outside of the vehicle and affixed in accordance with IMDG Code. When stowing and securing the cargo, the appropriate Codes must be strictly followed.

If some of the provisions mentioned in the list above (which is not to be considered exhaustive) are not in compliance, the Master can use his discretion to decide to reject non-compliant cargo. This should be done, however, with utmost attention and only if the Master has taken into consideration all negative consequences that could arise if he accepts the cargo. The Master must always remember that the cargo is paying his salary and that rejecting the cargo is always against the Company's interests. Nevertheless, if the Master considers that any particular cargo might put the safety of the ship, crew, and cargo at risk, he must not hesitate to reject this cargo.

Loading Vehicles

Having prepared the cargo compartments and accepted or rejected particular units, the cargo operations can start. Car carriers are loaded and discharged by the so-called roll-on/roll-off technique. This technique involves handling the cargo onto or off a ship primarily by horizontal movement.

It was mentioned earlier that the calculations for assessing the nose striking, rear striking, bottom striking, and top striking should be performed during the preliminary survey. This is an important procedure because during the loading, as statistics show, most damage occurs in the vicinity of the ramps. Therefore, attention should be paid to prevent the vehicle from striking its nose or rear near the base of the ramp, or from striking its bottom or top near the top of the ramp.

The maximum permissible working load of the ramps must be strictly followed. Considering that this load may vary from 70 to 300 metric tons (tonnes) and more, this is not a problem for the passenger cars, but it could become a problem in case of loading very heavy units, such as power plants, etc.

During loading, a sufficient distance between the vehicles should be kept. The maximum allowed speed on board must not exceed 20 km/h (12 mph). It is an obligation of the ship's management to strictly observe this and not allow higher speeds. Additionally, the speed must be reduced when approaching ramps or curves. The loading time of a car carrier is dependent upon the time taken to maneuver, stow, and secure the vehicles, but the speed at which the vehicles can complete their cycle depends on several factors, including:

- the gradient of each ramp and its width
- the bends, turns, and blind sectors to be negotiated
- the "vehicle envelope"
- the change of gradient of the ramps
- the traffic flow

The angle of the ramps is of great importance for smooth cargo handling. Unlike typical Ro-Ro or Ro-Pax ships, car carriers have larger and heavier ramps and when these ramps are lowered they are not horizontal but at some angle to the horizontal surface. The steeper the slope of the ramp, the more difficult cargo handling will be. Most of the ramps can be adjusted depending on the height of the quay and special buttress cylinders can achieve this adjustment. In addition, most of the ramps are restricted in their maximum angle of slope (up to 10°–13°). It must be borne in mind that, even if the slope does not prevent the loading of a normal passenger car, it may be prohibitive for high and heavy units, especially those that are being towed, such as trailers, etc. Therefore a reasonable angle of slope must be achieved by proper trimming astern. The ramps must be adjusted in such a way that they have the least gradient possible.

The "vehicle envelope" is the total space required by the whole vehicle and its load as it negotiates a change in gradient without fouling any obstructions above.

If too steep, a change of slope can cause the grounding of the vehicle. The equations for striking must be calculated in order to have clear view of the situation and to avoid any structural damage either to the ramps or the cargo.

It must be kept in mind that extreme tidal ranges in some ports may affect the slope of the ramp, which may cause cargo operations to be postponed and will entail negative consequences for the ship. It is very important that preliminary calculations for the slope are made when visiting such ports and sent to the stevedores in order to facilitate cargo operations.

During loading, all headlights of the cars must be on before driving into the hold. As a rule, sudden starts, stops, or turns must not be performed. Normally the cars should be driven into the cargo hold forward. In cases when the cargo hold is nearly full, the cars will be driven rear first in order to facilitate unloading. Personnel working inside car decks should wear suitable personal protective equipment, including high visibility garments as determined by a risk assessment. Where personnel are working in shadow areas, hand lamps and flashlights should be available for use.

Stowage of Vehicles on Board

As the cargo is being loaded, it must be stowed inside cargo holds. As a rule, the drivers just bring the cars inside the car decks and then the cars are stowed by stowing drivers. The relative expertise of the stowing drivers can either accelerate or delay cargo operations. If the labor is temporarily employed, as it is the case during holidays or summer season, the ship's management must be very vigilant for any damage, even the smallest incident, because these drivers are not as experienced in stowing cars on board. Special traffic guides should be posted to provide guidance by making clear signals by whistles, hands, etc.

Stowing of the vehicles can be performed in one of the three systems described earlier—clockwise, counterclockwise, or head-on—depending on the country of export. In all cases, the stowing should be conducted in such way that the front bumpers of vehicles are aligned, leaving the necessary space for lashing, unlashing, and lashing inspections. When the vehicles are of different lengths, they must be lined up in such a way that the front bumpers are aligned.

The hand brake or emergency brake should be fully engaged; this must be checked by ship's personnel for every car, as the hand or emergency brake can prevent the cargo from moving. For automatic transmissions, the gear must be in the park position; for manual transmissions it must be in a low gear or neutral. The tires must be positioned straight ahead. The windows must be rolled up completely upon completion of stowing. All headlights must be off.

It is advisable that the traffic guide opens and closes the driver's door when the vehicle has been stowed. The doors must not be locked. Car keys must be affixed at required places. The distances between the cars, as discussed earlier, must be strictly observed. It is absolutely prohibited to climb or sit on the vehicle, to place articles on the vehicle, to place elbows or hands on the vehicle, to lean against the vehicle, to tap the vehicle, etc., because it can damage the vehicle, entailing all negative consequences against the ship. Smoking is absolutely prohibited inside cargo holds.

Very often it is necessary to refill gasoline. In normal circumstances the problematic car must be towed outside, refilled and then driven back on board, but on some occasions it must be done on board. Irrespective of the fact that this is against the rules and must be avoided, it can be allowed only when all safety precautions have been taken and an appropriate risk assessment has been carried out, including the availability of fire extinguishers of powder or CO_2 type in the vicinity.

The stowage of the vehicles must be performed as stated in the Cargo Securing Manual. The road vehicle must be stowed in such a way that its chassis is kept as static as possible, thus not allowing free play in the suspension of the vehicle. This can be done by compressing the springs, by securing the vehicles to the deck, or by releasing the air pressure on compressed air suspension systems. On voyages, longer than twenty-four hours, the air pressure must be released. If practicable, the air pressure also should be released on shorter voyages.

When vehicles are stowed athwartships, special consideration should be paid to the forces and accelerations that may arise from such stowage.

When vehicles are stowed on inner ramps or an inclined deck, the wheels must be chocked before lashing commences.

Where jacks are used on a vehicle, the chassis should be strengthened around the jacking-up points and the position of the jacking-up points should be clearly marked.

Semi-trailers should not be supported on their landing legs during sea transport unless the landing legs are specially designed for that purpose and so marked. An uncoupled semi-trailer should be supported by a trestle or similar device placed in the immediate area of the drawplate so that the connection of the fifth wheel to the kingpin is not restricted.

When loading cars on inner ramps, vehicles should be stowed head-down when loaded above the main deck to which the stern ramp is affixed, and should be stowed head-up when loaded below the main deck.

The cars stowed near the sides of the cargo hold should be at least 50 cm distant off the sides. When opening the doors of such cars, special attention is required and very often special soft pads are fitted to the sides in order to prevent damage to the door.

Soft pads are often attached to the sides of cargo holds.

Safe passage should be left unobstructed.

Irrespective of the type of the cargo being stowed, all passages leading to the pilot doors must be kept clear. These passages are normally clearly painted and marked "Do not obstruct." Due to the length of the cargo, these passages can sometimes be obstructed. In this case, an alternative passage between the cars must be left. It must be borne in mind that, in some countries, pilots are very sensitive about this matter and they can even refuse to pilot the ship, creating negative consequences as a result.

Discharging

The cargo should be delivered at the discharging port in the same condition as it was loaded, so exercising due diligence during the discharge operations is very important. Most damage to the cargo is caused during discharging due to either high speed or lack of care from the stevedores' side. Therefore, special attention is always required from the ship's crew during this part of the voyage. The following should be discussed with the crew before commencement of discharging:

- the cargo decks and holds to be discharged in the particular port
- the number of units to be discharged
- peculiarities of the cargo to be discharged
- safety measures to be observed during discharging, such as smoking, high speed, fencing the opening with railings, operation of the ramps, etc.

In most ports, the cargo is unlashed by the stevedores upon berthing of the ship. If, however, it is required that the crew unlash the cargo, it should be done with utmost attention in order to avoid any damage to the cars. In all cases, the unlashing should be executed after the ship is berthed, as small impacts of the ship against the berth may cause the cargo to shift, which may result in damage.

Before commencement of discharging a pre-discharge meeting with the stevedores should be held and all safety aspects for smooth discharging should be brought to the attention of the stevedores. During this pre-discharge meeting the discharge planning should be discussed and a so-called "flow chart" (See chapter 12, Documents) should be ticked off.

During discharging all safety precautions should be strictly followed. Wearing reflective vests, safety shoes, and clean overalls gives a good impression to the shore laborers. A driving speed of 20 km/h (12 mph) should be respected during discharging.

Sawdust and rags should be deployed on car decks being discharged; in case of oil leakage from vehicles, these should be used for cleaning. It should be borne in mind that any injury to the stevedores due to oil slicks will be the ship's responsibility and will give rise to unpleasant claims against the ship.

Stalled cars should be towed off by special service cars or forklifts and not by cars that are part of the cargo. In no case should the cargo be used by the stevedores as taxi cars.

During opening and closing of internal ramps, the ship's crew must make sure that all safety precautions have been taken. The slopes of the ramps should be adjusted properly. All openings should be properly surrounded by railings and marked by safety cones.

The ventilation should be operating continuously in the "Port" mode. Fire detection systems should be disconnected, but when no cargo operations are being carried out they should be switched on at once.

If cars need a jump-start, the crew should take all safety precautions. As a rule, such cars should be towed off by a service car. In order to facilitate cargo operations, however, they can sometimes be started on board. In such cases, extra fire extinguishers should be deployed and all anti-fire precautions taken.

Upon completion of cargo operations the following should be checked:

- **Cargo discharged**: the total number of units and respective weight
- **Over-landing or short-landing of the cargo, using the appropriate checklist.** It is not uncommon for some cars to be over-landed or short-landed, which perhaps will give rise to claims against the Carrier at a later time. Upon completion of every cargo compartment, the cargo discharged should be crosschecked against the Stowage Plan. If cargo for more than one port is loaded on one car deck appropriate separation should be made.
- **Checking and signing the time sheet and/or Statement of Facts if necessary** (See chapter 12, Documents)
- **Issuing an Outturn Report for the cargo discharged** (See chapter 12, Documents)

During cargo operations all safety precautions should be taken. It is worth stressing once again that the cargo is paying the salary of the crew and therefore the crew should exercise due diligence, not only because this is expected by the Hague Rules, but also because safe transport of the cargo will improve safety for the crew, ship, and shore laborers and will add to the economic viability of the transport operations.

CHAPTER 5

LASHING MATERIALS

Loading and Securing Cargo

Lashing materials for securing the cargo are important for the safe and effective transportation of vehicles at sea. Taking into account the size of present car carriers and, especially, their height, it is necessary to examine the stress on vehicles due to anticipated vibrations and to provide adequate lashing to prevent vehicles from moving. The tendency of the cargo to slide or tip over depends on its size and shape, the position of the center of gravity, and the coefficient of friction between the cargo and the deck. There are many types of lashing equipment and many different types of dunnaging material available; it is an obligation of the responsible officer to choose the appropriate material for securing the vehicles properly and increasing the friction between the cargo and deck.

Securing Vehicles

Properly securing the cargo is one of the most important tasks that must be conducted before departure, as required by SOLAS chapter VI Reg. 5 (6). The cargo must be secured in the most appropriate way necessary to avoid any movement or shifting during the passage, even if the ship encounters boisterous weather. The movement of the cargo during the voyage can result from the ship's movements: rolling, pitching, yawing, swaying, surging, and heaving. It is not the subject of this book to elaborate on these movements, but for the purpose of explanation of the forces acting on the cargo some aspects of them must be highlighted.

Roll, pitch, and **yaw** are *rotational movements*; **sway, surge,** and **heave** are the *linear movements*. During a voyage, the ship experiences all six movements, but some of them may be stronger or weaker depending on weather conditions, wind, and sea. Considering their short, parallel body form, the impact of these movements are even stronger for car carriers. Depending on the area exposed to the wind, if it is comparatively strong and is blowing abeam, the ship will roll rather than pitch. If the wind is blowing from dead ahead or astern or from the port or starboard quarter, the ship will pitch rather than roll. Depending on the force of the wind, if the wind and sea are from the port or starboard quarter (the worst scenario for car carriers), the ship will roll and pitch heavily. In all cases, these movements of the ship combine to create three forces acting in three dimensions: vertical, athwart ship, and longitudinal.

The strength of these forces depends on the condition of the ship, i.e., her metacentric height (GMo), her dimensions, and, of course, the force of the weather conditions. If the ship is **stiff** (high GMo), the forces will be more severe and the respective accelerations will be larger. This could result in the unpredictable movement of the cargo with all the serious consequences and damages that result. If the ship is **tender** (small GMo), the forces will not be as strong but the issue of ship stability will become the primary concern. The larger the ship is, the smaller the accelerations will be.

These forces act throughout the ship and affect everything on board, including the cargo. However, they act on different parts of the ship with different power and the accelerations created will be different in force in different parts of the ship. It must be remembered that the acceleration forces act upon cargo units and they increase or decrease as the ship rolls and/or pitches in one direction and then in the other. This means that the accelerations are changing their force and direction constantly. These accelerations are transferred from the ship's structure through the lashings, the chocking, and the dunnage under the cargo. As long as the securing lashings are strong enough to counteract these accelerations the cargo will not move relative to the ship and the lashings.

Where are the strongest accelerations to be expected? As a rule, *the farther the cargo is from the center of motion, the larger the accelerations will be,* which means that *the closer the cargo is to the center of motion, the less vulnerable to the accelerations it will be.* To calculate the center of motion is a very difficult, even impossible, task. For the purpose of proper securing of the cargo, therefore, it is enough to place it as near to the center of gravity of the ship as possible, this latter being calculated precisely during the stability calculations.

Applying this to car carriers, we can conclude that the most severe accelerations acting upon the cars will be on the higher car decks and in the fore and aft part of each car deck. During the distribution of the vehicles on board for loading, therefore, it is necessary to assess the advisability of putting a vehicle (especially a heavier one) at some specific place on the car deck.

The position of the cargo on board also must be taken into account when considering the method and materials for lashing and securing it. In addition, the maximum permissible load (MPL) and the possibility for proper securing of the vehicle at a particular place must be taken into account.

Forces Acting on the Cargo during Sea Passage

In car carriers (being ships with large area exposed to the wind), two different forces will act on the cargo and on the securing devices: inertia and gravity. When the ship encounters heavy seas, she and her cargo will be affected by the six motions discussed earlier, which will cause dramatic shifts in inertia and gravity. When the ship takes a list at angle Θ, the gravitational force is experienced in two ways: $\mathbf{F_T}$ [the force acting athwart and causing the cargo to slide] and $\mathbf{F_V}$ [the force acting in vertical direction].

Frictional braking power: R. This is the power preventing the cargo from sliding due to the friction with the deck. In general this power can be derived from the following formula:

$$\mathbf{R = W \times \cos\Theta \times K} \quad [1]$$

Where:

K = friction coefficient

Θ = the angle of slope caused by the movement of the ship, generally by pitching

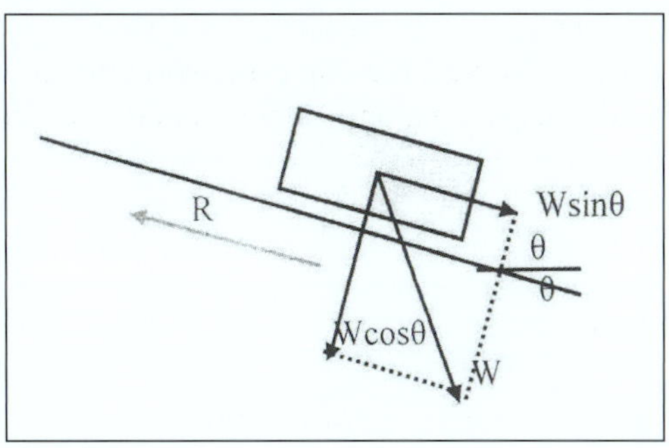

Forces

When the ship is rolling, pitching and heaving, $F_V = W \times \cos\Theta$. Thus we can derive from the following formula for R:

$$\mathbf{R = F_V \times K} \quad [2]$$

When the ship reaches her extreme value of list to either side due to rolling, she will start moving to the opposite side. At the moment of the largest angle of list, the cargo will be affected by the force of inertia (I):

$$\mathbf{I = m \times g}$$

Where:
m = mass of the vehicle/cargo
g = 9.81 m/sec^2

The direction of this force is the tangent to the movement of the cargo around the center of gravity of the ship (**G**). The force **I** can be expanded to $\mathbf{I_A}$ [acting athwartship and causing the cargo to slide to the lower side (if the cargo is not properly secured, of course)] and $\mathbf{I_V}$ [acting in vertical direction]. The values of these two forces can be expressed by the following formulas:

$$I_A = \frac{\mathbf{W \times h \times \Theta}}{\mathbf{15 \times T_R^2}} \quad [3]$$

$$I_V = \frac{\mathbf{W \times b \times \Theta}}{\mathbf{15 \times T_R^2}} \quad [4]$$

Where:
W = weight of the car
h = height of the car
b = breadth of the car
$\mathbf{T_R}$ = rolling period

To the force of inertia due to the rolling we can add the force of inertia due to the heaving of the ship. The latter has its maximum when the ship is at the top or the bottom of the wave. The respective values can be written down as:

When the ship is on top:

$$I_A{}' = \frac{\mathbf{W \times H_W \times \Theta}}{\mathbf{30 \times T_H^2}} \quad [5]$$

When the ship is on bottom:

$$I_V{}' = \frac{\mathbf{W \times H_W \times \cos\Theta}}{\mathbf{T_H^2}} \quad [6]$$

Where:
$\mathbf{H_W}$ = height of the wave
$\mathbf{T_W}$ = heaving period

The force of inertia greatly increases when the rolling period decreases (see [3] and [4]).

$\mathbf{I_A}$ depends on the distance between the center of gravity of the vehicle/cargo and center of gravity of the ship. If the vehicle/cargo is below the center of the gravity of the ship, then $\mathbf{I_A}$ will be directed toward higher side of the ship. The sum of the forces that are affecting the cargo and causing it to slide will be different for different car decks. The higher the car deck, the higher is the risk of the cargo sliding. In the same way, the lower the car deck (and respectively the cargo), the lower the risk of sliding because the two forces, the inertial force acting athwartship [$\mathbf{I_A}$] and displacing force acting in the athwartship direction [$\mathbf{F_T}$] partly compensate for each other.

Lashing Materials

Breaking Load

One very important issue that should be taken into account when it comes to lashings is their strength.

Normally lashings are (or should be) marked with their breaking load (BL), which is the maximum load the lashings can handle before they are no longer effective. In other words, this is the load for which the lashing is designed.

In the practice, however, the term "maximum securing load" (MSL) is widely used. This represents the strength of a lashing device as a percentage of the breaking load.

The Code of Safe Practice for Cargo Stowage and Securing (CSS Code) requires all securing equipment to be supplied with their nominal BL (breaking load) in kilo-newtons (Kn=102 kgf [kilogram force]=0.1124 tnf [ton-force]) [Refer to the CSS Code, Annex 13, Para. 4]. The same Para 4.2 of the CSS Code indicates that MSL (maximum securing load) is to be used as allowable load capacity of a device for securing cargo on board. In a table, being part of the same paragraph, the MSL of different materials is given as determined from their breaking load. For webbing lashings, the MSL is 50% of their breaking strength, as it is for chains. The SWL (safe working load) may be substituted for MSL for securing purposes, provided this is equal to or exceeds the strength defined by MSL.

The standard EN 12195–1:2000 for the European Union came into force in 2000, and provided a definition for the lashing capacity (LC). The LC is the strength of a lashing device as a percentage of the breaking load, a synonym therefore of the MSL.

This ratio between the BL and the LC (or MSL) is called the **safety factor**. Using the webbing lashing described above, for example, if lashing has a BL of 10.0 metric tons, its MSL (LC) is 5.0 metric tons. The safety factor, then, is 2. When lashings for specific cargoes are being selected, these factors must be taken into account.

Once the vehicles have been loaded and stowed they should be properly lashed. There is a variety of lashings available for securing the cargo on board. However, the lashings for the vehicles on board car carriers and Ro-Ro ships can be divided into the categories that follow.

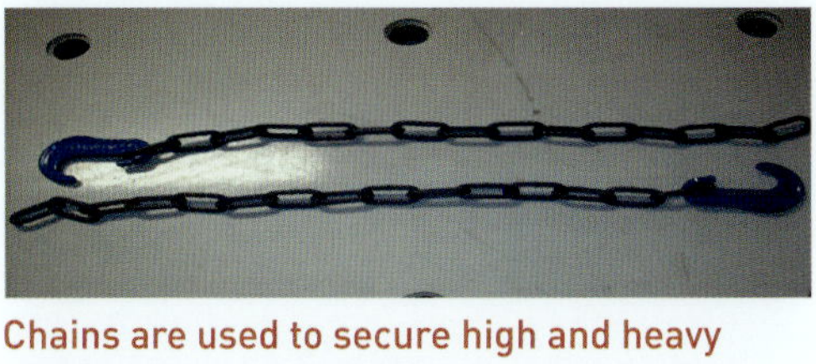

Chains are used to secure high and heavy cargo such as excavators and trailers. There is a variety of chains broadly used on board car carriers and Ro-Ro ships but generally the set of chain consists of: chain, tensioner, and extension handle for the tensioner.

13 mm: SWL = 10.0 t; MBL = 20.0 t
11 mm: SWL = 7.5 t; MBL = 15.0 t

Chains

Chains used for securing vehicles on board Ro-Ro ships are made of high-tensile steel. They can be either long-linked or short-linked. Both of these can use lever tighteners (shorteners). Manufacturers are obliged to supply the vessel with details of breaking strengths of the chains.

The CSS Code stipulates that the MSL of the chains is 50% of their BL. The chains can be 9, 11, or 13 mm, which is the measure of the diameter of the metal in the links. The BL of standard long-link chain of 13 mm is 20.0 metric tons (tonnes).

The high tensile, short-link chains are available in several grades with different characteristics. The chains are generally used for securing heavy units such as excavators, tractors, trailers, etc.

The main advantage of chains is that they do not stretch, though it must be remembered that the cargo can move slightly during the voyage, especially if the ship encounters boisterous weather, and this movement can cause the chains to slacken. When necessary, the chains can be tightened and slackened by tensioner, which often involves the use of extension handles.

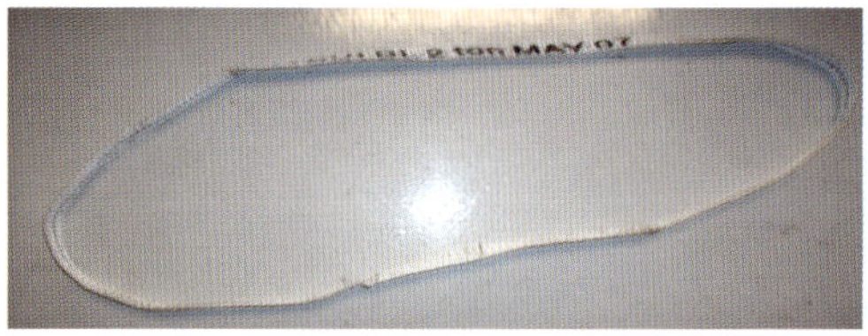

Soft sling. There is a variety of soft slings used for attaching hooks to the vehicles and their LC can vary. They should be light, flexible, moisture-resistant, and made of long-life strap material (normally produced from polyester). They should correspond to EN 1492-1.·

Chains are awkward to handle and require at least two persons in order to be applied and tightened correctly. The chains can be secured directly to the vehicle or can be used in connection with heavy-duty lashing slings. These slings act as shock absorbers and can minimize damage to the cargo attributed to the use of chains. However, it should be remembered that the lashing system will be no stronger than its weakest component, namely the sling. Lashing chains should be discarded if they have visible deformations, if their elongation exceeds 3%, or if the wear exceeds 10% of the nominal diameter.

Belt-Type Lashings (Claspers)

Belt-type lashings are generally used for securing cars with different breaking loads. They are made of polypropylene, polyamide, or polyester, and consist of a tensioning device, end fittings, and a textile strap. The tensioning device is a ratchet. The end fittings are usually coated hooks, designed to prevent damage to the cargo. Claspers are designed primarily for passenger cars and their breaking loads vary. In Europe, these lashings should comply with standard EN 12195. They should be light and flexible, moisture-resistant, and made of long-life strap material. The lashings should be suitable for use in the temperature ranges from –40°C to +120°C. These ranges may vary in a chemical environment. Polyester is resistant to most mineral acids, but is not resistant against alkalies. In case of contact with chemicals, the lashing should be removed from service.

Irrespective of the type of the lashing materials, they should be properly marked with their BL. When cargo-securing devices are designed, the IMO recommends the following accelerations to be taken into account:

Sea Area	Sideways	Lengthwise
Baltic Sea	0.5 x g	0.3 x g in combination with 1 ± 0.5 x g vertically
North Sea	0.7 x g	0.3 x g in combination with 1 ± 0.7 x g vertically
Unrestricted	0.8 x g	0.4 x g in combination with 1 ± 0.8 x g vertically

Web Lashings

Web lashing is a load restraint assembly consisting of a tensioning device, end fittings, and flat, woven textile webbing. The tensioning device can be either a ratchet or a buckle. The ratchet is a tensioning device that is used to engage the tension force in web lashings using hand-operated force applied with a handle. The buckle is a tensioning device, in which the tension force is applied by pulling the webbing. The end fittings are usually hooks of various types. Webbing lashings are generally manufactured from impregnated woven polyester, polyamide, and polypropylene fibers.

Web lashings have good stretch characteristics and sustain a pre-tension of up to 40% of their maximum securing load (MSL). According to the CSS, the maximum securing load (MSL) of web lashings is 50% of their breaking load. As a golden rule, the user should remember that web lashings that are not marked with the breaking load and applicability should never be used for securing vehicles.

When web lashing is used to secure pallets or cargo on trailers, protective sleeves or edges should be used in areas where the lashing passes over metal parts or where sharp edges pose the risk of cutting the webbing.

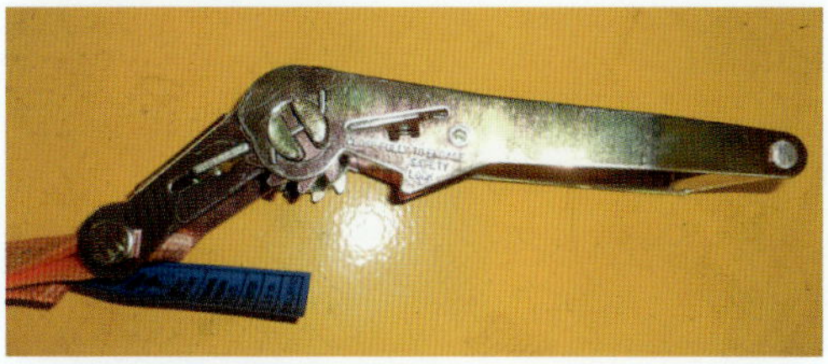

Tensioning device detail

Various web lashings widely used in Ro-Ro practice are shown here.

For tightening of this type of lashing, hand ratchets are used. It should be remembered that a spanner/wrench or bar must never be used to tighten a hand-powered ratchet tensioner due to the risk of personal injury. Only the maximum hand force of 500 N (50 daN on the label; 1 daN = 1kg) should be applied. This force is known as "standard hand force"(SHF) as defined by EN 12195–2 (European Standard for synthetic web lashings). As a tension indicator is usually not available, the tension force can be roughly estimated by applying the following rule: applying SHF of 50 daN to the ratchet must produce a minimum of 10% of the MSL. This tension usually disappears quickly if the web lashings are strained up to their MSL because of the vessel's motion, so regular retightening is required.

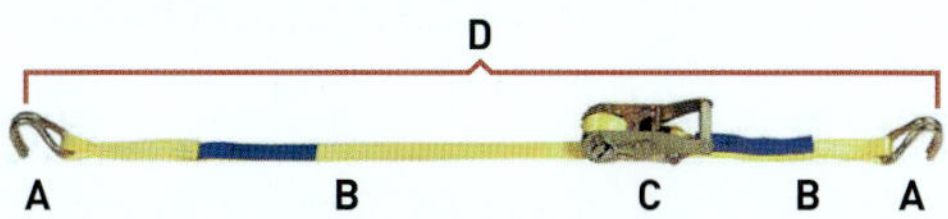

The main parts of web lashing:

A: End fittings (hooks). One end is attached to the vehicle and the other to the fixed securing terminal.

B: Webbing. It can be made of impregnated woven polyester, polyamide, and polypropylene fibers

C: Tensioning device (ratchet/buckle)

D: Assembly

Trailer web lashing: SWL = 5.0 t; MBL = 10.00 t
Length: 4.0 m

Some ratchets are fitted with tension force indicator. This device allows the operator to check the amount of tension applied to the load. It also enables the operator to check that the tension has not released during the transport due to the load settling or elongation of the webbing. *(Courtesy: Span Set)*

Trailer lashing: SWL = 10 t; MBL = 20 t
Length: 3.0 m *(Courtesy: LoadLok)*

Car lashing: SWL = 0.75 t; MBL = 1.5 t
Length: 200 mm
Width: 25 mm
(Courtesy: LoadLok)

Car lashing: SWL = 1.0 t; MBL = 2.0 t
Length: 200 mm **Width:** 25 mm
(Courtesy: LoadLok)

Car lashing: SWL = 0.75 t; MBL = 1.5 t
Length: 300 mm **Width:** 25 mm
(Courtesy: LoadLok)

Van lashing: SWL =2.5 t; MBL = 5 t
Length: 300 mm **Width:** 50 mm
(Courtesy: LoadLok)

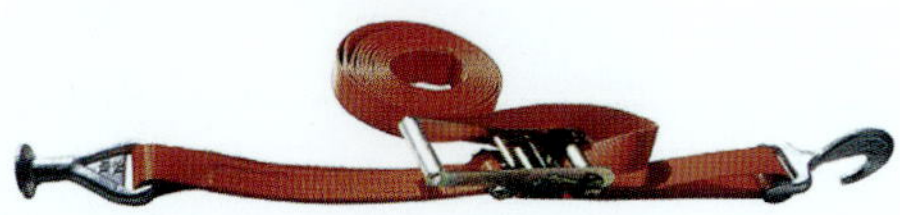

Trailer lashing: SWL = 6.0 t; MBL = 12.0 t
Length: 3.0 m
(Courtesy: LoadLok)

Inspection of Lashing Materials

Securing devices, including movable devices such as lashings, chains, and belts, should be checked periodically by the crew and replaced or withdrawn from service if they are found to be damaged. Lashings with visible signs of tears, cuts, nicks, and breaks in load-bearing fibers and retaining stitches should be removed from service. Lashings that are tie-knotted should never be used.

Deformations of tensioning devices and end fittings should be repaired as soon as possible and the respective lashing should be removed from service until the repair is completed.

The fixed securing devices should be examined as well and should be repaired in due time if they are not fit for duty.

Ro-Ro Equipment

Trailer horse (trestle): SWL = 50.0 t; MBL = 100.0 t.
Material: Steel, galvanized.
Dimensions: variable, depending on the manufacturer but generally: length: 1600 mm; width: 660 mm; height:1250 mmè

Trailer Horse (Trestle). A trestle is used for trailers and is positioned at the forward part of the trailer in order to ensure stability during the voyage. The trestles are of various BL and dimensions. They are made of galvanized steel.

Chocks. Chocks are used for cars as well as trailers, buses, etc. They are put under the tires to restrain any movement of the vehicle during the voyage. They can be made of plastic or rubber, the latter being more effective. The chocks can be either straight or curved.

Chocks

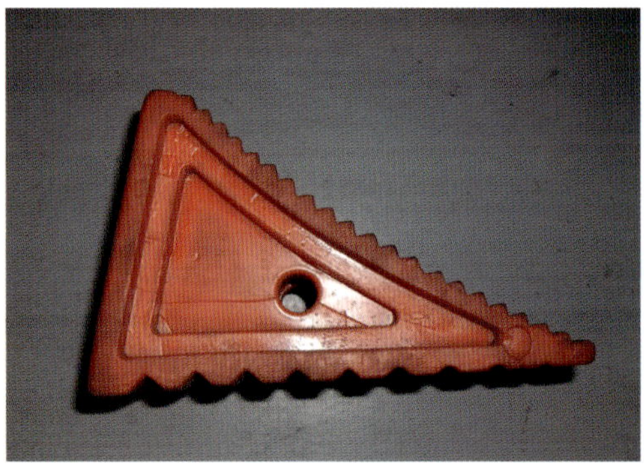

Chocks

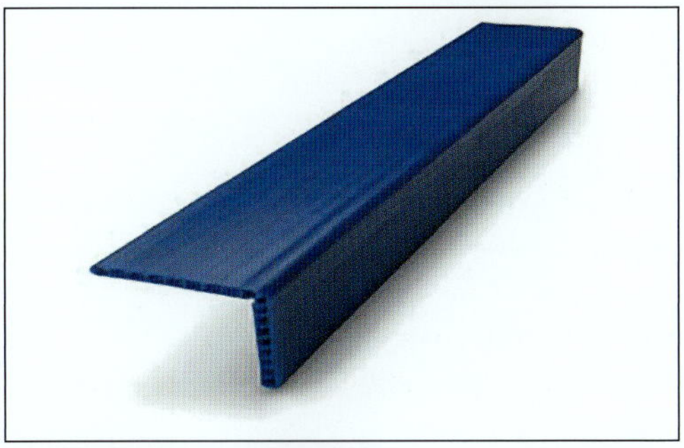

Edge protector profile

Protective sleeves

Trailer jack. MBL varies, but is usually about 30 t.
Height: 950–1350 mm
Weight: 35 kg

Storage Bins for Lashings. Storage bins are made of metal and used for collecting chains and web lashings.

Edge Protector Profile. These long, angular pieces are manufactured from polypropylene to protect edges of cargo, such as pallets, timber material on trailers, etc., and to avoid chafing damage that may lead to premature decay or degradation and result in failure. Dimensions can be adjusted by cutting.

Protective Sleeves. Made of resistant polyurethane, rubber, or polyester, they are used to protect the lashings against friction, abrasion, and damage from loads with sharp edges.

Trailer Jack. The trailer jack is made of galvanized steel. Its MBL varies, but is usually about 30–50 metric tons (tonnes). Dimensions and weight may vary. The trailer jack is placed under the roll trailers with cargo with total weight more than 30 metric tons (tonnes), as an extra support.

Fixed Securing Devices. As mentioned earlier, apart from lashing materials the ship must be equipped with fixed securing devices or lashing terminals. These devices should comply with international standard breaking loads. In general, the distance between the fixed securing points in fore-and-aft direction on Ro-Ro ships should not exceed 2.5 meters. Considering the increased accelerations in the forward and aft part of car decks, however, the distance between the fixed securing devices there should be decreased. The athwart ship distance between the fixed securing devices should not be less than 2.8 meters, but not more than 3.0 meters. There is variety of fixed securing devices but the most commonly seen types follow.

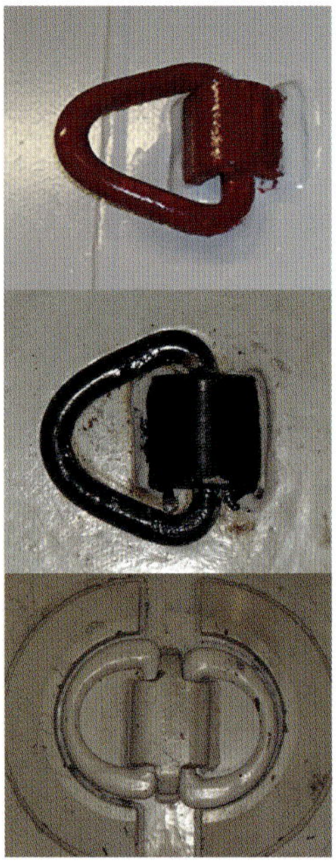

Single and double D-rings

D-ring. These rings are generally mounted on the sides and pillars inside car decks. Their main purpose is to secure high and heavy units, when it is not possible to secure them to the deck. As a rule their breaking load is between 15 and 20 metric tons (tonnes), but this can vary. D-Rings are made of drop-forged steel and can be either of single or double construction.

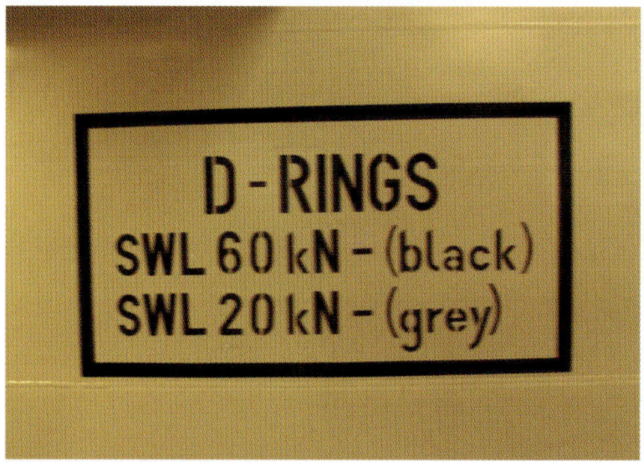

Marking of BL on ship's bulkhead"

Single-construction D-Ring: BL = 20 kN = 2 tonnes
Single-construction D-Ring: BL = 60 kN = 6 tonnes
Double-construction D-Ring: BL = 100 kN = 10 tonnes

It should be stressed that the yield strength of the weld connections must be at least equal to the intrinsic yield strength of the material welded. The SWL or BL should be conspicuously marked near the D-Rings.

Crinkle bars. The name originates from their form. These devices are mounted or welded on deck and are used for lashing of cars as well as high and heavy units. Normally these bars are made of mild steel with a yield strength of 235 N/mm^2. Again, the rule that the yield strength of welded connections should be at least equal to the intrinsic yield strength of the material welded applies. Crinkle bars can have either BL: 2.0 tonnes (SWL: 1.0 tonne) or BL: 6.0 tonnes (SWL: 3.0 tonnes).

Crinkle bars located on the deck are very susceptible to damage during the loading of heavy cargo. For this reason, it is a good practice that they be painted in a contrasting color.

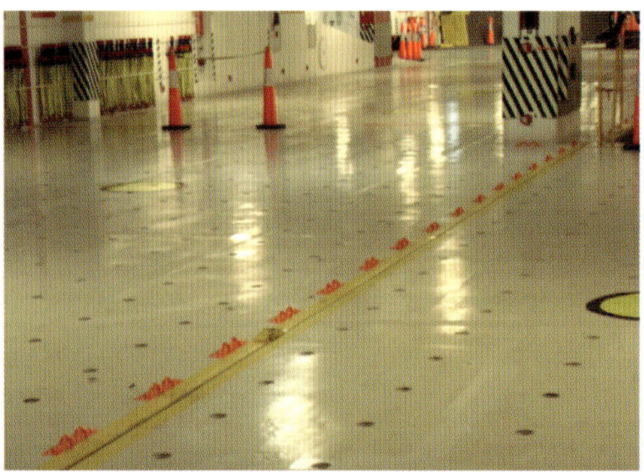

Orange crinkle bars show up on the deck.

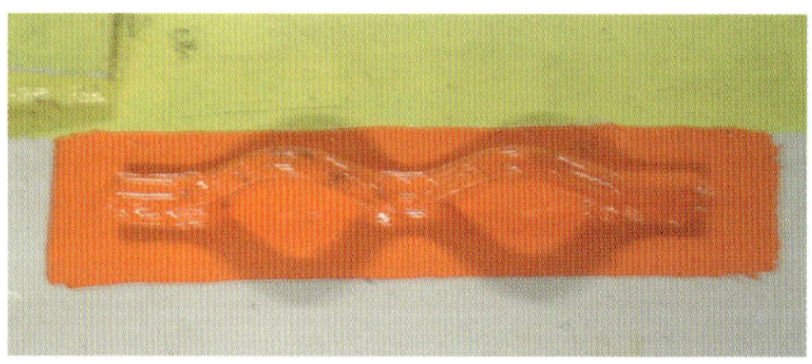

Crinkle bar

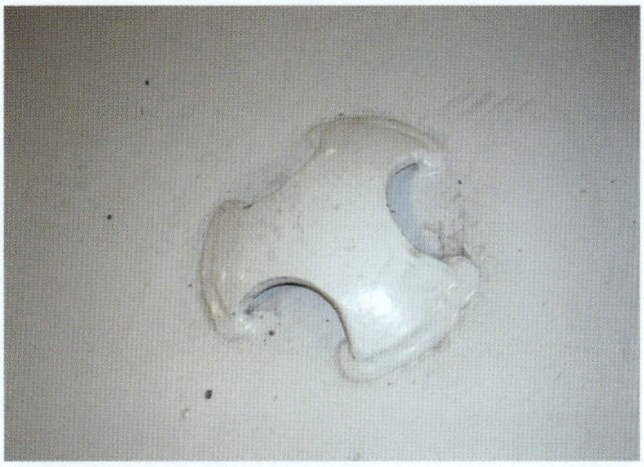

Elephant foot lashing pot

Lashing pot (elephant foot). This device can be used for lashing cars as well as high and heavy units. Normally it is fitted on car decks that cannot be holed, for instance on the lowest car deck or gastight car decks (wherever it is not possible to make any holes in the decks). The pots are welded to the car deck and their breaking load is about 30–40 metric tons (tonnes).

Lashing holes. As a rule, all car decks are holed so that the holes can be used as lashing terminals. It is very important for the Chief Officer and duty officers to keep in mind that snow or drops of water can fall down from upper decks to the lower decks through lashing holes. If this happens, appropriate contemporaneous evidence should be taken and a Letter of Protest be issued against Stevedoring Company.

The BL of the lashing holes may vary but usually is about 6.0 tonnes (SWL: 3.0 tonnes). The maximum securing load (MSL) of the lashing holes should not be less than 100 kN, but if "n" lashings can be secured to one hole, its MSL should be n x 100 kN.

Lashing cup

Lashing cups. Since lashing pots present some problems for loading passenger cars, they are fitted mostly on the lowest car deck (tank top), which cannot be holed. The other gastight car decks are holed, but there is another layer under the main deck, which guarantees gastightness; these holes form so-called lashing cups. Cups that fill with water or garbage must be cleaned during ballast voyage or whenever possible in order to avoid any claims against the ship. Cups with water or refuse would mean that the holds could be considered as not fit for loading as per Hague-Visby Rules, which would entail a lot of problems for the ship. During winter, the cups filled with snow or water can represent a more serious problem, namely the water inside can freeze and make the cups unusable. Again, if this happens, the ship can be considered unseaworthy due to unfit holds. The maximum securing load (MSL) of the lashing cups should not be less than 100 kN, but if "n" lashings can be secured to one cup its MSL should be n x 100 kN.

Cloverleaf lashing cup

Cloverleaf lashing cups. This type of lashing cup is fitted on most of the Ro-Ro ships. All information mentioned for lashing cups is applicable for cloverleaf cups as well. Up to four lashings can be attached at a same time to a cloverleaf cup. Their BL is 30.0 tonnes and the SWL is 15.0 tonnes.

Methods for Calculating the Number of Lashings

How Many Lashings Should Be Applied to Each Cargo Unit?

Paragraph 5, Annex 13 of the CSS Code provides a so-called "rule-of-thumb" method, which advises that the total MSL values of the securing devices on each side of a unit to be equal to the weight of the unit. This method does not take into account either the adverse effect of lashing angles or the favorable effect of friction. When using this method for assessing the efficiency of the lashings several requirements must be taken into account:

- All lashings must be of the same type so they have the same elasticity
- The number of lashings on each side must be applied in a balanced way, depending on the size and weight of the unit in question
- Some lashings should be put in fore-and-aft direction and some in the athwartship direction
- Lashings leading directly forward and aft and not having an athwartship component should not be included in the assessment. The same is to be applied for the lashings leading down from the unit at an angle more than 60°. These lashings can prevent tipping but not sliding.

This method ensures that, in normal circumstances, the cargo will not shift when the ship is rolling.

How Should the Lashings Be Distributed?

The 40:40:10:10 Rule suggests that the distribution of the lashings should be:

- 40% of the breaking strength of the lashing on port side
- 40% of the breaking strength of the lashing on starboard side
- 10% of the breaking strength of the lashing in fore direction
- 10% of the breaking strength of the lashing in aft direction

A second method for assessing the efficiency of the securing arrangements is the advanced calculation method. This method is time-consuming (it consists of four steps) and, thus, not very applicable on board Ro-Ro ships, when quick decisions have to be made. When a detailed assessment for a specific cargo unit is to be carried out, this method can be used. Details about it can be found in the CSS Code, Annex 13, Section 7. This method is not applicable to passenger cars. Also, it will not be applicable to a trailer with pallets on it if the exact position of the center of gravity is not known.

Another rule for determining the number of the lashings is the so-called "Three Times Rule." It states that the sum of safe working loads of all lashings should equal the static weight of the cargo unit, and that the breaking load is three times the safe working load. The safe working load, then, is calculated by dividing the sum of breaking loads of all the lashings by three. For example, a trailer of 15 tonnes can be considered as safely secured if the breaking load of all lashings is not less than 45 tonnes.

Irrespective of the method chosen for assessing the efficiency of the lashings, the general rule that the lashings be deployed in a balanced and efficient manner is valid. Of course, this is not always the case.

The weather conditions and the duration of the voyage must be taken into account when assessing the number of lashings. In all cases, when there is a smallest doubt about the number of the lashings, add more lashings to be on the safe side.

Also to be considered is the danger of the cargo sliding or tipping over. Cargo with a low center of gravity and a large base is likely to slide before it tips over. Cargo with a high center of gravity and a small base area is likely to tip over before it slides. Generally passenger cars will not tip over, but will most probably slide or shift. This is not the case, however, for trailers with cargo on top, where the possibility for tipping over is greater. Therefore the lashings must be deployed in such a way to address the greater risk, sliding or tipping over. When assessing the number and the required strength of the lashings the following issues should be taken into account:

Forces Counteracted by the Lashings

The lashings should prevent any movement of the vehicle. To do so, they must be able to counteract the forces that might cause the movement of a vehicle. As the forces acting on a vehicle have already been discussed, it can be easily concluded that the lashings should:

Counteracting the displacing force acting in the athwartship direction:
The force exercised by the lashing acting in direction opposition to the force created by the ship's motion will be $\mathbf{F_{CT}}$. This force, together with the frictional braking power (**R**), should counteract the force acting in the athwartship direction ($\mathbf{F_T}$), that is:

$$\mathbf{F_{CT} + R = F_T}$$

Thus we can derive the following equations for **FCT:**

$$\mathbf{F_{CT} = F_T - R = F_T - (F_V \times K)} \quad [7]$$

Where:
K = friction coefficient

If $\mathbf{F_{CT}}$ is negative, the frictional resistance is larger than the displacing force and the vehicle will not move, when not lashed.

Counteracting the displacing force acting in the vertical direction (F_V):
From equation [2] it is obvious that when $\mathbf{F_V}$ is negative the downward lashing force $\mathbf{F_{CV}}$ is required. $\mathbf{F_V}$ will be negative when the vehicle is jumping off the deck.

$$\mathbf{F_{CV} = F_V} \quad [8]$$

These forces operate in opposite directions.

Counteracting the displacing force acting in the fore-and-aft directions:
The fore-and-aft direction lashing force ($\mathbf{F_{FA}}$) can be obtained from [3], [4], and [5]. Thus:

$$\mathbf{F_{FA} + R = F_L}$$

$$\mathbf{F_{FA} = F_L - R = F_L - (F_V \times K)} \quad [9]$$

If $\mathbf{F_{FA}}$ is negative, the vehicles will not move when not lashed.

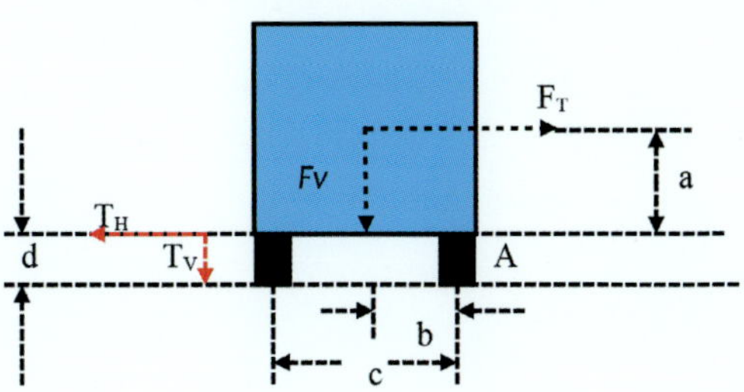

Counteracting tipping over:
It is not common for cars to tip over, but the situation is different with trailers or trucks with high centers of gravity. Considering the vulnerability of such cargo to tip over when the vessel is pitching or rolling heavily, special attention should be paid to the lashings deployed. The moment that tips over the vehicle ($\mathbf{M_T}$) can be expressed by the equation:

$\mathbf{M_T = (F_T \times a) - (F_V \times b)}$ [10]

Where:
a = vertical distance from the lower part (bottom) of the vehicle to its center of gravity, in meters
b = transverse distance from the middle of the vehicle to its side, in meters

The lashing force $\mathbf{F_{TO}}$ that prevents tipping over can be expressed as:

$\mathbf{F_{TO} = (F_{TH} \times d) + (F_{TV} \times c)}$ [11]

Where:
$\mathbf{F_{TH}}$ = horizontal component of the lashing force
$\mathbf{F_{TV}}$ = vertical component of the lashing force
d = vertical distance from the deck to the lower part of the vehicle, in meters
c = width of the vehicle, in meters

Another method for assessing the tipping and sliding forces acting in vehicle lashings when it concerns trailers was cited in the Annex to the Merchant Notice, but at present this Annex is withdrawn. In this method it was assumed that the vehicles and/or units of cargo stowed on Ro-Ro ships will be subjected to the following forces:

Force parallel to and across the deck = 1.0 W
Force normal to the deck = 1.4 W
Force in the longitudinal direction = 0.3 W

Where:
W = total weight of the unit

The forces preventing tipping are the vertical force and the lashings ($\mathbf{F_{LT}}$). Assuming that the moments causing tipping over are taken about point "A" – the outer edge of the wheel. Then the equation can be written as:

$\mathbf{F_{LT} \times L = (1.0\ W \times 0.67\ H) - (1.4\ W \times X)}$

$\mathbf{F_{LT} \times (X + Y) \sin\Theta = W\ (0.67\ H - 1.4\ X)}$

$\mathbf{F_{LT} = W\ (0.67H - 1.4\ X) / (X + Y) \sin\Theta}$ [12]

Where:
W = total weight of the unit
X = the horizontal distance from the outer edge of the outer wheel to the centerline of the unit
Y = the horizontal distance from the centerline of the unit to the lashing, the latter being secured to the deck
Θ = the angle between the lashings and the horizontal plane
L = $(X + Y) \sin\Theta$
H = the overall height of the unit

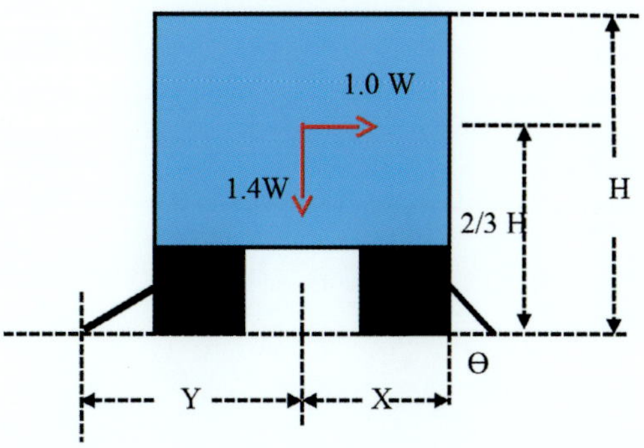

From the illustration, it is obvious that the distances H, X, and Y must be measured (or, better, taken from drawings if available). The angle Θ is the angle between the lashing and horizontal plane and must be measured as well.

The forces causing the vehicle to slide are calculated on assumption that the trailer is supported by wheels at one end and by a trestle at the other end (see Res. 581). The sliding is resisted by the frictional resistance between the trestle and the trailer and the tires and the deck. It is assumed that half the total force acts on each end of the trailer and that the coefficient of friction between the trestle and trailer frame is 0.2, and between rubber wheels and steel deck it is 0.4. (There is a table in the CSS Code, Annex 13, Section 7 giving the friction coefficients. This table indicates that the coefficient between timber and steel is 0.3, and that between steel and rubber is 0.4. The lesser frictions are used in the calculations so that the method will impose more stringent requirements regarding the number of lashings to be used.)

Friction Coefficient

The friction coefficient (μ) is defined as **the tangent of the angle to which that contact surface must be raised in order that movement between the two surfaces will occur as a result of gravitational force alone, without any other external forces acting**. There is a table in the CSS code giving the friction coefficients between different materials. The friction coefficient is independent of the size and weight of an object.

Wood, with a friction coefficient of 0.3, and rubber, with a friction coefficient of 0.4, are considered the most useful materials to be used between the cargo and steel deck. For comparison, the friction coefficient between steel and steel when dry is 0.1 and when wet it is 0.0.

So what can be expected when timber is put between a vehicle and a steel deck? The friction coefficient of 0.3 between the timber dunnage and the steel deck means that, irrespective of the size of the timber and its weight, it will start moving to the low side of the ship when the ship makes a list of 17° because 0.3 is actually the tangent of 17°. Of course, this only will be the case if no lashings have been fitted to the cargo. As the CSS Code is a compulsory regulation, the figures for friction coefficients must be considered as the official ones.

Dunnage

Dunnage includes different materials that are used to protect and separate the vehicles as well as decks. The purposes of the dunnage vary, including:

- Distributing the load of a heavy vehicle or cargo item across the deck
- Increasing the friction between the base of the cargo and the steel car decks (refer to the table with friction coefficients)
- Supporting one cargo being loaded on top of another

The dunnage on Ro-Ro ships is needed when high and heavy cargoes are loaded and stowed. The usual type of dunnage is timber bearers; their use will increase the friction between the base of the tractors or other vehicles, will distribute the total weight of the vehicle across the deck, and will protect the car deck from any structural damage that can occur.

The use of dunnage is impractical and unnecessary for passenger cars or other wheeled vehicles (the friction coefficient between the tires and steel is comparatively high) and, moreover, can cause damage to the passenger cars. This is not the case for tracked vehicles such as tractors, excavators, etc. Very often these vehicles have gross weights more than 40 metric tons (tonnes) and the use of dunnage is indispensable to protect the car decks as well as to distribute the weight of the vehicles across the car deck. The size of the wooden bearers can vary.

Dunnage should always be sound, dry, clean, and free of oil, grease, or other stains. A peculiarity of the dunnage used for high and heavy units is that it will be broken when used. Dunnage that is used and damaged is categorized as "cargo residues" under MARPOL Annex V and must be disposed of appropriately. Furthermore, if the dunnage is to be delivered to shore facilities, many port authorities require a certificate proving that it is not infected by any insects or has been treated by special chemicals to exterminate them. The Master must insist that suppliers of dunnage material deliver a certificate guaranteeing that the dunnage is free of any insects.

In order to prevent the proliferation of differing import regulations, the International Plant Protection Convention (IPPC) secretariat, part of the Food and Agriculture Organization (FAO) of the United Nations, has issued ISPM 15 (International Standards for Phytosanitary Measures) "Guidelines for Regulating Wood Packaging Material in International Trade."

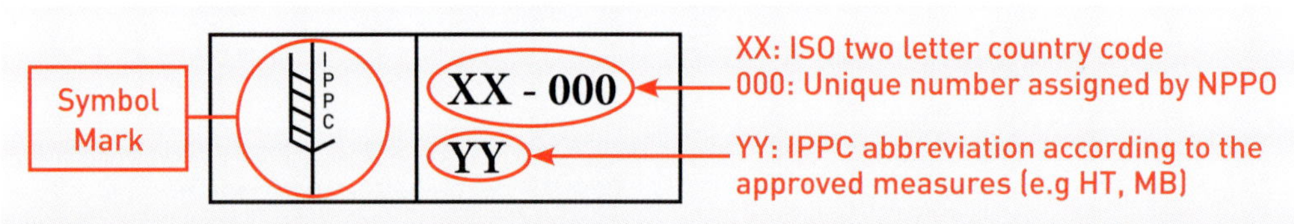

Labeling according to ISPM 15

All dunnage should be marked in this way. In this example the markings indicate: KR-South Korea; No:37279; HT–Heat Treatment.

These guidelines require that the wood packaging material, including dunnage, should be heated to a wood core temperature of 56° C for a minimum of 30 minutes. Heat treatment is indicated by the mark "HT." The wood packaging material should be fumigated with methyl bromide. The treatment is indicated by the mark "MB."

Dunnage materials should be marked, including, at the least, the IPPC symbol, the ISO two letter country code, a unique number assigned by the NPPO (National Plant Protection Organization) to the producer of the wood packaging material, and the IPPC (International Plant Prevention Convention) abbreviation for the approved measure used (e.g. HT, MB).

Markings should be legible, permanent, not transferable, and placed in a visible location.

Lashing of Vehicles

Cars

It is very important that the cars be equipped with appropriate lashing points. Some countries require these lashing points to be clearly marked. Vehicles without lashings points should be rejected for loading because they are not safe for transportation.

Immediately upon loading, the cars must be secured. Some Charterers require the cars to be left unsecured for short sea voyages. Although this is understandable from their point of view (in order to cut cost and avoid time delays), it is absolutely unacceptable for the ship management to allow this. There have been many claims against Ship Owners for cars that were damaged due to failure to lash the cargo or lashing it inadequately. Moreover, SOLAS Ch. VI requires that the cargo be properly lashed before the ship leaves the quay.

There are a number of general rules to be followed during lashing:

- The cars must be lashed immediately upon boarding and parking and unlashed on arrival at the discharging port. The lashing and unlashing operations are normally performed by shore gangs, but it is not uncommon for the ship's personnel to conduct these operations. If this is the case, special attention should be given to avoid any damage to the cars; in case of damage, the ship might be held responsible.
- The lashings used for securing a vehicle must not touch any other part of the vehicle except the lashing points.
- Vehicles must be lashed at a 20° to 40° angle to the longitudinal direction of the vehicle in order to prevent any movement during the voyage.

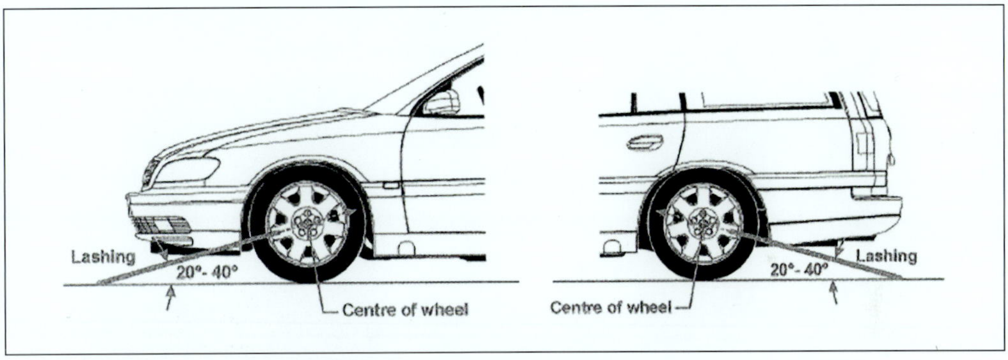

Proper lashings of car wheels to the deck

- The lashings used for securing the cars must be enough for the weight of the car.
- Vehicles must be lashed either on the wheel rim or on the towing hooks, according to the manufacturer's instruction. It is sometimes necessary for the cars to be lashed to the wheels using their aluminum or steel rims. In order to lash the car on the rim, fit the loose nylon loop around a wheel spoke and insert the hook into the loop with the hook opening facing downwards. For the lashing to be effective, the lashing must be attached to the lower part of the wheel, and it must be aligned with the center of the wheel. If those conditions are not respected, the wheel might turn and the lashing might become loose during transport.

- When lashing hooks are present the lashings must be secured there. The following must be strictly abided by:
  - *The shorter end of the lashing must be hooked in the lashing hook of the car.*
  - *The other end of the lashing must be anchored to the ship's deck.*
  - *The lashing is to be locked by pulling at an angle.*
  - *At least two lashings must be attached to a lashing hook.*

- In all cases, the number of lashings should be in accordance with the manufacturer's instructions.
- The cars should not be tightened down onto their springs.
- During the winter season the number of lashings can be increased.

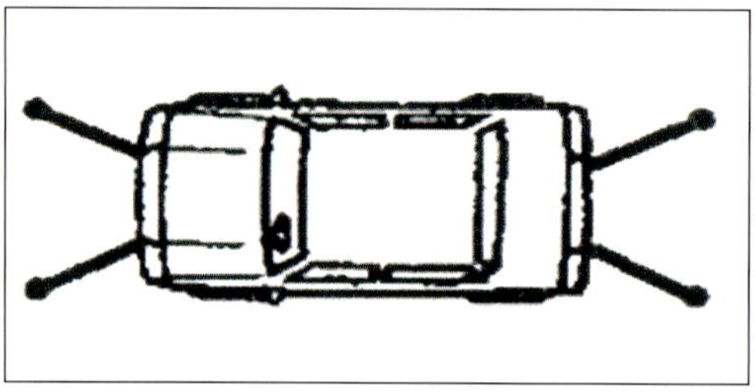

Lashing of passenger car in fore-and-aft direction *(Courtesy: Stamco Ship Management)*

- Normally, when the cars are stowed in fore-and-aft direction, the number of lashings are two lashings in front part and two lashings in back part of the car.

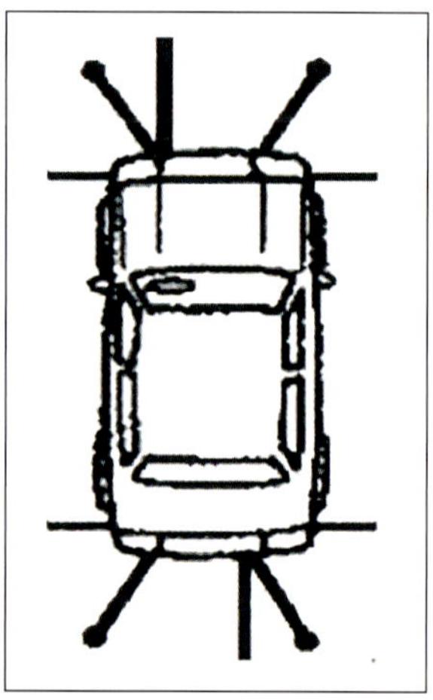

Lashing of passenger car in athwartship direction *(Courtesy: Stamco Ship Management)*

- When the cars are stowed athwart ships then the number of lashings should be increased to three lashings in front part and three lashings in back part of the car. In addition chocks should be placed under the wheels.
- When the cars are stowed on ramps the number of lashings is three or four on the upper part of the car (depending on the manufacturer's requirement) and two lashings on the lower side. Wedges/chocks should be put under two of the wheels.

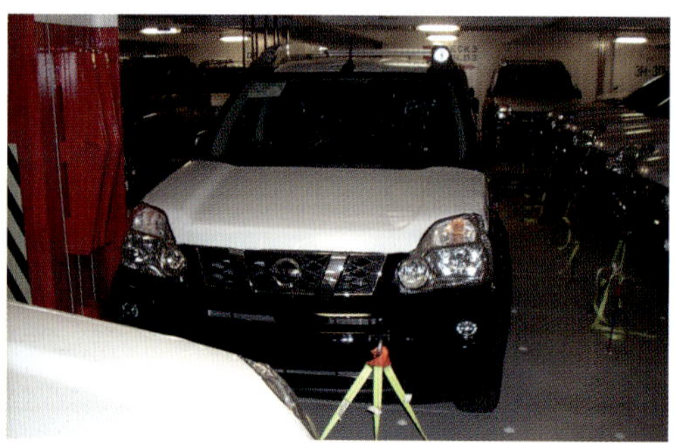

Proper lashing will guarantee safety of the cargo during the voyage and allow the inspection of the cargo.

The summarized requirements for the lashing can be found at: http://www. ecgassociation.eu.

High and Heavy Units

Properly securing high and heavy units is of utmost importance. Unfortunately, there are many cases where improper lashing of heavy units has led to severe structural damage to the ship and/or damage to the surrounding cargo. Considering the heavier weight of high and heavy vehicles, it is logical that they will require more lashings and sometimes (depending on the type of the cargo) special securing. In general, the rules that apply to the lashing of high and heavy units is the same as those for the lashing of cars and vans. Special attention must be paid to avoid any damage to the vehicle.

Buses and Trucks

Buses, trucks, vans, etc., with gross vehicle mass up to 10 metric tons (tonnes), must be secured by web lashings, not by chains. Buses, trucks, vans, etc., with a gross vehicle mass more than 10 tonnes should be secured by chains. There is a requirement for lashing points to be clearly marked.

A distinction needs to be made between securing points and lashing points. A securing point is an area on the vehicle that is suitably reinforced to withstand lashing forces. Securing points may have more than one lashing point.

A lashing point is that part within a securing point to which a lashing may be directly attached. It is not permitted to have more than one lashing at each lashing point. Each lashing point must be painted in contrasting color to the securing point.

The symbol for marking a lashing point

An information plate measuring 200 mm x 150 mm must be affixed permanently on both sides of the vehicle 1.6 meters or less from the front end. The height from the ground to the plate's lower edge must be 1 to 1.5 meters where possible. The information plate shall comprise a number indicating the number of lashing points per side and an anchor symbol.

The number of lashings that should be used for securing large units can be obtained in the ways mentioned earlier. However, the minimum number of securing points on each side of a cargo unit should be as follows:

- Gross vehicle mass between 3.5 and 20 tonnes: at least 2 securing points
- Gross vehicle mass between 20 and 30 tonnes: at least 3 securing points
- Gross vehicle mass between 30 and 40 tonnes: at least 4 securing points

Thus, if the weight of the truck is 10 tonnes and we use web lashings of SWL: 5.0 tonnes (MBL: 10.0 tonnes) we should put at least two web lashings on the front and back sides of the truck in order to guarantee safe securing of the vehicle. However, if we use web lashings of SWL: 2.5 tonnes (MBL: 5.0 tonnes), we should put at least four lashings on front and back sides in order to secure the unit in a safe manner. In other words, **the total breaking load of the lashings on each side should be at least equal to the weight of the unit and the number of lashings should be at least two on each side.**

Roll-On/ Roll-Off Ships—Stowage and Securing of Vehicles, "Annex 1: Vehicle Lashing Arrangements" suggests a method for securing cargo on Ro-Ro ships on short sea voyages. Special graphs show the minimum number of lashings of a given strength for a range of roll periods and a range of vertical heights above the waterline. There are four graphs for four different typical trailers that are commonly transported in short sea voyages in Northern Europe. GVMs (gross vehicle masses) cited are: 10, 20, 30, and 32 metric tons (tonnes). By entering the roll period on the horizontal axis and the height of the trailer above the waterline on the vertical axis of the appropriate graph, the minimum number of lashings per side can be obtained.

When securing buses, special attention must be paid not to lash around electrical cables, tubes, and other non-approved lashing points.

Draw bar combination

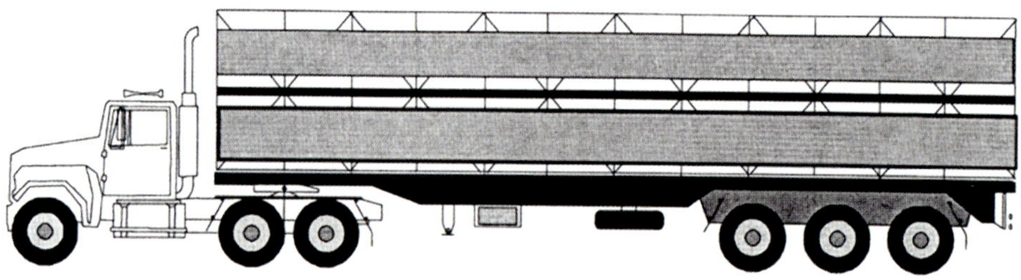

Van body trailer attached to the truck

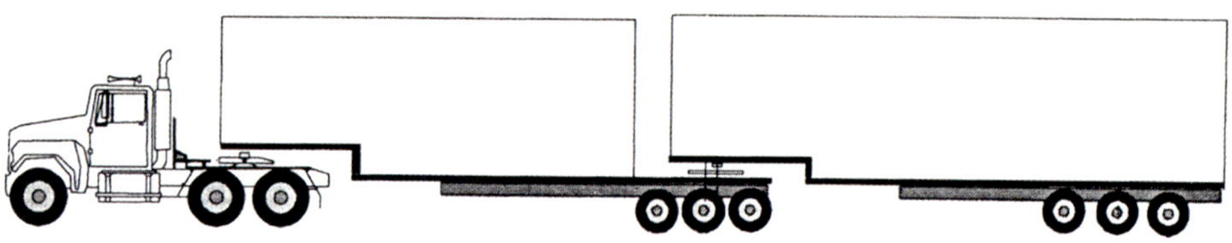

Draw bar train

Road freight vehicles, road tank vehicles, or road livestock vehicles, having a gross mass of 3.5 metric tons (tonnes) or more, must be fitted with securing points complying with the requirements of ISO 9367-1, "Lashing and securing arrangements on road vehicles for sea transportation on Ro-Ro ships—part 1," and the Master must ensure that they are so equipped. Examples of the types of vehicles that need to be fitted with such securing points, including a draw bar combination, a van body trailer attached to the truck, and a draw bar train, are illustrated.

The following vehicles are not required to be fitted with such securing points meeting the requirements of ISO 9367-1:

- Road freight, road tank, and road livestock semi-trailers, with or without a tractor unit, less than 3.5 metric tons (tonnes)
- Road freight, road tank, and road livestock vehicles that are not intended for transport on Ro-Ro ships, but are being freighted for delivery purposes only, without payload
- Passenger vehicles, e.g. cars, minibuses, buses
- Motor homes or caravans
- Oversize vehicles
- Railway wagons

If chains are used for securing of vehicles, the hooks of the chains should never be attached directly onto the chassis. Soft slings (of the appropriate SWL) should be used in order to protect the vehicle from any damage. It is not uncommon for a more stringent requirement to be applied, such as covering the chain with a protector. This practice, however, is normally applied to new vehicles only. When it comes to the second-hand vehicles this practice is usually overlooked.

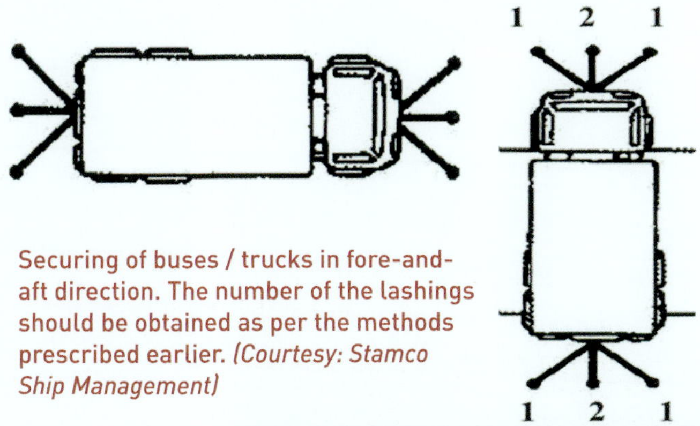

Securing of buses / trucks in fore-and-aft direction. The number of the lashings should be obtained as per the methods prescribed earlier. *(Courtesy: Stamco Ship Management)*

As a rule trucks and buses over 10 metric tons (tonnes) should be stowed in fore-and-aft direction. The distance between them is subject to manufacturer's instruction, but otherwise the standard distances detailed earlier can be used.

The lashing of trucks

Tractors, Excavators, and Trailers

In all cases, this type of cargo should be loaded and stowed on special, strengthened decks. Normally there are two or three decks specially designed for loading of heavier cargoes. These are provided with liftable panels in order to allow loading of higher cargo.

Loading excavators. Note the ropes surrounding the excavator's track to protect the deck.

Lashing of tractors should be performed in the same way as buses and trucks. If they are fitted with tires, web lashings should be used for securing them. The same principles should apply.

Because excavators are tracked vehicles, they require special attention when being stowed and secured. When being loaded or discharged, the excavators can damage the deck and the ramps. Therefore it is essential that ropes (hawsers) or rubber mats are used to avoid any direct contact between the tracks of the excavators and the decks and ramps.

Excavators should be stowed in fore-and-aft direction. They are secured by chains, the number of which is obtained by the methods prescribed earlier.

If the weight of the excavator is less than 10 tonnes it can be secured by web lashings of proper BL.

Lashings of excavators

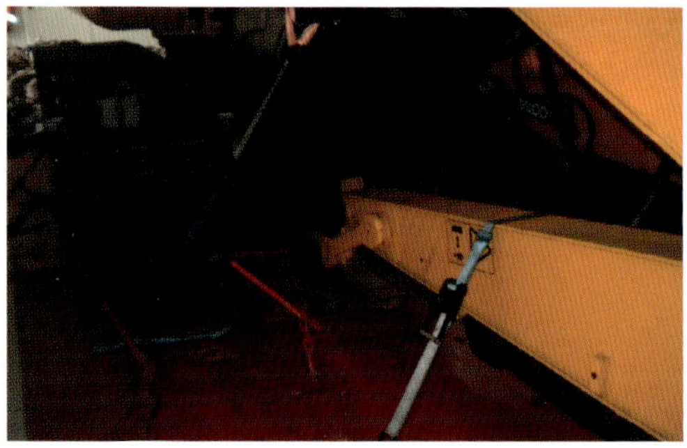

Lashing jib

Once parked the battery of the excavators should be disconnected or put in the off mode, and the jib should be properly stowed on deck. Failure to disconnect the battery can result in delays at discharging because of dead batteries, and an improperly secured jib can cause damage to the surrounding cargo. In addition, tracked vehicles should be stowed on dunnage material, ropes, or rubber mats in order to reduce the friction between the track and the deck and to distribute the weight of the vehicle properly.

In the illustration, the bucket of the excavator is lowered and secured to the deck, and the jib is secured with web lashings to avoid any movement during the voyage. It is common practice for the stevedoring companies to overlook the use of dunnage underneath the bucket. Here the presence and attention of the duty officer is very important.

Tractors can be stowed either in fore-and-aft direction or athwart ship. Tractors with weight more than 10 metric tons (tonnes) should be secured by chains and tractors with weight less than 10 tonnes can be secured by webbing lashings of proper BL.

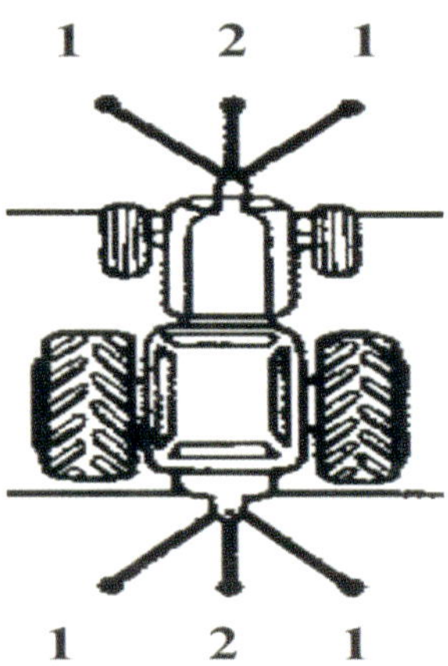

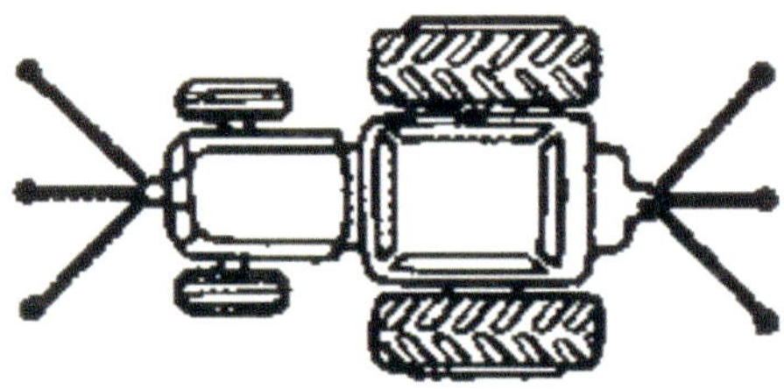

Above: Securing of tractors in fore-and-aft direction. The number of the lashings or chains should be obtained using the methods prescribed earlier. *(Courtesy: Stamco Ship Management)*

Left: Securing of tractors in athwart ship direction. The number of the lashings or chains should be obtained using the methods prescribed earlier. *(Courtesy: Stamco Ship Management)*

Loading and Lashing Project Cargo

Today, it is a very common practice for project cargo to be shipped at sea by car carriers or Ro-Ro ships. This is dictated primarily by two things: car carriers are very suitable for the shipment of such cargo when it is on trailers and loaded and stowed on board on basis of the roll-on/roll-off principle; and Ship Owners welcome this type of cargo, because the freight paid is much more than for other cargoes. Nevertheless, the transportation of project cargoes needs special attention. The weight of such cargo, which can include wind farms, power plants, yachts, and even small airplanes, can vary considerably. This requires special consideration when securing it on board.

Generally, the same principles described earlier for the calculation of the number of lashings and securing points can be used. In addition, it is important that the cargo be secured to the trailer (if stowed on a trailer) at the same time it is secured to the deck. It is absolutely unacceptable to secure the cargo only to the trailer and not to the deck. For securing project cargo, chains are the most suitable means. They must be tightened by tensioners and checked and re-tightened during the voyage at reasonable intervals. Very often, due to its height and shape, the project cargo may need to be lashed to points that are not specially designed for this purpose. In this case, special edge protectors can be used to prevent any chafing damage to the cargo.

This machine was driven on board by a trailer, then discharged and stowed by a crane. The dunnage was properly arranged underneath.

If the project cargo consists of power plants or big cranes reaching up to 60–70 metric tons (tonnes) in weight, it should be secured directly to the deck. If web lashings are used for this purpose their lashing capacity (LC) and their number should be significant. If chains are used for lashing, it sometimes may be necessary to attach the hook of the chain to a sling, due to the lack of securing points. In that case, the ship's crew must ensure that the chains are properly tightened. It must be kept in mind that, due to vibrations during the voyage, the chains secured to the slings can slacken much more easily than the chains secured directly to the securing points. This will require more frequent checks of the cargo during the voyage.

When project cargo is involved, its loading and securing on board is normally supervised by a port captain. The final decision for proper securing of this cargo, however, is the responsibility of the Master and Chief Officer and, therefore, their expertise is vital. They have the right to disregard the instructions of port captain when they consider specific lashing arrangements to be unsafe. In all cases, they must refer to the Cargo Securing Manual approved for the ship.

Loading Boats

Boats should be secured not only to their trailer but also to the deck. In rough seas nobody can predict how the lashing will act, so putting more lashings and securing the cargo to the deck will guarantee that the cargo will be safely secured during sea passage. Moreover, improper lashing of the cargo makes the ship unseaworthy and in case of any damage during the voyage, the Carrier will be held responsible.

If the boat is on a cradle, dunnage must be placed under the cradle.

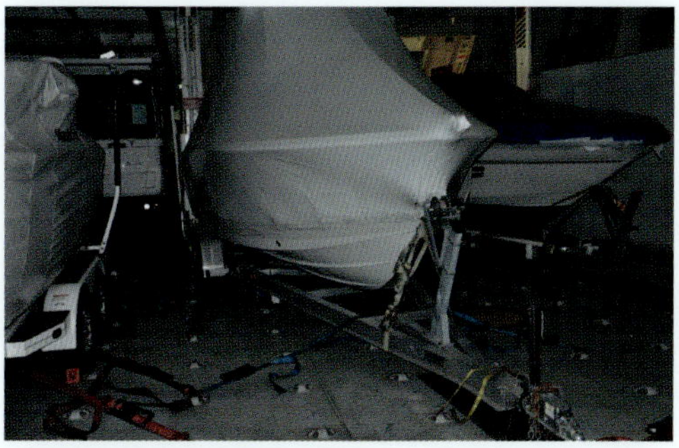

A stowed yacht on a trailer

Loading and Securing Pipes

The loading of pipes on board car carriers is not uncommon nowadays. The lashing can be problematic, especially if the ship is not supplied with wires. Methods and techniques for securing and lashing of pipes should be thoroughly studied well in advance and reference to the respective codes and publications should be made.

Loading a dam pipe on trailer

Transferring the pipe from the trailer and stowing it on the deck

The illustrations show the process of loading of a dam pipe on board a car carrier. The pipe is delivered on a trailer, and moved to the deck using a heavy forklift. Placed on dunnage and properly chocked, it is finally lashed to the deck with wires.

The pipe properly stowed and secured on deck

Another issue to be considered when loading high and heavy cargoes is the strict supervision of the handling and securing of these cargoes. Unfortunately, there are many examples of bad handling, bad stowage (not as per the Stowage Plan approved by the Chief Officer), missing keys, etc., that can delay cargo operations at the discharging port. At all times, a crewmember should be present, preferably a duty officer, attending cargo operations and compiling contemporaneous evidence if necessary. If keys are missing or bad or inappropriate lashing is being made by the Stevedoring Company, etc., the crew member can identify these issues immediately and the ship administration (the senior staff including the Master, Chief Officer, etc.) can issue a Letter of Protest against the Stevedoring Company, thus protecting the Owner's interest.

Loading and Securing Trailers

Gooseneck of a tug master

Roll-trailers are specifically designed to alleviate the problems of transporting "loose" cargo that is unsuitable for containerization. These trailers are used to safely transport cargo on Ro-Ro vessels, at terminals, and at industrial and military sites. Originally created for the movement of products such as steel, paper, and cables, roll-trailers are also ideal for the transport of high-value cargo such as yachts, vintage cars, etc.

Roll-trailers are driven on and off the ship by a tractor or a so-called "tug master" with a gooseneck rig. Coupling of the tug master to the trailer can be done in a few seconds. The specially shaped tongue of the gooseneck is inserted into the coupling mouth of the trailer and then raised. During lifting, the tongue is automatically locked into the coupling mouth, which creates a tight connection to the trailer. The trailer is then lifted from the ground at the forward end and is ready for transport.

Trailers or mafis can be of the following type:

	20-foot	40-foot	60-foot	80-foot
Length	6.10 m	12.19 m	18.50 m	24.0 m
Width	2.50 m	2.44 m	2.50 m	2.80 m
Height	0.62 m	0.75 m	0.85 m	1.03 m
Capacity	25.0 t	60–120 t	90.0 t	100.0 t
Tare Weight	2.9 t	6.8 t	11.4 t	20.0 t

Stack of roll trailers secured to the deck by web lashings

Mafis should be marked with their ID number, tare, and SWL.

Very often stacks of several trailers need to be transported by sea. In this case, the trailers should be secured to each other with web lashings or chains and the stack should be secured to the deck according to the approved lashing methods. It is very important that the wheels of the trailers are properly chocked in order to avoid movement during the sea passage. It is strongly recommended that these units be secured to the deck with chains of heavy-duty web lashings.

Another problem when loading or discharging trailers is the small clearance between the trailer and the deck or ramp. Despite the fact that the gooseneck can increase the height of the mafi, sometimes this is not sufficient. It is therefore very important that the angle of the ramp is properly adjusted. The cargo on the trailer should be properly secured as well and it should be monitored all the way from the quay to the deck. Though they present some challenges, the advantages of using the trailers are obvious: simple one-man operation; fast automatic coupling; and fast operations for heavy and non-movable cargoes stowed on the trailers.

When securing trailers the following important issues should be considered:

- The number of lashings should be calculated using the methods prescribed earlier.
- Lashings should be placed symmetrically on both sides.
- There should be rubber or wood between the forward part of the trailer and deck.
- Roll-trailers should always be stowed in fore-and-aft direction.
- The cargo on trailer should be secured to the deck as well as the trailer.

It is important to calculate where the center of gravity of the cargo is. This will allow the prediction of which phenomenon is likely to occur: sliding or tipping. High cargo stowed on a trailer and loaded in fore-and-aft direction will be more sensitive to tipping in transverse direction.

Tipping Centers

Tipping centers are points around which the tipping of the cargo or vehicle can occur.

In the forward end of the trailer the tipping will take place around the outer edges of the trestle (when a trestle is used). The forward part of the roll trailer is very often resting directly on the rubber mats over the deck. At the wheel end of the trailer, the tipping will take place around the centers of wheel bogies. If the friction coefficient is larger than 0.5, the trailer will overturn instead of slide.

The support width in the forward part of the trailer is larger than in the wheel end, so the risk of tipping is less in the forward part than in the aft (wheeled) part. The risk of tipping at the wheeled part will increase based on the cargo stowed there.

The risk of tipping can be estimated by the vertical distance from the tipping point to the center of gravity and the horizontal distance from the tipping point to the center of gravity. If the ratio of vertical/horizontal distance is more than 1.6, there is a risk of transverse tipping.

As the center of gravity of the cargo cannot be changed, the position of the tipping point must be changed to reduce the risk of tipping over, thereby reducing the ratio. The tipping point can be changed by using extra dunnage or even by adding some supporting jacks (if possible). The dunnage or jacks should be located in front of the wheels, situated so that the distance between them and the aft part of the trailer is about 3.0 meters.

Sideways tipping as a result of slack lashings can represent a very serious problem, especially in boisterous weather. The crew should check the lashings during the voyage. Irrespective of frequent checks, lashing should be properly done.

Very often the web lashings or chains are secured over the top of the cargo to the deck. This will provide some security and will help to prevent the cargo from tipping. However, this kind of securing is not very efficient as the tipping can take place inside the lashings, especially when web lashings are used.

Securing of trailer with cargo. The cargo stowed on the trailer should be lashed to the trailer, but also to the deck. It is preferable for trailers with heavy cargo on them to be secured by chains. Lashings can damage the cargo, so, especially if the latter is valuable, protective edges can and should be used.

It is a better practice to secure the lashings on deck, pass them over the cargo, and finally secure them to the D-rings on the sides of the ship. When doing this, protective sleeves should be used on the lashings passing over the cargo.

In short, to prevent sliding of a trailer, low, horizontal lashings should be used. To prevent tipping over, vertical lashings should be used.

In addition to chains, webbings, etc., a trestle or a trailer horse is used for securing semi-trailers, the wheelless end of the semi-trailer being supported by the trestle during the transport. Semi-trailers are conventionally provided with their own legs, by means of which the wheelless end can be supported ashore, but these legs cannot usually sustain the combined load and forces that act on them (from the unit and its cargo) as a result of the movements of the vessel during sea transport. Therefore a trestle or equivalent is needed to support the semi-trailer during sea transport. The trestle is usually made of steel.

Loading and Securing Side-Curtain Trailers

Curtain sides are an advanced development for greater efficiency in transportation and haulage of cargo. Curtain sides or taut liners are designed to provide fast and easy access to the cargo in the freight area of the vehicle, while keeping it secure and sheltered.

Curtain sides are a combination of flatbed transportation, allowing for unloading from the side of the vehicle, with the added protection you would expect from a dry van. The curtain sides or taut liners contain retaining straps that allow the curtain to be pulled back to one side when released, thus allowing convenient loading or unloading of cargo. This provides an ideal method of transporting large loads, while protecting the goods from the elements in a convenient and efficient way. They also allow the transporting of goods that are large or have irregular shapes, such as oversized materials, building components, and particularly fragile, sensitive goods. They can accommodate large, bulky goods while containing them neatly, securely and sheltered from the environment.

Guide to Truck Trailer Dimensions

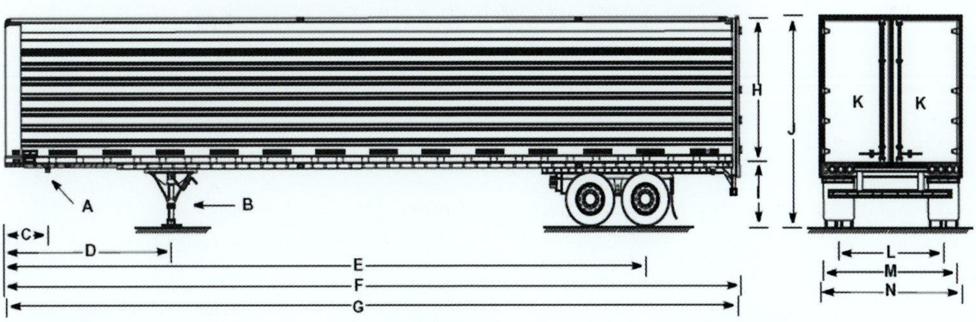

A Kingpin
B Landing Gear
C Distance to Kingpin
D Distance to Landing Gear
E Wheelbase
F Length Overall
G Length Interior
H Door Opening
I Floor Height
J Height Overall
K Swing Doors
L Track
M Width Interior
N Width Overall

The transportation at sea of side curtain trailers with cargo poses a particular problem: the side curtains cannot be used for securing the cargo unless the trailers are certified for that purpose.

The shifting of the cargo inside the trailer is the most common type of damage during the sea transport. To prevent this, the cargo should be firmly and tightly packed inside the trailer, ensuring that cargo movement is reduced to a minimum. After testing, some side curtain trailers may meet the performance standards for securing of cargo in the lateral direction for lighter cargo only. To be so certified, the curtain deflection must not exceed 100 mm.

Lashing side curtain trailers should be performed following the principles outlined for other trailers. The significant difference is that the cargo cannot be secured to the deck and no lashings can pass over it. Despite the fact that the stowage of the cargo inside the side curtain trailer is not the responsibility of the Carrier, it is good practice to check it during the securing process, when possible.

The trestle should be in the forward part of the trailer. If the center of gravity of the cargo inside is high, a risk of tipping exists and should be assessed.

Loading and Lashing Palletized Cargo

Special attention should be given to the operation of forklifts on board the vessel. Only skilled drivers should operate them, especially when driving on slopes or ramps, and when breaking out the first pallet or crate. In all cases, sufficient personnel should be available to guide the driver. The speed of the forklift should be restricted to 25 km/h as recommended by ILO.

When loading palletized cargo, especially milk-powder, etc., the forks on the forklifts used on board as well as ashore must be shorter than the length of the pallets. This is to prevent the forks damaging the pallet stowed behind the one being lifted or moved, which, in fact, is the most frequent cause of damage to this type of cargo. In addition, the wall of the tower on each forklift must be completely flush, as otherwise the cartons will be dented when the pallets are picked up in the shed and when they are stowed on board. When stowing pallets, they must be, as much as possible, stowed against a flush bulkhead and never against obstacles or edges of any kind. The pallets must be placed exactly on top of each other, and always in straight lines.

Do not use plywood sheets between the pallets when stowing the milk powder, as this often will cause damage to the cartons.

When loading other kinds of static cargo, like unpacked machinery, etc., it must be ensured that the lifting, stowage, and lashing operations do not cause any kind of damage.

Some cargo may be delivered for sea transport in special crates. The crate should meet some requirements:

- It should have a solid bottom frame.
- The top and sides should withstand the lashing force needed to secure the cargo.
- Goods should be bolted to the frame.
- There should be lashing points in upper and lower part of the frame.
- Lashing points in the upper part should not be lower than the center of gravity.
- The crate should be properly marked with its center of gravity, wood treatment stamp, lifting point, port of discharge, port of transit (if any), gross weight, size, and address of consignee. Some additional information, if applicable should be marked as well.

Crates with cargo

Needless to say that the cargo inside the crate should be properly stowed and secured.

Special stands of square sectioned wood sometimes can be made in order to chock the cargo of crates or boxes against ship's structure or other cargo. This method of securing the cargo is known as "tomming off."

Loading and Lashing Wagons

Loading, securing, and transporting railway wagons at sea is a quite big challenge. Wagons are shipped by specially designed train ferries and such ferries operate mainly in the Black Sea (Varna-Ilychevsk), the Baltic Sea, and others. The loading of wagons takes place at special terminals equipped with rails. There are three different gauges of the rails in Europe:

- Europe : 1435 mm (the most popular)
- Finland: 1524 mm
- Russia: 1520 mm

Once the wagons are loaded they should be properly secured. There are different types of hooks and brackets fitted on the wagons that can be used for securing of the wagons on board train ferries.

- Tow hooks
- Tow hooks with hold-down brackets
- Hold-down brackets

Tow hooks must be able to withstand a force of 50 kN in direction within a spherical sector. The yield strength of the hook is 225 N/mm^2.

There are two different types of lashing widely used for securing of wagons on board train ferries. The first is direct fastening to a single hook; this hook allows a lower maximum securing load. The second type is fastening with a loop around the neck of the hook; this hook allows an increased maximum securing load.

The hold-down brackets should be dimensioned in such way to allow a maximum securing load of:

- 50 kN in a spherical sector from 0° to 45° downwards in the longitudinal directions
- 50 kN in a spherical sector from 0° to 30° in the transversal direction
- 80 kN in the spherical sector from 45° downwards in one of the wagon's longitudinal directions to 45° in the other
- 80 kN in the spherical sector 0° vertical to 30° outwards in the transversal direction

These criteria apply to all types of hold-down brackets, whether combined with a tow hook or a pure hold-down bracket design.

Any load on the wagon should be properly secured as well.

When transporting wagons on board car carriers, the wagons can be loaded and discharged by air shuttle trailers or rubber tire bogies. An air shuttle trailer is designed for the loading and discharging of assembled railway wagons. It is fitted with rails on top and a pneumatic system, so the air shuttle can lower and raise a trailer to and from the ground level. In this way, the need for lifting the cargo is eliminated. The air shuttle lifts the wagon and transports it to the stowage position on board. There the trailer is lowered and properly secured. Only two air shuttles are required for loading and discharging wagons, one in the loading port and another on the discharging port. An air shuttle has a maximum pay load about 47.5 metric tons (tonnes). Its size depends on the type of wagons being transported. It has been designed by Wallenius Wilhelmsen.

Loading and Lashing of Non-self-propelled Vehicles

Vehicles equipped with a designated towage appliance are classified as non-self-propelled vehicles. They are considered vehicles when in towable condition with inflated tires and brakes in working condition.

Loading of Heavy Bulk Cargo

Heavy break bulk cargo (pallets, bags, etc.) that is not fit for stowing inside containers, can be transported on board car carriers when stowed on bolsters. Bolsters or flat beds are metal platforms that can be either 6 or 12 meters (20 or 40 feet) long. Bolsters are loaded and discharged with heavy-duty forklifts. Dunnage, properly treated, should be situated under the bolsters. The cargo stowed on the bolster should be secured to the bolster and to the deck. Bolsters are secured to the deck by means of chains. Loading capacity of a bolster is 23.5 metric tons. It is 2.44 meters wide and its height when stowed on deck is only 0.23 meters.

Loading and Lashing SECU (Stora Enso Cargo Units)

A SECU is a type of inter-modal container built to transport break bulk cargo, such as paper. A SECU is larger than a standard 12-meter (40-foot) ISO container, measuring 13.75 x 3.43 x 3.43 m. This container can carry up to 79.5 metric tons (tonnes). These containers are very popular in the Baltic trade and are mainly used for the transport of paper. They are being shipped on board Ro-Ro ships and therefore these ships should be properly designed to receive, stow, and secure them.

Loading Cargo on Weather Deck

The latest generations of car carriers can accommodate certain oversized cargoes on their weather decks. However, considering the uniform load of the weather deck, such cargo must be comparatively light. Lifting gears used for lifting such cargo should be of approved type and in good order and condition.

CHAPTER 6

TRANSPORT REGULATIONS

The safe transportation of vehicles at sea is based on compliance with certain rules imposed by the Cargo Owner, the Ship Owner, or relevant international legislation. The Master should be well aware of such regulations and strictly abide by them. It is important to mention that transportation of vehicles destined for the USA should comply with 49 CFR and the cargo destined for other countries should comply with the IMDG Code. The regulations imposed by IMO and USCG are the most important ones and in this chapter they will be further analyzed.

IMDG (International Maritime Dangerous Goods) Code

The most important document concerning the carriage of vehicles at sea is the International Maritime Dangerous Goods Code (IMDG Code).This is because all vehicles have some fuel in their tanks and, therefore, can be considered dangerous. Vehicles (automobiles, motorcycles, trucks, tractors, etc.) are considered dangerous when carried as cargo if the engine or fuel tank contains class 3 flammable liquid fuels or if the battery cable is connected. The extent of danger is determined by the quantity of fuel in the tanks.

The IMDG Code requires that vehicles assigned for sea transport be inspected and that the following points be observed:

- If leakage is found during the inspection, the vehicle should not be accepted for shipment.
- The fuel tank of a vehicle or mechanical equipment should not be more than one-fourth full.
- Vehicles or mechanical equipment stowed in a hold or in a freight container should have their battery cables disconnected and isolated from the terminals.

On board the ship the following issues should be checked:

- Portable fire extinguishers with a total capacity of at least 12 kg of dry powder or its equivalent should be provided for the cargo spaces.
- "No Smoking" signs should be conspicuously displayed in way of each access to the hold or compartment.
- Freight containers and CTU (Cargo Transport Unit) containing vehicles should have "No Smoking" signs at their access doors.

- Portable electric lights or equipment used in the stowage area should be explosion-proof. Lighting shall be of a type suitable for use in an explosive petrol and air mixture atmosphere. (SOLAS Ch. II-2 Reg. 20/3.2.1)

Vehicles are not considered as dangerous per the terms of IMDG Code when the vehicles have their tanks empty, when the engine is run until it stalls due to lack of fuel, when both battery cables are disconnected, and when no other dangerous goods are present in the vehicle.

Since the spaces on Ro-Ro ships and car decks on car carriers are specifically suited for carriage of motor vehicles with fuel in their tanks for their own propulsion, the provisions for carriage of vehicles should not apply. Vehicles can be stowed on deck (garage deck if any) or under deck, with their ignition off, if the tank is not filled to such an extent as to create a possibility of spillage. In particular, stowage under deck is permissible provided the tank is drained prior to loading so as not to leave more than five liters in the tank.

It is important to ensure that no additional spare jerry cans of fuel are carried. The flash point of gasoline is -43° C and the quantity of gasoline and the fuel in spare jerry cans, if any, would represent a great fire risk for the ship in case of spillage.

Transportation of Vehicles as Stipulated by CFR

Vehicles shipped to the USA come under the Code of Federal Regulations (CFR), where they are described as "Other Regulated Material" under 49 CFR, Part 172.01. Under 49 CFR the vehicles are considered as non-hazardous if they comply with the following conditions:

Vehicles using fuels with a flash point of under 100° F (37.8° C)

- The fuel tank is empty.
- The engine was allowed to run until it stopped by running out of fuel.
- Both battery cables are disconnected.
- Other hazardous materials are not carried by the vehicle.

When shipped as non-hazardous materials under these regulations, a certificate stating the above details should be obtained from the Shipper and submitted to the Master

Vehicles using fuels with a flash point of over 100° F (37.8°C) but under 200° F (93.3°C)

- The tank contains less than 416 liters.
- Both battery cables are disconnected.
- Other hazardous materials are not carried by the vehicle.

When shipped as non-hazardous materials under these regulations, a certificate with these details should be obtained from the Shipper and submitted to the Master.

The vehicles can be transported in freight containers as well. These vehicles are not considered as dangerous under CFR. However, if vehicles transported in freight containers are considered hazardous materials and they are transported in non-ventilated containers, warning labels should be affixed on container doors. If they are transported in ventilated containers, it is not necessary to affix such warning labels. If the vehicles are considered hazardous materials under CFR, leakage of oil should be checked before loading and vehicles showing leakage should not be loaded. The fuel should be less than one-quarter of the tank capacity. In addition, two portable dry chemical fire extinguishers of more than ten pounds should be placed at a point with easy access to the place where vehicles are loaded. Vehicles using fuels with a flash point of under 100° F (37.8°C) should not be loaded in the same hold or area with other hazardous materials.

Transportation of Dangerous Goods Loaded on Vehicles

When loading vehicles consisting of dangerous goods, the Master should conduct a thorough inspection of the vehicle. It would be very useful if the Master refers to MSC 1/Circ. 1202, "Inspection programmes for cargo transport unit (CTU) carrying dangerous goods." The vehicle should be properly labeled and supplied with the appropriate documents: a Dangerous Goods Declaration and a Vehicle Packing Certificate (See chapter 12, Documents).

Using this circular as a guide to inspecting the cargo, the Master should decide whether to accept or reject the cargo in question, depending on the condition of the cargo presented for shipment. If the vehicle is not clean and dry and is not fit to receive dangerous goods, if the vehicle is not properly marked/labeled as required for the respective class of dangerous goods, or if the packages have not been properly secured inside the vehicle, the Master is in position to reject the cargo. If the doors of the vehicle are locked, they should be of such a design that they can be opened without delay in case of emergency.

Special attention should be paid to the labeling of the cargo. If the Master fails to note the improper labeling as required by the IMDG Code and the vehicle has been loaded, there is a risk that this cargo will be rejected for discharge at the destination port.

Once the vehicles packed with dangerous goods have been accepted for loading, they should be properly segregated by using the segregation instructions as stipulated in IMDG Code.

The following classes of segregation are applicable for vehicles with dangerous goods stowed on board Ro-Ro ships:

Away from:

- On deck: at least 3 meters fore-and-aft and athwart ship stowage allowed
- Under deck: at least 3 meters fore-and-aft and athwart ship stowage allowed

Separated from:

- On deck: at least 6 meters fore-and-aft and athwart ship stowage allowed
- Under deck: at least 12 meters or one bulkhead

Separated by a complete compartment or hold from:

- On deck: at least 36 meters fore-and-aft and athwart ship stowage allowed
- Under deck: two decks or two bulkheads

Separated longitudinally by an intervening complete compartment:

- Allowed only on deck, fore-and-aft direction stowage, at least 48 meters

If the vehicle deck does not meet the requirements of the IMDG Code for such stowage, the cargo cannot be loaded there. The closing arrangements between the vehicle deck where these cargoes are loaded and the accommodation or machinery spaces should be securely closed in order not to allow any dangerous vapors or liquids to gain access to these spaces. As a general practice on car carriers, vehicles loaded with dangerous goods are stowed on the strengthened car decks.

No dangerous goods are allowed on or inside passenger cars.

The respective vehicle—either trailer or road tank—should be properly labeled as required by IMDG Code. Vehicles containing flammable gases or liquids having a flashpoint of 73.4°F (23°C) or less and transported on deck should be stowed "away from" any source of ignition.

Used portable tanks or road tank vehicles must be equipped with a Gas Free Certificate, showing that the vehicle is no longer considered as dangerous cargo. In Europe, this document is known as European Cleaning Document (ECD). Details can be found at www.eftco.org.

APPENDIX TO DOCUMENT OF COMPLIANCE SPECIAL REQUIREMENTS FOR SHIPS CARRYING DANGEROUS GOODS

Document No.: 5972
DNV Id. No.: 24838

DANGEROUS GOODS IN PACKAGED FORM

Cargo spaces indicated with numbers corresponding with the table below

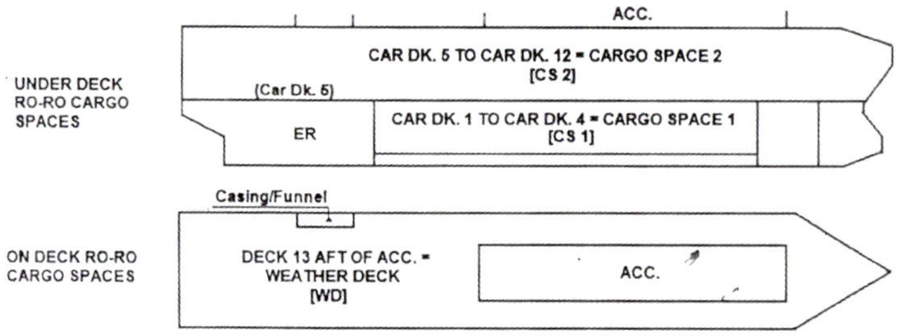

Class	Cargo spaces:	CS 1	CS 2	WD								Footnotes
1.1–1.6	Explosives	-	-	-								
1.4 S	Substances and articles which present no significant hazard	P	P	-								-
2.1	Flammable gases	P	P	-								1) 3)
2.2	Non-flammable, non-toxic gases	P	P	-								3)
2.3	Toxic gases	P	P	-								3)
3	Flammable liquids. Pg I and II Flash point <23°C	-	P	-								4)
3	Flammable liquids. Pg III 23°C ≤ Flash point ≤ 60°C	P	P	-								3)
4.1	Flammable solids, self-reactive substances and desensitized explosives	P	P	-								3)
4.2	Substances liable to spontaneous combustion	P	P	-								3)
4.3	Substances which, in contact with water, emit flammable gases.	P	P	-								3)
5.1	Oxidizing substances	P	P	-								2) 3)
5.2	Organic peroxides	-	-	-								
6.1	Toxic substances. Liquids	-	P	-								4)
6.1	Toxic substances. Liquids. Flash point <23°C	-	P	-								4)
6.1	Toxic substances. Liquids. 23°C≤ Flash point ≤60°C	-	P	-								4)
6.1	Toxic substances. Solids	P	P	-								
8	Corrosive substances. Liquids	P	P	-								
8	Corrosive substances. Liquids. Flash point <23°C	-	P	-								4)
8	Corrosive substances. Liquids. 23°C≤ Flash point ≤60°C	P	P	-								3)
8	Corrosive substances. Solids	P	P	-								
9	Miscellaneous dangerous substances and articles	P	P	-								

P Indicates PACKAGED GOODS PERMITTED
- NOT ALLOWED
See notes and footnotes on last page.

DET NORSKE VERITAS 1864
DARBU

DET NORSKE VERITAS, VERITASVEIEN 1, NO-1322 HØVIK, NORWAY, TEL INT: +47 67 57 99 00, TELEFAX: +47 67 57 99 11
Form No.: DG47.71b Issue: October 2007 Page 2 of 3

Ro-Ro spaces. The drawing shows "Under deck Ro-Ro cargo spaces" and "On deck Ro-Ro cargo spaces" on a 6,000-unit car carrier. CS1 (Cargo Space 1) and CS2 (Cargo Space 2) are separated because on some car decks packed goods of various classes are permitted, while on others this is not the case.

Cargo ships of 500 GT and over, passenger ships constructed since September 1, 1984, and cargo ships of under 500 GT constructed since February 1, 1992, are required to carry a Document of Compliance if engaged in the carriage of dangerous goods on international voyages. More recently, the format of that document has been amended to show the spaces that have been categorized for the stowage of dangerous goods and to limit its validity to five years. Owners whose ships have documentation over five years old should consider reviewing its validity.

Transportation of Military Cargo

Military cargo can be transported by sea only with the permission of the head office of the Company. Arms, ammunitions, and cargo that is not listed as military but looks like it are not accepted at all.

Australian Regulations

There are no special provisions in the Australian regulations that treat vehicles as dangerous objects. Transportation of vehicles using LPG as their fuel is subject to the same regulations applicable to vehicles powered by gasoline engines.

Australia does have one of the strongest quarantine measures in the world. Ro-Ro machinery, vehicles, etc., shipped to Australia, are subject to inspection by Australian Quarantine and Inspection Services (AQIS).

All cargo is inspected upon discharging and must pass the inspection. AQIS require the cargo to be presented in a clean condition. All vehicles should be thoroughly clean from soil and road grime, plant matter, and seeds. The most important points to be checked include the following:

- Wheels, wheel guards
- Spare tire and boot (trunk)
- The underside of the vehicle
- Chassis rails
- Under seats

Such an inspection is not the responsibility of the Carrier. It should be performed by the consignee at the discharging port. However, the role of the Carrier is to supervise the loading of the vehicles and to alarm the Stevedoring Company in the case of doubt.

US Regulations

The transportation regulations for vehicles, discussed earlier, are stipulated in CFR.

Many cargo units are packed in wooden crates, stowed on trailers, and delivered in the destination port. US regulations concerning the wood being used as packaging material, including dunnage, are very stringent and should be strictly adhered to. (See also chapter 5 for further details about dunnage.)

Another issue that should be considered is Asian Gypsy Moth. If car carriers have visited any of the six ports, Ooita, Hiroshima, Hannan, Sakata, Hachinhe, or Hakodate, where this moth lives, they are subject to inspection when visiting US ports. If the ships visit during the high-risk period (from July through September), they must be certified as AGM-free or risk delays in US ports.

Details about the regulations concerning AGM can be found at: www.aphis.usda.gov/plant_health/plant_pest_info/gypsy_moth/downloads/vessel-certification.pdf.

Details about the inspection of the ship with regard to AGM prevention can be found at: www.aphis.usda.gov.

Age Restrictions for Vehicles

Some countries have imposed age restrictions for importing vehicles. These restrictions are not of concern for the Carrier, but are of particular interest for the ship operators.

The following countries have imposed restrictions:

- **Angola:** No second-hand vehicles are permitted for import.
- **Barbados:** The age of the vehicles should not exceed twelve years.
- **China:** No second-hand vehicles are permitted for import.
- **Cyprus:** The vehicles should not exceed five years.
- **Dominican Republic:** The vehicles should not exceed five years.
- **Iraq (Umm Qasr):** The vehicles should not exceed one year, but there is no restriction for high and heavy units.
- **Jordan (Aqaba):** High and heavy units should be left-handed.

Transportation of Animals on Ro-Ro Ships

Council Regulation (EC) no. 1/2005 on the protection of animals during transport and related operations (The Regulation) is the main document applying to the carriage of live animals in vehicles on board Ro-Ro ships.

The Regulation came into force on January 5, 2007, and is applicable in all EU Member States

The Regulation is applicable to all vertebrate animals. However, in case of transportation of pet cats and dogs additional advice can be obtained from a Defra booklet entitled "Protecting the welfare of pet dogs and cats during journeys—Advice to Owners."

The Regulation only applies to commercial transport.

It is worth saying that Ro-Ro ships do not require inspection and approval before they are used to carry animals. Ro-Ro vessels should meet the additional provisions of The Regulation as stipulated in Annex I Chapter II 3.1.

The vessel and her fittings should be designed, constructed, maintained, and operated so as to avoid any injury and suffering, and to ensure the safety of the animals.

An enclosed deck used for animal vehicles must be fitted with a forced ventilation system that has an alarm and an emergency power source.

The animal vehicle should be suitable for Ro-Ro use. The vehicle and its fittings must be designed, constructed, maintained, and operated so as to avoid injury and suffering, and to ensure the safety of the animals. It must be able to withstand the stresses caused by the movement of the vessel at sea, and the center of gravity of the loaded vehicle should be as low as possible.

The animal container should be securely attached to the vehicle, and both the container and the vehicle must be adequately secured to the vessel. One securing point should be fitted close to each corner of the container, and others at intervals of not more than three meters along each side.

Animal shippers must ensure that the vehicle is suitable for carriage on Ro-Ro vessels and that water, feed, and rest intervals for the animals can be complied with.

Ship Owners must ensure that the vessel has suitable facilities for transport of animals in vehicles and that the Master is competent and has received specific instructions for Ro-Ro transport of animals.

The Master, officers, and crew of a Ro-Ro vessel should be trained in their duties and be competent to perform them with respect to carriage of animals. The Master, loading officers, and ship's staff under his authority must ensure:

That the animal vehicle is:

- Suitable for Ro-Ro use
- Is stowed and secured in a well-ventilated position
- Is given sufficient protection from the weather

That the weather conditions for the voyage:

- Are such that the animals will not be injured or suffer

All carriers should be authorized by the competent authority when the journey exceeds sixty-five kilometers. Such authorizations are valid for not more than five years and must be either for journeys up to eight hours (Type 1) or for long journeys (Type 2).

If it is to be stowed in enclosed deck, before loading a vehicle carrying animals, the Master should be satisfied that a ventilation system is fitted with a failure alarm and an adequate secondary power source. The air change capacity should normally not be less than twenty air changes per hour. However, a minimum of ten air changes per hour may be sufficient when only a limited number (five or less) of animal vehicles is carried.

The animal vehicle should be loaded in a way that it can be positioned in a suitable position to ensure the safety of the animals. Animal vehicles should be properly secured before the voyage commences.

Vehicles carrying adult cattle on two tiers should be transported on board a ship that has an effective stabilization system.

Of utmost importance for the transportation of animals on Ro-Ro ships is the combination of temperature and humidity. A combination of high temperature and high humidity within an animal compartment can quickly cause distress or even death. The table below shows the acceptable combinations of temperature and humidity.

Temperature	**24°C**	**26°C**	**28°C**	**31°C**	**35°C**
Humidity	**100%**	**75%**	**50%**	**25%**	**0%**

Ventilation arrangements differ from ship to ship and from vehicle to vehicle. If the vehicles lack effective mechanical fan ventilation, the following should be noted:

- Two-tier and single-deck vehicles with adequate ventilation and height may be stowed on any suitably ventilated vehicle deck.
- Three-tier vehicles have limited ventilation and headroom. Therefore they should be stowed in totally enclosed vehicle decks when the ambient temperature in the vehicle deck is below 20° C. If the ambient temperature is 20° C or above, the three-tier animal vehicles should be stowed on open or semi-open vehicle decks.
- Four-tier vehicles are not considered suitable for Ro-Ro use. This is because they have very restricted ventilation and headroom within the livestock tiers.

The level of lighting at the loading point and in the vehicle deck should be sufficient for inspection and care of the animals. Lighting within the vehicle may be part of its fittings or of the portable type.

In the event of emergency treatment or the necessity to slaughter sick or injured animals, the Master should have a procedure for getting advice from a veterinarian.

If safety regulations permit, a vessel carrying animals on a voyage exceeding three hours must have a suitable means of emergency slaughter on board.

CHAPTER 7

CARGO HANDLING EQUIPMENT

Ro-Ro ships are loaded/discharged according to the roll-on/roll-off principles. This requires special cargo handling and access equipment. In order to allow the cargo to be driven on, car carriers are equipped with special ramps connected to the ship by hinges.

Considering the type of cargo being loaded and discharged on Ro-Ro ships, the cargo equipment on board includes internal and external ramps with different SWL, trailer lifts, retractable decks, and movable bridges. Shipboard management must be familiar with this equipment and its operation if they are to conduct the cargo operations in the safest and most effective manner.

Ramps

To avoid accidents and damage to ship cargo, it is most important that all ramps must be operated by well-trained and authorized ship's personnel.

Purpose

The external ramps are used as doors leading in and out of the ship. Their main purpose is to allow loading and discharging of vehicles, but, at the same time, they act as watertight doors.

The recess of the external ramps is very close to the water level, so, if the watertightness of the ramp is not complete, the ship is subject to flooding. To fulfill this latter purpose, the ramps must be designed in such a way to guarantee their watertightness. This is usually done by using special rubber gaskets that surround the perimeter of the ramp. A steel compression bar compresses this gasket.

From a legal point of view, ramps that are not watertight will render a vessel unseaworthy and not in accordance with the Hague-Visby Rules or Hamburg Rules, depending which are in force, as stipulated in the Charter Party (C/P). In order to allow the crew to become acquainted with the ramps and their operation, the manufacturer must issue an operation manual, which should be approved. Operation procedures for the ramps should be understood by the crew in charge, who should strictly abide by them. However, some precautions are in force regardless of the manual:

- No personnel are allowed close to and beneath moving objects.
- No personnel are allowed close to moving operation equipment such as wires, winches, etc.
- All personnel operating the ramps must be very well trained. Only authorized personnel are allowed to operate the ramps.
- All personnel working close to ramps should wear reflective vests.

As a general rule the equipment must be kept in good working condition, which is the responsibility of the officer in charge. It is of vital importance that the Planned Maintenance Schedule is strictly adhered to and the appropriate records required by SMS and/or manufacturers are regularly kept. Greasing is one of the most important tasks, especially if the ship operates in cold climates. (*See Maintenance*)

The ramps are usually described by their dimensions, which consist of the following:

- Total length
- The length of different sections, if any
- Width of the driveway in the narrowest part
- Width of the ramp
- Slope of the ramp
- Slope of different sections, if any
- Allowable quay heights with maximum slope
- The maximum distance between ship and berth that allows safe use of the ramp
- Maximum working load, which is the maximum load that can pass over the ramp at the same time. It varies between 30 to 300 t.

Types of Ramps

Generally the ramps can be divided into two main groups depending on the driving mechanism:

- Hydraulically operated ramps
- Electrically driven ramps

Both types can be fitted either with wires or cylinders.

Depending on their location and the purpose, the ramps can be divided into two categories:

- External ramps, acting as doors and ensuring the watertightness of the ship
- Internal ramps, acting as way for distributing the vehicles inside the ship

Ramps can be divided as stern and side ramps, depending on their location on board. Ramps located partially or totally below the freeboard deck and with a clear area greater than 6 m[2] should be provided with an arrangement for remote control located above the freeboard deck.

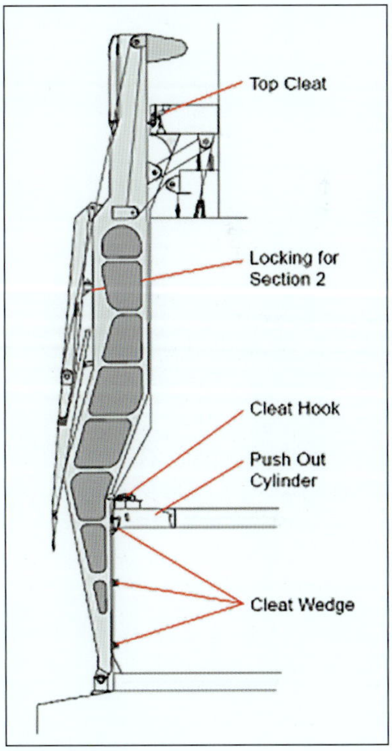

Stern ramp layout

Hydraulically Operated Ramps

Lowering or heaving the ramp is conducted either by means of wires or cylinders.

It must be kept in mind that this is a general description of a hydraulically operated ramp with wires. In each case, the particulars of a ramp will be different and the operation manual should be read carefully.

Hydraulically Operated Ramps with Wires

These ramps normally consist of two sections connected to each other. The first section is the section attached to the ship's hull by means of hinges. The second section is the one lies on the pier when the ramp is lowered. Finger flaps are attached to the ends of both of these sections, as well as to the connection between them, in order to provide smooth transition between ramp and ship and to distribute the forces between the ramp and the quay.

The ramp is lowered or heaved using a wire, one end of which is connected to the main winch and the other to the first section. The main winch is normally of the drum type and is driven by a high-torque, low-speed, hydraulic, radial piston-type motor.

Another very important part of the winch is its parting brakes (band-drum type). These brakes are spring-actuated and are released through hydraulic pressure.

When the ramp is being lowered, the second section is spread out by a jigger winch or by a spreading wire that is coiled onto the spreading drum. Another feature is a so-called launching cylinder, which pushes out the ramp from the stern to the point where it starts falling by gravity. During closing, this hydraulic cylinder has a cushioning effect when the ramp passes the equilibrium point.

IACS (International Association of Classification Societies) defines a "securing device" as a device that is used to keep the ramp/door closed by preventing it from rotating about its hinges or about pivoted attachments to the ship. Devices that secure the ramp weathertight to the coaming are operated by sets of cleating cylinders.

A "locking device" is defined as a device that locks a securing device in the closed position. Devices that lock the ramp to the hull are operated by locking cylinders.

When the ramp is on the pier its height can be adjusted for the height of the pier, taking into account the tidal tolerance. The adjustment is made using two buttress cylinders placed on the first section. These cylinders are located symmetrically on each side of the ramp. When the ramp is down and the height is adjusted according to the height of the quay, the correct slope of the ramp can be maintained by a so-called quay detector, which measures the distance to the quay. In this case, the main winch and jigger winch (spreading wire winch) are working as automatic, self-tensioning winches—in other words they are fed with pre-set and respective spread pressure to keep wires tight and reduce quay pressure.

Main winch: The main winch for operating the wire. There can be one or two main winches depending on the size of the ramp. As required under SOLAS, the date when the wires are put in operation or when the ends are turned must be permanently marked; in the picture, the date is stenciled with red paint.

Quay detector: If quay detector detects low clearance between ramp and quay or vice versa, it allows the buttressing cylinder to increase the angle between both sections of the ramp automatically.

Needless to say, a very steep slope is to be avoided because it could lead to damage to the cars, especially to high and heavy units with small clearances. In order to avoid this, the duty officer must observe the slope and keep the vehicle envelope (which was explained in chapter 4) as wide as possible. There are many instances of cargo operations being discontinued by the stevedores due to steep slopes and small vehicle envelopes. In fact, all the damages and problems will be borne by the ship.

Another issue to be considered is tidal clearance. The ramp will be moving up and down, so the slope will change accordingly. It is important that the ship management has all tidal calculations and expected changes in ship's draft at hand so the ramp can be adjusted as soon as possible upon berthing, in order to avoid any delays. The slope can be measured by a slant ruler or special slope indicator (inclinometer) mounted on the ramp.

Buttress cylinder: At the left in the picture is the jigger winch for spreading the second section of the wire-operated ramp. Also we can see the finger flaps mounted on the connection between the first and second sections. Buttress cylinders can adjust the slope of the ramp depending on the height of quay—low, normal or high

When the ramp is closed, it is locked to the hull by a set of locking cylinders. The ramp is secured to the coaming by a set of cleating cylinders, making a watertight connection. Watertightness of the ramp is guaranteed by means of rubber packing compressed by a compression bar.

Other parts of the ramp equipment include: a safety valve block on the winch motor for automatic stopping in case of hose or pipe failure; one set of load control valves on the jigger winch to hydraulically stop the second section; two load control valves, one on each buttressing cylinder; and electric solenoid valves, safety relief valves, and pressure reduction valves usually located in the steering gear room.

The ramp is operated from a control stand, which should be equipped with procedures for correct operation as well as indicators for different stages of the operating process, i.e., start, stop, when the second section is folded, when the ramp is closed and locked, etc.

Stern ramp: A typical layout of a wire-operated ramp

All winches are hydraulically operated. The hydraulic unit consists of several pumps, an oil tank, and flexible hoses and pipes. One or two pumps are used for filtration or cooling of the unit. The corresponding electric motors are equipped with anti-condensation heating.

The oil tank is essentially a box equipped with covers for cleaning, visual level indicator, temperature sensor (which automatically will stop the electrical motors if the temperature is too high or too low), one level sensor, filter, filter indicator, and air filter. There is a draining plug at the bottom.

The maneuvering time of this type of ramp varies according to the ambient temperature, but it is generally about 15–20 minutes.

Normally, external ramps are wire-operated. This is because wire-operated-ramps are more reliable than hydraulic ramps.

Some of the internal ramps are coated with anti-skid paint. This paint requires special attention because it can be easily damaged. It also poses the risk of scratching the cars during loading/discharging because of the stones/sand embedded in the paint.

Maintenance of Hydraulically Operated Ramps with Wires

Maintenance of these ramps includes not only the ramp itself, but also the associated equipment. Therefore consideration must be given to the most common failures of the wires, ramps, and hydraulic equipment, and to the ways of avoiding them.

The maintenance of wire-operated ramps must be conducted as per the Planned Maintenance Schedule and manufacturer's instructions.

Greasing the Wires

The most important maintenance item for this type of ramps is the greasing of the wires. Appropriate methods for internal lubrication are outlined in Australian Standard™ AS 2759-2004, "Steel Wire Rope—Use, Operation and Maintenance."

The following principles are applicable to greasing the wires:

- **The greasing should be applied as soon as the wire is put in operation and then at regular intervals in order to avoid corrosion or dryness.**
- **The appropriate type of grease should be used, as prescribed by the manufacturer.** Where the wire is exposed to the corrosive action of water (e.g., the spreading wire), it should be greased with a continuous layer of high-viscosity grease. However, the type of the grease depends on the size and construction of the wire rope, type of equipment on which the rope is used, and the operating conditions of the wire.
- **The grease should not be applied in excessive quantities.**
- **When the old grease contains impurities, it should be removed and disposed of as required by MARPOL (not thrown overboard).** It must be kept in mind that in some countries PSC officers regularly check the storage of the old grease corresponding to the records for Planned Maintenance Schedule as required by ISM Code.
- **Before a lubricant is applied to the wire, the wire should be thoroughly cleaned.** There are different methods for cleaning the old grease, including: by hand, using wire brushes or scrapers; with dry compressed air (attention should be paid when using compressed air, as it tends to blow the impurities between the strands of the wire); or by rubbing down with a light flushing oil that is free of kerosene. When the old grease is removed, it is advisable to apply wire oil, because it has good penetrating abilities and acts as anti-corrosive fluid. After evaporation of the fluid, a thin, colored, greasy preventive film will remain.
- **New wire grease should be applied using painting gloves or a brush.** The grease should be the one recommended by the manufacturer. The drum section can be lubricated by hand using a brush or an oil can. In order to prevent corrosion, special attention should be paid when greasing the sheaves and any other places that are difficult to reach.

Inadequate lubrication can result in corrosion, heavy abrasive wear, fretting between wires, and stiffening of the wire. The recommended greasing interval is usually not more than three months.

Inspection and Maintenance of Wires

The wires used to operate the ramps are galvanized, which provides protection against the corrosive action of the sea. Very often, the wires have IWRC—independent wire rope core. The wire can be identified by its construction, normally the number of strands in the rope and the number of wires in each strand. The most common type of wire used for ramps is IWRC 6 x 24, which denotes a 6-strand rope, with each strand having 24 wires. The helix or the spiral of the wire is known as the "lay" of the wire. The most common lay is called regular or ordinary lay, which has wires that are twisted in one direction and strands that are twisted in the opposite direction to form the rope. Ropes with ordinary lay are less likely to untwist or kink. Such ropes are also less subject to failure from crushing and distortion because of the shorter length of the exposed outer wires.

The wires have the following characteristics:

- **Strength (often referred to as minimum breaking force or minimum breaking load):** the minimum load required to break the wire
- **Resistance to rotation**
- **Resistance to abrasive wear:** Abrasive wear takes place between the wire and sheave, and between the wire and the drum winch. In order to reduce the abrasive wear, wires with relatively large outer wires should be selected.
- **Corrosion resistance:** As mentioned earlier, the wires are galvanized to reduce the corrosion.

The ratio of the breaking strength of a wire to the total applied load is the safety factor. The minimum safety factor of wires for lifting gear used on board is a 5:1 ratio.

Normally the wires are to be changed every five years or when the external wires are heavily corroded and there is reason to believe that internal corrosion exists. When corrosion is observed, the wire should be examined thoroughly and replaced if necessary. The new wire should be of the same type as the replaced one, with the same length and safety factor. The wires are subject to annual and five-year surveys. Details of the surveys are recorded in the vessel's Register of Lifting Appliances and Cargo Handling Gear. A current standard, DIN 15 020 (Safety operation of wire ropes) stipulates the criteria for discarding wire ropes.

External Inspections

During the external inspections, the following should be verified:

- **Reduction of nominal rope diameter due to loss of core support or internal or external corrosion or wear of individual outside wires.** The diameter should be measured in the circumscribing circle in six or more places on the wire
- **Number of broken outside wires and degree of distribution or concentration of broken wires**
- **Corroded, pitted, or broken wires in way of end connections.** When corroded wire ropes become fragile, their strength dramatically reduces. If only the surface is rusty, the rope may be all right, but the condition requires extreme caution if the corrosion has progressed.
- **Corroded, cracked, bent, worn, or improperly applied end connections**
- **Severe kinking, crushing, or distortion of rope structure.** The best way to prevent kinking is to find signs of kinks and prevent them.
- **Evidence of exposure to heat**
- **Valley breaks.** As the IWRC fails, the outer strands lose their radial support. This allows the wires of the outer strands to bear against each other tangentially. The resulting inter-strand nicking restricts the movement of the strands within the rope. Without this freedom of movement, secondary fatigue breaks will develop at the strand tangent points in the wires

of the outer strands. Because these fatigue breaks develop in the valleys between the outer strands, they are also called valley breaks.

- **The wire rope retains an adequate safety margin**
- **All sheaves are rotating freely and properly greased**

One of the methods for visual inspection is the rag-and-visual method. This method is simple. If the rope is covered by a rag and then moved, the broken wires will snag the rag. This will be indication for external damage.

Prohibition of Use of Unsuitable Wire Ropes

The wire ropes should be discarded in the following cases:

- Their strands have been broken to 10% of the total number within a pitch
- Their diameter has been reduced by 7% or more of the nominal one. Although wires of six-strand construction hold up to 90% of their strength in the outer strands, it should be borne in mind that the core provides the support that maintains the wire's efficiency and performance.
- They are conspicuously deformed or corroded
- They are buckled
- They have significant built-up corrosion
- They are pinched
- There are visible wire and strand fractures

Reduction of wire diameter: In this particular case the reduction of diameter was more than 15%, clear grounds for replacement of the wire.

Internal Inspections

A wire can be opened for internal inspection only when it is completely relaxed. While trying not to damage the strands or core, open the wire in six or more places, by working a marlinspike between two strands. Carefully rotate the spike to expose the core and underside of the strands. Inspect for internal corrosion, broken wires, or core failure. Particular attention should be paid in areas close to the end fittings, areas of the wire that pass over sheaves or are coiled onto drums, and areas that remain exposed to seawater. Only qualified personnel should be authorized to inspect wires. There is also a non-destructive method for discovering internal defects of the wire using electro-magnetic testing devices.

Regulations concerning the testing, certification, and thorough examination and inspection of wire rope will be implemented by the competent authorities in accordance with the requirements of ILO Convention 152: articles 21 to 26.[4]

Wires should be tested by the manufacturer, referred to as a "mill test," and the appropriate certificate should be issued and available on board. ILO Convention 152: 1979, "Occupational Safety and Health" (dock work), articles 21 to 26, requires the following information to be entered into the certificate:

- Name and address of the manufacturer
- Identifying number of each coil
- Diameter of wire
- Straight line breaking strength
- Knotted breaking load or, alternatively, the elongation in a 10-inch test piece
- Number of strands
- Number of wires per strand
- Type of core
- Lay of wire
- SWL

The elongation in such a test piece is not to be less than 7%. It is the responsibility of the person using the wire to check that each coil is referenced on the mill certificate and is adequate for the intended use.

Additionally, a certificate for the wires, showing their specifications, should be available on board.

Greasing through Nipples

Greasing through nipples should be performed according to the Planned Maintenance Schedule and manufacturer's instructions. Such grease nipples are located on all hinges, cleats, locking devices, and flaps. The responsible officer must ensure that the greasing is done with utmost care and attention, because improper greasing can lead to failure and hamper proper operation. There is a greasing plan in the Operation Manual and this must be strictly followed. The grease must be of the appropriate type and can be applied by grease guns or, on the cleats and locking devices, by brushes. Grease guns should be calibrated to measure the amount of grease applied, and clean to avoid mixing of types of grease.

Moving parts of stern ramp, properly greased through grease nipples

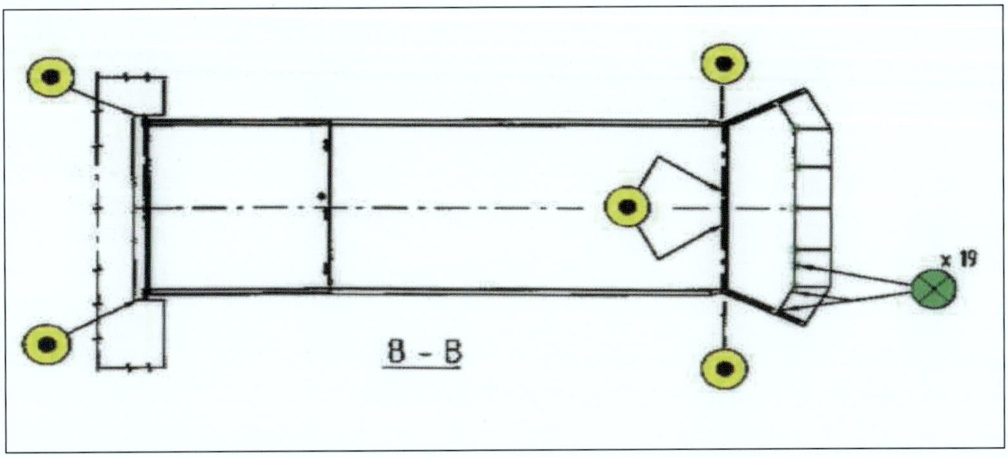

Lubricating plan for the ramp

Inspection of Hinges and Pins

This inspection should be conducted as per Planned Maintenance Schedule and recorded accordingly. Special attention should be paid to the pins, especially if the ship is old. They should be checked for corrosion and proper positioning. The most common accidents have happened due to such pins being extracted from their proper positions.

Hinges of stern ramp

Maintenance of Rubber Packing

The weathertightness of the ramp is guaranteed by rubber packing compressed by compression bar, so this packing should be regularly inspected and maintained. During inspection of rubber packing, the person in charge should verify that the rubber is undamaged. If it is damaged, it should be replaced when the ramp is open. In order to protect the rubber packing and to guarantee a longer service life, a thin film of manufacturer's approved grease (Vaseline) should be applied on a regular basis. The retaining channels for the rubber packing should be inspected as well.

Maintenance of Anti-Skid Paint

Before commencement of cargo operations and especially during ballast voyages, the condition of anti-skid paint should be checked and new paint applied if damage is found. It should be stressed that the process of mixing, applying, and curing of such paint is time-consuming and, therefore, it must be completed well in advance of the commencement of cargo loading operations.

Maintenance of Hydraulic Unit

The hydraulic system of the cargo-handling equipment requires utmost attention. Regardless of the type of ramps, they are generally operated by a hydraulic power pack with the oil being supplied via flexible hoses and piping. In case of malfunction either in the pumps or in the piping (such as ruptured pipe or hose), the cargo handling equipment will not operate as required, which will lead to delays and even uncontrolled movements of the ramps. Therefore proper maintenance is crucial.

Inspection of the hydraulic unit should comprise the following:

- Oil level in the tank is to be checked daily; the level gauge should be to the required level. Checking must be performed when the power pack is off.
- Electrical indicators of all filters should be checked regularly as specified in the manufacturer's guidelines.
- Brake adjustment of drum-winches should be checked regularly as specified in the manufacturer's guidelines.
- Contamination of the oil should be checked regularly, as specified in the manufacturer's guidelines.
- All flexible hoses should be checked and replaced in case of wear or damage. (If the connection between the hose and piping is covered with anti-corrosive tape, any corrosion or wear might be overlooked.)
- Electrical circuits should be checked regularly, as specified in the manufacturer's guidelines.
- Oil leakages and seepage should be dealt with on spot.
- It should be kept in mind that any oil leakage could lead to oil pollution, which may result in the ship being detained.

Piping and hoses located outside the ship's hull should be checked before any opening or closing operation of the ramp.

Hydraulically Operated Ramps with Cylinders

Hydraulically operated ramps with cylinders do not have wires but are lowered down and heaved up using hydraulic cylinders. At the beginning of the lowering of the ramp, a launching cylinder pushes the ramp out to the point where it starts falling by gravity.

Hydraulically operated stern ramp: Typical layout of a hydraulically operated ramp

The hydraulic power pack of cylinder-operated ramps is the same as hydraulic wire-operated ramps, if both types are installed on board, and the principles of operating ramps with cylinders is the same as wire-operated ramps. The ramps are equipped with finger flaps, which are connected to the main part of the ramp by hinges. The finger flaps provide a smooth transition between the ramp and the ship and distribute the forces between the ramps and the pier. Maintenance and inspection is the same as hydraulic wire-operated ramps, with exception of the inspections of the wires.

Emergency Operation of Ramps

Hydraulic ramps can be operated in the emergency mode. In this mode, the computer program is by-passed and there are no visual and audible alarms on the control panels. Normally emergency operation is executed by a hand pump with two separate connections that are fitted to the respective connections of the ramp's control panels. The first valve is for unlocking and lowering the ramp; the other is for closing and locking the ramp.

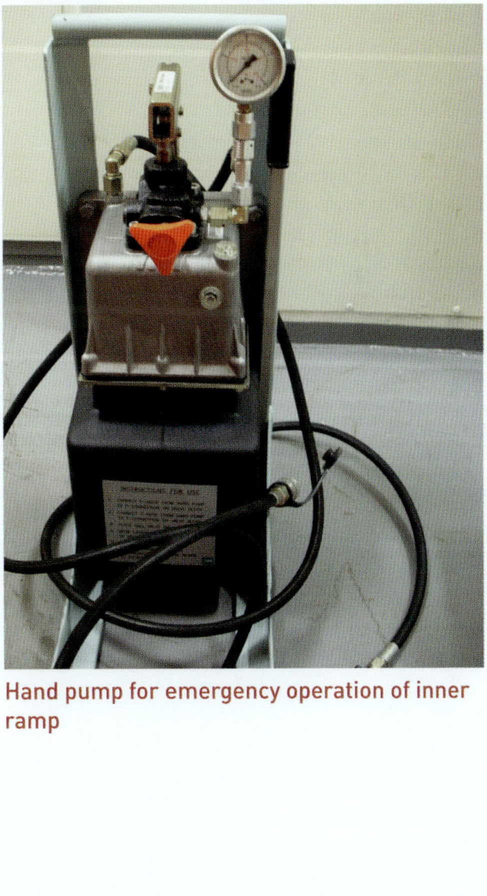

Hand pump for emergency operation of inner ramp

The operation for opening and closing the ramp in the emergency mode must be executed with utmost attention. The procedure for emergency operation of the ramps must be strictly followed and well known to the responsible officer. On the most modern generations of ramps, the emergency operation can be conducted from the PLC (Programmable Logic Controller) cabinet after redirecting control from the control room of the ramp to the PLC cabinet.

The internal ramps can be operated in the emergency mode as well, using a hand pump and the same principles for opening and closing as described above.

Electrically Driven Ramps

Electric ramps have the same construction as hydraulic driven ramps, but are operated electrically. The use of electrical power has some advantages. All ramps are operated from panels located on car decks and are controlled by PLC. The electric drive principle removes the necessity of hydraulic pipes and reduces the risk of oil pollution significantly. Electric actuators replace the hydraulic cylinders for locking and cleating. Electric driving systems are environmental friendly and easy to maintain. They save energy, as no continuous operation is needed. Also electric drive systems are not affected by cold or ice as hydraulic drives are.

Side Ramps

Side ramps can be either hydraulically operated or the electric type. A peculiarity of side ramps is that their height can be adjusted from main deck level to one or two decks higher. There are ports in the world where only side ramps can be used. The Master should receive information about the ramp to be used in advance. In addition, when preparing the Stowage Plan, the Chief Officer should take into account the port rotation as well as the possibility of using side or stern ramps only.

When lowering the side ramp, there is a risk of touching obstacles on the quay. Therefore, it is absolutely necessary that a crewmember is on the pier when the side ramp is lowered.

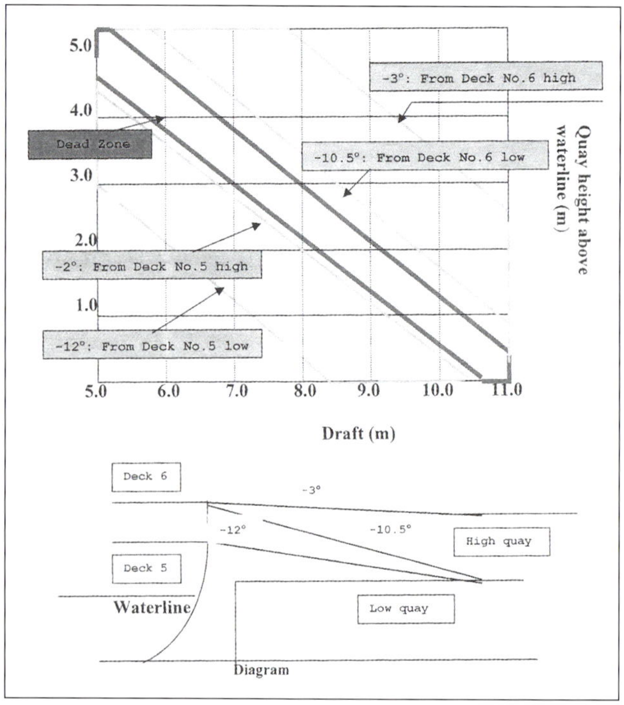

Safe range of angles: This diagram should not be used for estimating angles in real situations—it is intended for explanation only!

Side ramps should be marked with their SWL, which should never be exceeded. Due to their reduced SWL, side ramps, as a rule, can be used for loading and discharging of passenger cars only, not for loading and discharging high and heavy units. There is a diagram in the operation manual for the range of angles within which the side ramp can be operated safely (such diagrams are given for the stern ramp as well). The layout of the ramps and the angles to the pier also can be taken from the General Arrangement Plan.

Such diagrams are given in the operational manual for the ramps. From the diagram, the Chief Officer can obtain the range of working angles for stern or side ramps. The data necessary for using such a diagram are the height of the quay (it should be obtained well before arrival from the Agent) and the draft of the ship. The diagram illustrated here shows the range of working angles of a side ramp. The use of this ramp has been chosen because side ramps can be adjusted for two or more car decks, depending on the stowage and height of the quay, and therefore a variety of angles are available. On the drawing only the extreme angles for low and high quay are given. There is a dead zone in between, in which the ramp cannot be used.

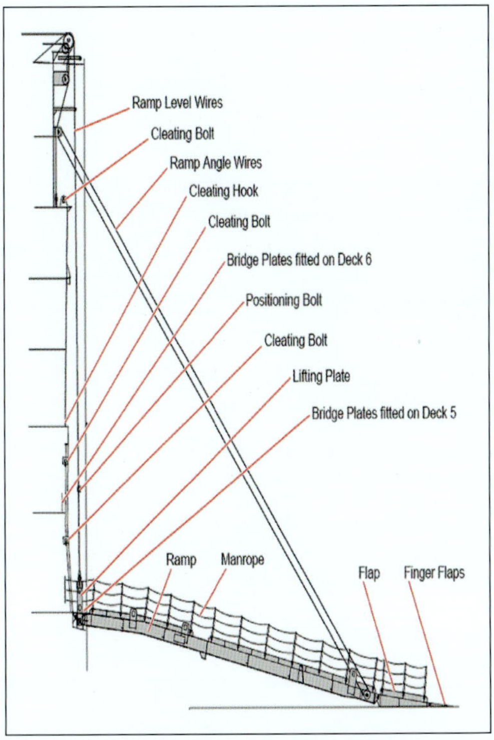

Side ramp layout *(Courtesy: MacGregor)*

Ramp supports on upper deck: Lack of greasing could lead to the supports becoming stuck and resulting in problems when positioning the side ramp in the upper position. Note the greasing nipples.

Side ramps can be adjusted to the respective car decks by so-called jigger winches. Once the ramp has been raised to the upper deck, it will rest on supports (which are subject to the Planned Maintenance Schedule). Failure to perform the proper maintenance on side ramps may lead to accidents and have serious consequences.

Hinges should be properly greased

The hinges connecting the ramps to the hull are designed to counteract the forces and moments to which the ramp is being exposed in case of trim and list caused by uneven loading or discharging. Proper and timely greasing of the hinges is necessary to keep them operable and should be included in the Planned Maintenance Schedule. The extreme values of trim and list should be cited in the operational manual of the ramps. Normally the list should not exceed ±3° and the trim may be up to ±2°.

Inspections of Side Ramp

A side ramp is a very important part of a car carrier's equipment because it is used for cargo operations and to ensure weathertightness of the ship. Therefore it requires proper and timely maintenance as stipulated in the Planned Maintenance Schedule. The main items that require inspection:

General layout of side ramp

Thimble of lifting wire attached to the side ramp

- **Hoisting and lifting wires** (level deck wires). Refer to Inspection and Maintenance of wires for general wire inspection criteria.
- **Hoisting wires that lift or lower the side ramp**
- **Lifting wires that are used for lifting the side ramp to upper decks**

The specifications of lifting wires can vary, but normally they have larger diameter than hoisting wires. Due to the type of cargo and rotation, lifting wires are infrequently used. Proper greasing of the lifting wire is essential, therefore.

Lifting wire properly greased

The sheaves of lifting wires should be greased as well.

Inspection of Supports for the Upper Position of the Ramp

As the side ramp requires lifting in only a few ports in the world, the use of these supports will be limited and sometimes they will not be used for a long time. To avoid becoming stuck or frozen, they should be greased as per Planned Maintenance Schedule.

Inspections of Locking Devices

Locking devices should be regularly greased with brushes to avoid any friction. During inspection locking devices should be checked for maximum thickness diminution (should be within the limits imposed by the Classification Society but not more than 15% below the "as-built" thickness or the maximum corrosion allowance of the Classification Society). If cracks are found, an examination using a non-destructive testing method should be carried out.

Inspections of Manual Locking Devices (if Fitted)

In addition to the automatically operated locking devices, most of the side ramps are fitted with manual locking devices. Their primary maintenance consists of the proper greasing of the thread, which should be performed at regular intervals. During inspection of locking devices, they should be checked for maximum thickness as described above.

Manual locking device

Inspection of the Jigger Winch

Jigger winches are used for heaving and lowering the side ramp to and from the upper deck. During a visual inspection, all hoses and piping should be checked for any leakage. If necessary, they can be protected with anti-corrosive tape. Jigger winches also can be used on stern ramps to spread the spread wire and fold the second section of the ramp.

Jigger winch on a side ramp. Notice that two hoses are protected with anti-corrosive tape.

Inspection of Shed Structure of the Ramp

Visual inspection of the structural items of the side ramp should be performed at intervals stipulated in the Planned Maintenance Schedule. Structural parts, especially when exposed to the environment, may wear down and their strength may become impaired. Maximum design clearance between securing and supporting devices should not exceed 3 mm.

Side ramp

Maintenance of Rubber Packing

Weathertightness of the ramp is provided by the rubber packing (or other soft material), which acts on a compression bar. Therefore, both the rubber packing and compression bar should be inspected and maintained. Check the rubber packing for damage and if it is found, replace it. In order to protect the rubber packing and to guarantee a longer service life, it should be smeared with a thin film of Vaseline on a regular basis. However, the greasing of rubber packing should be done only if recommended by the manufacturer. The channels for rubber packing should be inspected as well.

Slewing Ramp

A slewing ramp has a main advantage that the ship can be berthed without the need for dedicated shore facilities. Slewing can be to port or starboard. The ramp can also be used in the fore-and-aft directions.

Generally a slewing ramp is of the same construction as a stern ramp. However, there is an additional slewing unit, which allows the ramp to rotate. The slewing unit can be either operated by dedicated winches or directly by hydraulic cylinders.

The time for deploying the ramp may vary depending on the ambient temperature; it is normally within 15–30 minutes.

Internal Ramps

In order to allow for the movement of cars inside the ship (between different decks), several internal ramps are installed, depending on the size of the ship. Alternatively, some ships are equipped with lifts to move vehicles between decks. Generally, all internal ramps are hydraulically or electrically operated. The SWL of these ramps should never be exceeded. The SWL must be marked (stenciled or by label) close to the ramp in question. When the ramp is closed, it has the same SWL as the deck to which it is hinged.

Some ramps can be hoisted or lowered when loaded with cargo at its maximum SWL, but this operation should be performed ONLY when in port.

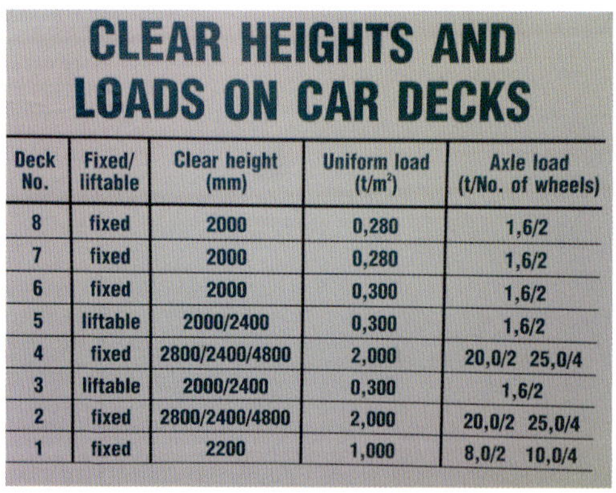

CLEAR HEIGHTS AND LOADS ON CAR DECKS

Deck No.	Fixed/ liftable	Clear height (mm)	Uniform load (t/m²)	Axle load (t/No. of wheels)
8	fixed	2000	0,280	1,6/2
7	fixed	2000	0,280	1,6/2
6	fixed	2000	0,300	1,6/2
5	liftable	2000/2400	0,300	1,6/2
4	fixed	2800/2400/4800	2,000	20,0/2 25,0/4
3	liftable	2000/2400	0,300	1,6/2
2	fixed	2800/2400/4800	2,000	20,0/2 25,0/4
1	fixed	2200	1,000	8,0/2 10,0/4

Placard showing clear heights on car decks

Some of the internal ramps are required to be gastight and watertight. Watertightness is achieved by a rubber gasket (or other soft material) that acts against a compression bar and completely surrounds the perimeter frame of the ramp.

The internal ramps are connected to the deck by hinges. As mentioned earlier, there are two or three strengthened car decks designed for loading of heavy cargo. Some of the internal ramps may be fitted with covers that are hydraulically or electrically operated, thus allowing free and unobstructed access of the taller cargo to the strengthened decks. When closed, these ramps will be locked and cleated by locking devices. These locking devices consist of locking cylinders and locking devices.

When the ramp is lowered, it must be surrounded by safety fencing, such as railings, and clearly marked by reflective cones and signs. There are many accounts of accidents that involve cars falling due to improper marking of the boundaries of these openings.

Boundary railings should be rigged to block access to the open ramp. However, the use of lashings instead of ropes should be avoided.

The maneuvering time for operating internal ramps is generally between five and eight minutes, depending on the ambient temperature and hydraulic system.

When a ramp leads to movable decks, it can be positioned in two places depending on the position of the retractable decks. (See Movable Decks)

No cargo operations are allowed while internal ramps are being opened or closed. Only authorized personnel are to operate the ramps and at least two persons should be involved in this operation: an operator who operates the ramp from the control stand and a watchman who oversees the operation and keeps an eye out for any unauthorized movements. All internal ramps are operated from control stands and sometimes the view from these stands is obscured, which can be dangerous.

Proper fencing and marking of all openings is a must during cargo operations.

Internal ramp in open position with the legs resting in their sockets

Legs of internal ramp resting in their sockets (close-up)

When hydraulic cylinders (legs) support the ramp in its open position, special attention should be paid that the cylinder is resting properly in the socket. When the legs are properly seated they will activate a sensor, which will activate an alarm on the control panel. However, a visual check for improper seating is necessary as well. This could happen, for example, if the ramp is covered with anti-skid paint, creating the possibility that the small stones, which are mixed into the paint, are dislodged and fall into the sockets. This could cause a risk of the legs not resting properly in their sockets. Before lowering the ramp, the sockets should be checked and cleaned if necessary.

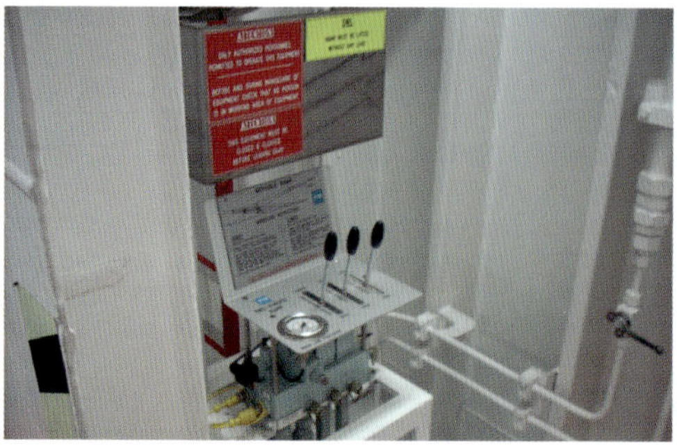

Control stand for an internal ramp. Pay attention to the warning indicators, which should be checked during inspections.

There should be signs that clearly indicate the SWL of the ramp, as well as signs stating that all locking devices should be engaged before the ship leaves the pier. As a rule all internal ramps are fitted with a lock. The position of this lock on hydraulically driven ramps is on the hydraulic pressure line isolation valve. As such, only authorized personnel can handle the ramp.

All internal ramps should be fitted with audible and visual alarms.

Some of the internal ramps are painted with anti-skid paint. The anti-skid paint increases the coefficient of friction between the tires and the deck but requires special attention during preparation of the ship for loading. Special attention should be paid when sweeping ramps before the commencement of the cargo operations in order to avoid scratches to the cars.

Anti-skid paint is applied on this slope.

The deck in front of the internal ramp is painted with green anti-skid paint. The ramp is painted with Bimagrip™ anti-slip paint.

Suspension hinges

The responsible officer must be well-acquainted with procedures for the emergency opening and closing of the ramps. (See Emergency Operation.)

Some internal ramps are wire-operated and can be adjusted to two positions: the car deck position and the full-up position, if the upper car deck is liftable. These ramps are supported by suspension hinges, to which the ramp is locked when in stowed position (either car deck position or full-up position). The illustration shows suspension hinges for locking such ramps when in the car deck position (corresponding to the normal/middle position) and hinges for locking the ramp when in the full-up position.

When hoisting the ramp to the car deck position, especially if cargo is loaded on the ramp, the operator should pay extra attention. Normally when the ramp is in car deck position, an indicator or alarm will inform the operator that the ramp is in the required position and the suspension hinges should be locked. On some older ships, however, such alarms do not exist. Therefore the presence of extra lookouts is indispensable to determine when the suspension hinges are in position for locking. When the ramp is in the required position, the lookouts should inform the operator, who should then lock the ramp. If the lookouts overlook this moment, the ramp will continue to rise until the roofs of the cars collide with the overhead structure. Much cargo damage has been caused by failure to lock the ramp at the appropriate time.

Inner ramp in up position

The angle of the ramps depends on the type of the vehicles that will use them; normally angles are between 8° and 9.5°. In order to meet the required slope, the maximum vertical distance between the decks should be measured and the length of the ramps adjusted in proportion to this.

In order to smooth the passage of the vehicles and avoid grounding of longer trailers, the ramp ends are provided with knuckles.

Two-way Ramps

Two-way ramps are provided with flaps and hinges at both ends. In this way, the hinge can be fixed to the upper deck at either end, allowing the opposite end to be lowered. This ramp can be operated by wires or hydraulic cylinders. The ramp can be lowered or raised when fully loaded. This ramp also acts as a watertight/gastight door when closed.

Ramp Covers

Ramp covers can be either end-hinged or side-hinged.

End-hinged cover in stowed/locked position

End-hinged ramp cover: Normally this ramp cover consists of one section and is opened by hydraulic-cylinders. When open, the cover is secured by locking wedges supported by the hull structure. In its open position, the height of the opening is enough to allow unobstructed passage of vehicles. When closed, the cover can be watertight, gastight, or both. A rubber gasket, fitted around the perimeter of the cover, ensures watertightness and gastightness. In closed position, the cover has the same SWL as the deck it belongs to. It is absolutely prohibited to hoist the cover with cargo on it. When the cover is open, the appropriate safety precautions should be taken. The cover is operated by control panel located nearby. Sensors indicate whether the cover is open or locked.

Side hinged ramp cover: This type of cover can be mounted only when sufficient vertical and transverse stowage space is available. In its open position, the cover is locked by devices supported by the hull on the upper side or by a locking mechanism in the hinge part of the coaming. This cover consists of one, two, or three sections, which are opened sequentially. When closed, the cover can be either watertight, gastight, or both. Watertightness and gastightness is ensured by a rubber gasket, fitted around the perimeter of the cover. In closed position the cover has the same SWL as the deck it belongs to. It is absolutely prohibited to hoist the cover with cargo on it. When the cover is open the appropriate safety precautions should be taken. The cover is normally operated by control panel located nearby. Sensors indicate whether the cover is open or locked. Indicators are located close to the cover as well as on the bridge.

Inspection and Maintenance of Inner Ramps

The inspection of inner ramps is the same as for stern and side ramps. Hinges, locking and securing devices, as well as sealing arrangements are subject to inspection and maintenance as per Planned Maintenance Schedule. Operating panels, sensors, and audible and visual alarms are to be inspected and tested, as well. Sheaves and wires of wire-operated ramps should be properly inspected and greased.

Hydraulic cylinders should be checked for leakage; if leakages are found, the problem should be fixed as soon as possible.

Testing the Ramps

SOLAS 74, as amended 2009, Ch. II-2, B-2, Reg. 16, requires all watertight doors to be tested with a head of water they might sustain in a final or intermediate stage of flooding. Apart from the required water hose test the following tests for checking the watertight integrity of the ramps and doors can be performed as well:

- **Visual:** during and after opening of the ramp
- **Hose test:** (water test—see above)
- **Chalk test:** Apply chalk to the compression bars when ramp is in its tilted position. As the ramp is closed, contact marks will be left on the rubber surfaces. When reopened, the lack of chalk on the rubber surfaces will clearly indicate the areas with little or no contact.
- **Ultrasonic method:** This method can detect even the smallest deviation. The operator using the equipment should be certified and the equipment should be calibrated at regular intervals. Ultrasonic tightness testing allows for "dry" testing and identifying areas that lack compression with pinpoint accuracy.

Indicator Panels

Indicator panel on the bridge

Separate indicators—visual and audible—are positioned on the bridge. When ramps or doors are opened an audible alarm sounds. The visual indicator shows a red light when the ramp or door is open or not properly closed; when doors or ramps are properly closed, the indicator becomes green. The power supply for these indicators is independent of the power supply for operating and closing the ramps and is provided with a backup supply.

There is a "harbor/sea voyage" switch, as well. This should be set to "harbor" mode when engines are stopped and to "sea voyage" mode before departure. When properly set, an audible alarm will sound if the ship leaves the quay with open or improperly closed side, stern, or internal ramps.

Signals from the indicator panel are recorded by the Voyage Data Recorder (VDR).

The panel is subject to inspection and testing. It should be checked for proper functioning and the following items should be checked:

- Lamp test on the panel
- Verification that it is not possible to switch off the indicator light on the panels
- Verification of fail-safe performance

- Proper visible and audible alarms are working on the bridge panel and on the operating panels
- Confirmation that power supply for the indicator system is supplied by the emergency source or another secure power supply independent of the power supply for operating doors and ramps
- Proper condition of sensors; they should be protected from water and ice formation, and free of mechanical damage

Cargo Lifts (Also Called Trailer Lifts)

Cargo lifts can be used for moving the cargo vertically between different car decks. Usually cargo lifts are used on Ro-Ro trailer ships; their use on board car carriers is very limited because the use of lifts increases the time for loading and discharging considerably. Cargo lifts can still be seen on some older car carriers today, and often on Ro-Ro ferries trading in North European waters. Generally, the lifts are used for lowering and lifting vehicles (trailers) into and out of the lower hold spaces. However, the use of lifts is time-consuming and, therefore, fixed ramps and slopes are preferred for loading and discharging. When lifts are installed, their maintenance should be covered by the Planned Maintenance Schedule.

On trailer ships, the lifts are the only solution for transferring trailers between decks when the space is too limited for the trailers to operate.

Generally, a lift consists of a lift platform, which is suspended by a four-point double wire arrangement in conjunction with a jigger winch. They are usually about 13–16 meters in length and 3.5–4.2 meters wide. The maximum load is about 50 metric tons (tonnes). Normally the hoisting/lowering time of the lift platform between the decks is about one minute.

When designing a trailer lift, the vehicular access onto the platform must be considered. In the lower position, the lift is on the main Ro-Ro deck and access flaps are required at the ends of the platform to facilitate the movement of vehicles between the deck and the platform. These flaps can be either attached to the platform or part of the ship's deck.

Safety is of paramount importance during the operation of lifts. Railings or barriers should surround the lift longitudinally. In addition, on both drive-on ends there should be automatically actuated protection barriers. There are trip devices under the platform that, when activated, will stop the operation of the lift immediately.

Emergency stops of the "dead man" type are located on each deck. Rotating lights and sound alarms are activated when the lift is moving.

Bow Doors and Ramps

There are two types of bow doors: visor doors or side-opening doors.

A visor door is opened by rotating upwards and outwards about horizontal axis using two or more hinges near the top of the door and connected to the door by longitudinally lifting arms.

Side opening doors are opened by rotating outwards about vertical axis using two or more hinges near the outboard edges. These doors are normally arranged in pairs.

As the name indicates, the bow door is on the forward part of the ship and is used for facilitating loading/discharging of vehicles. The door consists of one or two sections. When there are two sections, they swing outward from the door aperture and are stowed outside the ship's hull when in the open position. Operation is by hydraulic cylinder(s) with swinging maneuvering arms hinged to each door section and the hull.

Safety is one of the most important issues concerning the bow doors. The inner door should be watertight. The watertightness is ensured by rubber gasket fitted around the perimeter of the door and, in case of two sections, between both sections.

In closed position, the door is locked by hydraulically operated cleats to the ship's hull. Locking devices are mounted in the lower part of the door sections and the hull.

Audible and visible alarms are activated when the door is being opened or closed. In addition, there are sensors that indicate whether the door is closed or open.

In some instances, there are fitted inner bow doors behind the bow visor. These doors can have either one or two sections. The doors and the ramp are separated in collision-safety mode. The ramp acts as a bumper in the case of frontal collision and transfers the forces horizontally to the upper deck.

During the annual surveys of ramps (internal and external), covers, and lifts, the following items should be thoroughly checked:

- Documentation of the ramps and doors, i.e., operating manuals; it should be verified that an approved copy in the language of the ship is available on board
- Structural condition of the ramps, covers, and doors
- The condition of the shell surrounding the ramps, covers, and doors (cracks, deformations)
- Locking devices
- Supporting devices
- Hinges and bearings
- Sealing arrangements

The ramps, covers, and lifts should be checked for proper operation. This should include the following:

- Proper working of the hinged arms and hinges
- Securing, supporting, and locking devices
- Securing the ramps, doors, and covers in open position
- Proper sequence of the interlock system for the opening/closing system and the securing and locking devices
- Mechanical lock of securing devices
- Proper locking of hydraulic securing devices in the event of a loss of the hydraulic fluid
- Correct indication of the open or closed position of ramps, covers, and doors
- Presence of a notice plate near each operating panel with instructions that all securing devices should be closed and locked before leaving the harbor
- Proper functioning of indication and monitoring panels

Liftable Decks

As mentioned earlier some of the car decks on car carriers are strengthened for the loading of high and heavy units. To achieve this, it is necessary that the decks above the strengthened decks are lifted to ensure sufficient clearance for taller units.

Normally there are two or three strengthened car decks on board car carriers. Hence, there are two or three liftable decks. In other words, the number of liftable car decks is equal to the number of strengthened decks. A liftable deck consists of steel panels of various dimensions and weights of about 20–21 metric tons (tonnes). Panels are built according to the open construction design with the top plate being stiffened by angle bars and supported at the ends by girders. No anti-skid paint is applied to these panels. Because of their structural design, deck panels will not be

Marking of deck panels

watertight or gastight. Each panel is clearly and conspicuously marked by number and location. In the photo, for example, 3D-89(C) below the panel is part of deck 3, panel 89, in the center (fore-and-aft direction).

On the panel arrangement plan sent by Charterers to the vessel, the panels are always identified by their number to avoid confusion or misunderstanding. Upon receiving of the Stowage Plan or the cargo to be loaded, the Chief Officer should consider the position of the panels. On most car carriers, the Stowage Plan and panel arrangement plan are received simultaneously. The Chief Officer needs only to arrange the correct position of the panels. On some occasions, however, the Chief Officer receives only the cargo to be loaded. If this cargo is homogeneous, i.e., only cars, the panels will not be arranged. They will stay in their stowed position. When the cargo consists of high and heavy cargo the Chief Officer must prepare the Stowage Plan as well as panel arrangement plan. These should then be sent to the Cargo Owners/Charterers for approval.

In the upper load position and in the stowed position deck panels are supported by semi-automatic locking devices or suspensions/hooks. In the lower load position, deck panels are supported by fixed supports or foldable suspensions. For this reason, all panels that are secured in upper position by hooks are holed and fitted with a bar to which the hook is fixed. Special attention should be paid when lifting such panels, because improper fixing of the hooks can lead to the panels falling down, resulting in damage or accidents. The hooks and foldable suspensions are operated by special ropes passing through roller guides. Maintenance of these ropes and roller guides should be included in the Planned Maintenance Schedule. When the respective foldable supports are not being used, they should be in the vertical (upright) position in order to avoid cargo damage.

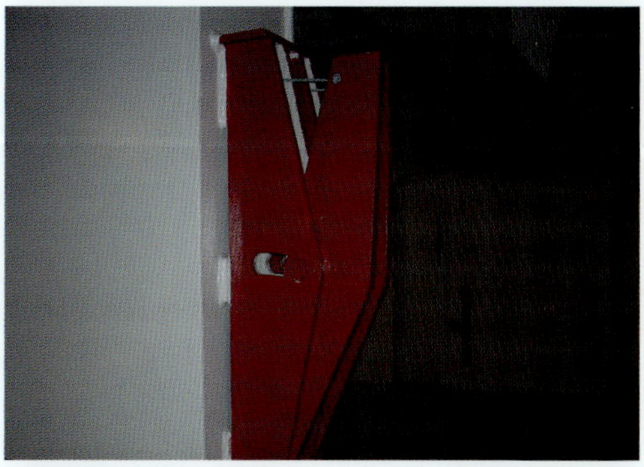

Foldable suspension

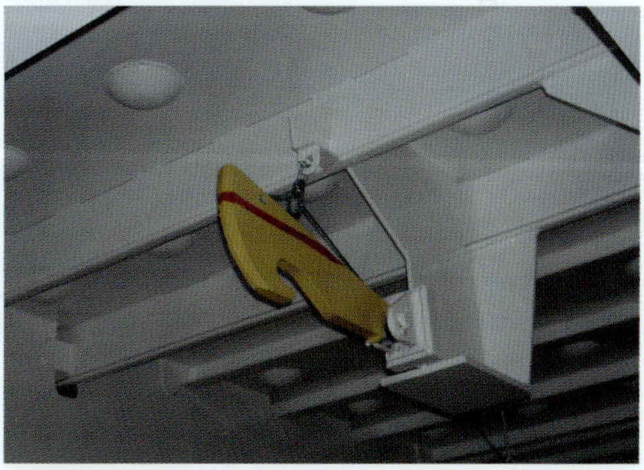

Foldable hook

Fixed suspension

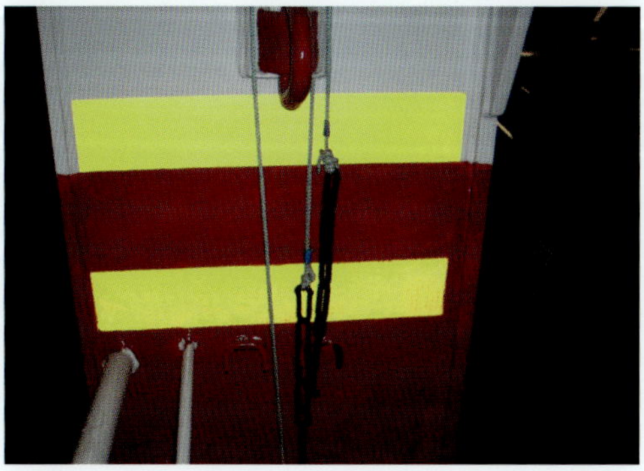

Ropes for operation of foldable suspension and hooks

Positions of deck panel

The illustration shows two different stowage positions for a panel—the normal stowed position and "one step" position. As a rule there are three positions of panels: "normal;" "one step"("middle up"); and "up" (in upper position). When the panels are in normal position, they act as a normal car deck designated for loading of cars (2.4 meters). When the panels are in the "one step" position, vans with height of no more than 2.8 meters can be loaded on the strengthened deck below. In the one-step position, the liftable deck panels can be used for loading, if movable bridges are used (see "Movable Bridges" later in this chapter). When the panels are in the up position, cargoes with a height up to 5 meters can be loaded on the strengthened deck below, but the liftable deck cannot be used.

Deck panels are lifted and lowered by special machines called deck lifters. There are various designs of deck lifters, but the principle is the same—they consist of a special hydraulically or electrically operated frame that raises or lowers the panels.

Deck lifters in operation

Deck lifter in stowed position

Circles for deck lifters are painted in contrasting colors on deck.

No one is allowed to stand under the operating frame of the lifter when it is lifting or lowering the panels. The lifter should be positioned in special circles that are marked in contrasting paint on the deck. This is necessary to ensure safe and proper operation. Improper positioning can cause the lifter to topple over, with consequent damage to the lifter and the panels.

While Ro-Ro ships have no deck lifters, they are equipped with various systems for hoisting or lowering the liftable decks. Some systems comprise hydraulic jigger winches and wire systems, and some make use of electric winches.

Externally mounted jigger winch: In this type of installation, the jigger winch is mounted either vertically in the ship's side structure or horizontally on the overhead deck, with the operating wires being connected to the liftable deck and running through pulleys on the deck head. In this arrangement, the piping supplying hydraulic oil to the cylinder of the jigger winches is fixed in place.

Integrally mounted jigger winch: For systems where an externally mounted jigger winch assembly cannot be installed, the winch unit can be incorporated into the platform's supporting structure. The operating wires extend from pulleys on the platform to fixed points on the deck head. The hydraulic oil supply to the operating cylinder of the jigger winch is through heavy-duty flexible hoses.

In addition to the jigger winch-operated systems, there is an alternative in the form of a fixed cylinder-operated hoistable car deck system, where a hydraulic cylinder is at each of the four corners of a panel. With this arrangement there are no wires involved, the platforms being raised and lowered directly by operation of the cylinders. As with the other systems, the necessary securing devices are provided for the panels in both their raised and lowered positions.

Maintenance of Liftable Panels

Liftable panels require special attention and careful inspection in order to avoid damage to the cargo and the ship. The inspection and maintenance should be performed in accordance with the Planned Maintenance Schedule. However, it is strongly recommended to inspect the panels and their supports before any panel operation takes place.

Inspection of the Pin of the Supporting Block

There are many cases on record of cargo being damaged by falling panels during heavy weather. The chief reason for this is that the pin of the supporting block becomes loose and falls out. Therefore, the pins of all panels should be inspected before any panel operation.

The pins of supporting blocks must be checked before any operation, before the ship goes to sea, and after encountering heavy weather to ensure that pins are in place and are secured

On other occasions, the supporting safety pin is secured by a hitch pin. (See illustration)

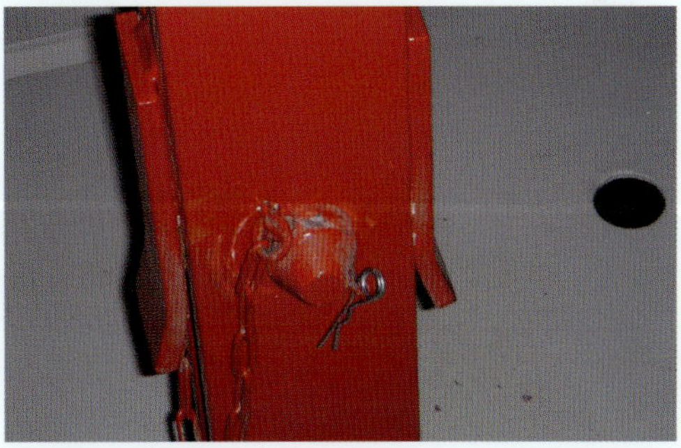

Pin in the supporting block

Inspection of Panels for Cracks

The inspection of panels should be performed at regular intervals as per the Planned Maintenance Schedule, covering all the elements specified in it. Cracks are some of the most common structural damages on panels, resulting from improper distribution of the shear forces and bending moments throughout the whole panel. Such cracks are more likely to exist on older ships. In order to avoid the progress of the cracks throughout the deck (especially the transverse web and girder), it is recommended that these cracks be repaired.

Crack in panel structure

When carrying out inspections special attention should be paid to the supporting bracket parts and adjacent structures. The cross-area between deck girders and deck transverse near the supporting brackets should be examined thoroughly to confirm the presence or absence of cracks. Any damage should be promptly and properly repaired and advice of class should be called in. This is a consultation from the class society about certain technical issues on board. If a repair is needed, an approval of class or certification should be obtained. In some cases, where there is a deviation from the rules, a disposition can be obtained.

Inspection of Welded Parts between Deck Plates and the Web of Transverse

The inspection must ensure that there is nothing wrong with the welded parts between deck plates and the web of transverse. Special attention should be paid for any corrosion or breaks in the welded parts.

Inspection of the Web Transverse of a Liftable Car Deck

The inspection must ensure that there is no abnormal deterioration of the web transverse of the deck or in the cross area between the webs of transverse and longitudinal girders.

Inspection of a Liftable Deck Plate

One of the most unpleasant structural damages to the deck plate is the bend of the plate. Fortunately, it is more probable that such damage will be found on older ships. Bundling and wave deformation also can be found during inspection.

The strength of the deck plate and web/girder is an area called the "minimum effective breadth"(MEB). In order to avoid damage to the deck plate, there should not be any deformation within this minimum effective breadth. As a rule, MEB is equal to one meter across the transverse web/girder.

There are two types of deck plates: longitudinal and transverse. The longitudinal type has small girders fitted lengthwise. In this structural type, the forward, rear, and middle transverse webs increase the bending moments and should be subject to close up examination.

In the transverse type of deck plate, the centerline girder and the side girders increase the bending moments, in addition to the webs. They should be the subjects of close examination.

When rubber straps are damaged, replacements should be requested.

Inspection of Guides and Suspensions

The guides of the ropes operating the suspensions should be free rotating and properly welded to the deck. The condition of the ropes should be checked and if any are torn or damaged they should be replaced. The ropes are fitted with rubber straps at the working end. The condition of these straps should be checked and they should be replaced in case of damage.

Inspection of the Covers of Openings for the Hooks of Deck Panels

As already mentioned, some of the panels are held in position by hooks. These hooks are attached to the panels by pins fitted in openings. When such panels are in their normal position, the openings are covered to avoid personal injury or damage to the cars. Such cover plates are attached to the panels by hinges. The inspection of these covers should include a check for structural damages to the covers as well as the condition of the hinges. Before commencement of any lifting operation these covers should be opened and checked. Failure to do so might result in damage to the cover and panel when the panels are being heaved up.

Bent cover for a panel opening

Inspection of Liftable Decks before Lifting

Before commencement of lifting, the responsible officer should perform a thorough inspection to make sure that all surrounding protective railings are removed. If this is overlooked, there is a possibility that panels may not be properly positioned due to the presence of detachable stanchions. If the panel is in the "middle-up" position instead of the "full-up" position while being used for cargo operations, this could lead to accidents. Once the operation of lifting the panels is completed, the responsible officer should check the adjacent panels to ensure they are protected with railings.

Inspection of Supporting Bracket Parts and Their Adjacent Members on Liftable Decks

Deck panels consist of an efficient strengthened structure that comprise the deck plate, transverse, girders, and longitudinals. They are supported by four or six supporting brackets and adjacent members that are vulnerable to heavy stresses, especially in boisterous weather.

These heavy stresses can lead to severe cracking and the brackets can be detached from the ship's structure. Close-up inspection of the supporting brackets and their adjacent members should be carried out to ascertain if there are any cracks. Special attention should be paid to paint blisters, paint cracks, etc., which may be an indication of excessive stress.

If any problem is found, it is recommended that a hammer test be performed to inspect the structure underneath the suspect areas. If any deficiencies are found during the hammer test, it is recommended to perform non-destructive testing with dye penetration (color check).

Inspection of Guide Shoes (Pieces)

The guide shoes of the panels should be inspected before any panel operation. When a ship is designed, the width of these shoes is precisely calculated. Due to continuous adjustment during the lifetime of the panels, however, this width is subject to change. If it widens, the panel and the landing area between the supporting block will be reduced, which can lead to the panel falling. On the other hand, guide shoes that are not wide enough will create difficulties when adjusting the height of the panel. This can lead to bending the panel and structural damage. In such cases, applying grease on the pillars where the guide shoes touch will help during height adjustment.

Touching area between the supporting block and panel, when the clearance of the guide shoe is properly calculated

Guide shoe of proper clearance

Scratches to the pillar due to reduced clearance of the guide shoe

Inspection and Maintenance of Deck Lifter

Normally, deck lifters are included in the equipment insured by the hull and machinery policy. The inspection and maintenance of deck lifters should be performed as per the manufacturer's manual. Special attention should be paid when operating the lifters; only well-trained personnel should be assigned to operate them. The sound and visual alarms should be checked regularly to ensure that they are in working condition. Deck lifters should only be used when the trim does not exceed 3° and list is less than 2°. When not in use, the deck lifter should be parked with the hand brake applied, the outrigger frame lowered down horizontally, the power off. Like any other equipment, deck lifters should be inspected regularly and the following items should be checked:

- Clutch and brake operation
- Hydraulic oil tank and fuel tank for leakages
- Hydraulic lines for leakages
- Condition of the wiring
- Condition of the battery and charger
- Condition of the outrigger frame (cracks, deformations, etc.)
- Outrigger cylinders (rods) for leakages

Before departure, deck lifters should be parked in a designated area and properly secured. Their batteries should be disconnected and chocks should be placed under the tires.

Movable Bridges

When the panels of one deck are positioned at a different height, it is necessary to use special bridges (called movable bridges) to allow safe and proper transportation of vehicles. The edges of these bridges should be painted in a contrasting color and be very visible. They have to be fixed in such a way to ensure safe passage of vehicles from one level to another.

Movable bridges

Needless to say, all safety precautions should be taken when movable bridges are in use. Bridges should be fenced by railings and marked with safety cones and barrier tape. A crewmember should be assigned to guide the cars through these movable bridges. The ship's crew must exercise due diligence to make sure that all precautions have been taken before commencement of loading or discharging that uses movable bridges. When not in use, these bridges should be stored in a place where they do not obstruct the normal cargo operations. They must be secured with lashings to avoid any movement during sea passage. Normally these bridges do not require special attention, but the routine inspection for rust spots or signs of corrosion should be performed before use and at intervals as per the Planned Maintenance Schedule.

CHAPTER 8

DAMAGE TO THE CARGO

When the cargo is damaged during the sea passage, the Master should try to collect all contemporaneous evidence related to the damage. In this chapter, we will analyze the most common causes of damage to the cargo on board Ro-Ro ships, preventive actions to avoid such damage, and how the Master can protect himself (and the Ship Owner) against any possible claims.

Introduction

As stipulated in the Hague Rules, Article III, Rule 2, the Carrier has the obligation "properly and carefully load, handle, stow, carry, keep, care for, and discharge the goods carried," from the time they are entrusted to the Carrier until the moment they are delivered to the receiver. In other words, it is the Carrier's responsibility to deliver the cargo in the same condition as it was entrusted to it. This means that any damage to the cargo caused by improper loading, stowage, transportation, and discharging will be the Carrier's liability.

There are some circumstances, however, when the Carrier will not be held responsible for the damage of the cargo or, at least, for not delivering the cargo in the same condition as loaded. These circumstances are incorporated in Hague Rules, Article IV, Rules 1 and 2. The Carrier, though, will be responsible to ensure that all his obligations under the rules have been met.

The causes of damage to the cargo can range from improper cargo handling and insufficient care for the cargo during the voyage to a crew that is not sufficiently qualified for handling certain types of cargo. It is important to note that, if the crew is not properly qualified for working on board a Ro-Ro vessel, it is very easy for claimants (in case of cargo damage) to prove that the ship was not seaworthy at the outset of the voyage. The Master must ensure that every crew member is fully aware of his responsibilities and duties during cargo operations and while on passage.

Facing a large range and variety of causes of damage, the Carrier must always endeavor to protect its interests. These protective measures include ensuring proper cargo handling, taking care of the cargo during the voyage, and compiling contemporaneous evidence related to the damage. It is of utmost importance that any damage to the cargo during cargo operations be duly recorded and documented (pictures should be taken including date and hours).

The Master must be aware of any special terms in the contract of carriage or any special by-law rules concerning the transport of vehicles or cargo handling operations in the respective ports. Normally the manufacturers of vehicles issue special instructions that are to be followed during cargo handling operations and during the voyage. This information should be received well in advance from the Owner's Agents or P & I representatives.

In almost all cases where damage to the cargo is involved, the Carrier will be considered guilty for not exercising due diligence and will need to prove that it has performed its obligation of taking care of the cargo. Only accurate records, contemporaneous evidence, and proof that manufacturer's instructions have been duly followed can defend the Carrier against claims.

If it is obvious during loading that some of the vehicles are damaged or are not in a condition for transportation, the Master is in position to reject the cargo. Acceptance of damaged cargo for sea transport is only justified if the cargo condition is described as such in the relevant cargo documents. In no case should such cargo be accepted for sea transport if its transportation will put the safety of the ship, the other cargo, and the crew at risk, regardless of the clauses inserted in the relevant documents. It should be kept in mind that the Master, under Section 5 of ISM Code, has the responsibility to reject any cargo that may jeopardize the safety of the ship and the crew.

Types of Cargo Damage

Cargo damage can be divided into three main categories: damage caused by human intervention, damage caused by inherent vices, and damage caused by *force majeure* circumstance.

Damage Caused by Human Intervention

The most common type of damage is that resulting from human mistake or lack of attention. The damage can be caused either by the stevedores or by ship's crew and may include scratches to the cars, paint damage, damage by soot, damage by rust, cargo damage prior to loading, and more.

Damage Caused by Stevedores

Vehicles regularly become damaged while being handled by stevedores during loading, discharging, or when the vehicles are outside the ship. Typical stevedore damage include the following.

Scratches to Cars

Scratches are among the most commonly seen damages to cars. It is of vital importance that all cars being loaded on board are thoroughly checked. If some scratches are detected during the inspection, an appropriate Damage Report should be issued by the Chief Officer. If scratches are detected by the stevedores at the discharging port, and if these scratches are not properly detected and documented by the ship's staff at the port of loading, a cargo claim will be filed against the ship. As a rule, the Ship Owner is insured for cargo liability claims with a P & I club. Nevertheless, more damage and claims will result in premium increases, which will affect the Ship Owner's profit. Therefore, the ship's staff must pay particular attention to such damage. If scratches are detected, the cargo operations should be stopped, evidence (pictures or video films) compiled, and appropriate Damage Report issued.

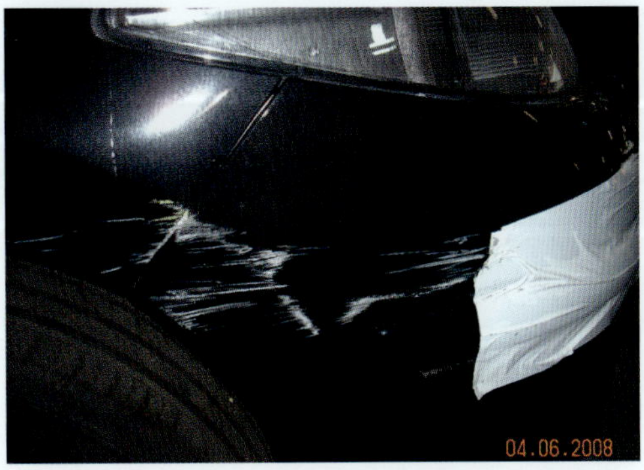

Among the most common damages to cars are scratches.

Drivers wearing jewelry, like rings, also may cause scratches inside the vehicles. Therefore, during the pre-operation meeting with stevedores, it is essential that they are advised not to wear any rings, accessories, or zipped overalls that can damage the car.

Special attention is to be paid when the stevedores open the doors and enter the cars. It was mentioned earlier that the minimum distances between the cars and the ship's side should be observed (at least 50 cm). Even so, depending on the stowage, plastic protectors should be fitted and adjusted to the height of possible contact points as a preventive measure for avoiding damage to the doors.

Flat Tires

This is another type of damage frequently seen during loading and discharging of vehicles, but it can also occur during the voyage, so special attention should be given to flat tires during routine inspections while the ship is at sea. If the ship's staff detects a flat tire during loading, cargo operations should be discontinued and the tire should be replaced with a spare tire. In such case, the Chief Officer should issue a Damage Report. A flat tire is a deflated tire that shows no signs of physical damage. A punctured tire is a deflated tire that shows physical damage caused by a nail or other sharp object.

Flat tire

If a flat tire is discovered during routine checks of the cargo, the appropriate Damage Report should be made. In such a case, the Carrier will need to prove that he has exercised due diligence in taking care of the cargo and that the damage was beyond his control. In order to prove this, the Carrier should present appropriate records that the ship was seaworthy at the beginning of the voyage and that due diligence was exercised during the voyage. If the Carrier is in position to prove that such damage is beyond its control then Hague Rules, Article IV, Rules 1-2 will apply and he will not be held responsible for the damage in question.

Broken Windows

Broken windows are frequently seen as well. The actions to be taken when discovering broken windows are the same as prescribed above: cargo operations should cease, contemporaneous evidence should be taken, and a Damage Report should be issued. Considering the extent of such damage, the probability of a broken window not being discovered is small. However, if the crew overlooks such damage and fails to document it, the carrier will be held liable for the damage.

Broken window

Such damage can also take place during the voyage due to inherent vice (factory fault). In that case, the ship's crew should make the appropriate entries in the logbook, take pictures, and notify the Cargo Owners. During longer voyages and due to ship's vibrations, the windows of some cars sometimes cannot withstand the inherent tension and break by themselves. It should be kept in mind that when a window breaks due to inherent tension, it tends to expand slightly but remains in the window frame. However, when glass is found scattered throughout the vehicle, the damage was probably caused by an external force or impact.

Broken Parts

Another category of damage caused by stevedores includes broken parts of the vehicles such as bumpers, lights, mirrors, etc. As a rule, this damage cannot happen because of inherent vice, therefore it is essential that the ship's crew pay particular attention to this type of damage. If this damage happens on board or is discovered by the ship' s crew during loading, operations should cease, pictures taken, and an appropriate Damage Report issued by the Chief Officer.

Broken front bumper due to lack of care of the driver

Other types of Damage Caused by Human Intervention

Dents: Inward deformations of the surface irrespective of the paint being affected or not

Scuffs: A mark on the surface that does not affect the paint. Scuffs are minor enough that they can be buffed or compounded out.

Chipped paint: Small areas of missing paint, less than 0.5 cm

Cars Covered by Dust

It is very common for new cars to be loaded while being covered by dust. In such a case, appropriate remarks should be inserted in the Mate's Receipts, pictures should be taken, and Cargo Owners notified.

Car covered by dust

This is a challenge, because it is very difficult to detect scratches or minor damages when cars are covered by dust. As neither the Master nor the crew has the physical possibility to check all dust-covered cars in detail, to protect the Owner's interest it is necessary to report this condition in the loading documents. As a rule, such report should be entered either on the Bill of Lading or in the Mate's Receipts, which are the most appropriate documents for describing the apparent condition of the cargo at time of shipment. One peculiarity of Ro-Ro vessels, and especially car carriers, is that normally no bills of lading are presented to the Master (they are sent directly to final destination). That is why such remarks are to be inserted in any documents presented by stevedores and in the Mate's Receipts.

To report this condition, include a phrase like:

> **CARS STOWED IN THE OPEN BEFORE LOADING. ALL CARS DIRTY—COVERED WITH DUST**

Damage to the Vehicles Due to Unsecured Ramps

Despite the fact that the stevedores are driving the cars when such an accident happens, the Carrier will be held responsible. This is due to the fact that the Carrier will be considered to be in breach of the Hague or Hague-Visby Rules (depending which are applicable) by not ensuring fitness of the ship for loading. This damage may result in total constructive loss of the cargo and personal injury, which is one of the most serious types of accident claims. It is very difficult for the Carrier to defend himself against this, unless it can be proven that all preventive measures were taken before commencement of cargo operations (preferably this should be done by providing evidence such as pictures).

As was mentioned earlier, a pre-operation meeting with the stevedores should be held before commencement of cargo operations. During this meeting all openings on deck and position of the traffic cones should be brought to the attention of the stevedores. Driving routes from stowed positions to the ramp should be discussed. Written evidence of such a meeting will be very useful in defending the Carrier in case of accident. In any case, the ship's staff must ensure that all openings, ramps, etc., that constitute a risk to the injury of cars or persons are properly fenced by railings and clearly marked by reflective cones or tape. No deck panels should be lifted and lowered during cargo operations. However, if some panels must be handled, utmost attention should be exercised.

Nose-Hitting of Vehicles

This damage can be caused when the ramps are very steep or the clearance between the vehicles and the ramps is very small. Irrespective of the fact that the stevedores are driving the vehicles, adjusting the slope of the ramps is the responsibility of the ship's staff. Normally the external ramp's slope is arranged before commencement of cargo operations, but because of tidal changes this may change. The ship's staff should monitor the tide and the external ramp's angle and adjust it as necessary. This can be done by adjusting the buttress cylinders or by appropriately trimming in very high tides. The drivers should proceed very carefully in order to avoid such damage. In addition, rubber matting should be placed on the flaps in order to absorb any impact and mitigate the damage if nose-hitting occurs. The ramp slope has a maximum angle of 13° and can be measured by slant ruler. It should be kept in mind, however, that the slope of internal ramps cannot be adjusted; the drivers must reduce speed when approaching such internal ramps.

Roof Damage to the Cars Due to Reduced Height of the Car Deck

The cargo should be stowed as shown on the Stowage Plan, which should take into account the heights of the car decks. Even so, during the pre-operation meeting with the stevedores, the actual height of the car decks should be confirmed and stowage of the vehicles agreed. The clear height of the car decks is marked on each entrance and inside each car deck.

It should be kept in mind that very often there is a discrepancy between the actual height of the car deck and the height given in ship's particulars. Therefore, the responsible officer should measure the actual height of the car decks and compare it with the given one in order to avoid damage of this kind. During cargo operations, areas where the height of the deck reduces should be clearly marked to avoid cars entering areas with insufficient overhead clearance.

Damage to the Vehicles Due to Improper Lashing

Depending on the terms of the contract of carriage, either the stevedores or the crew will be responsible for the lashing of the cars. In Ro-Ro practice, normally Group F from INCOTERMS 2009 is applied. The most common type of terms adopted in Ro-Ro practice is FIO/FIOS "Free In & Out and Stowed." In this case, the Carrier is free of expenses concerning loading, stowage, securing, and discharging. These expenses are transferred to the buyer and the stevedores handle all operations. (Sometimes CPT—"Carriage paid to…"—is applicable, due to the fact that, on Ro-Ro ships, ship's rails serve no practical purpose. CPT means that the seller pays the freight for the carriage of the goods, as well as any additional costs due to events occurring after the time the vehicles have been delivered to the Carrier, until the cargo is transferred from the seller to the buyer.)

The stevedores are obliged to stow and secure the vehicles in the most effective and safest manner, and the ship's staff is responsible for supervision of the stowage and securing the cargo. It means that the crew must ensure that the vehicles are properly stowed and secured and lashings are properly tensioned before the ship leaves the quay. In addition, SOLAS CH. VI requires the cargo to be properly secured before the ship leaves the berth.

Unfortunately, it is very common to find that the stevedores have not fulfilled their obligation for securing the vehicles in the proper way. In that case, the Master must show his professionalism in dealing with stevedores in a polite but effective manner. It must be kept in mind by ship's staff that they are not in a position to tell the stevedores how to secure the vehicles because in doing so they would accept liability. However, the securing of vehicles must be performed as per the ship's Cargo Securing Manual; the ship's staff can give some advice to the stevedores on how to secure the cargo but not insist.

If there are any concerns that the securing of the vehicles is not conducted as required as per the Cargo Securing Manual, the Master should make an appropriate entry in the logbook, take pictures, and lodge a Letter of Protest against the stevedores. If the Master considers that the cargo is not secured or is secured in such a way that could endanger the ship, cargo, and crew during the voyage, he is in position to insist on proper securing with all extra expenses to be borne by Charterers. In that case, there might be a conflict of interest, so the Master should be sure that the cars are not properly secured. If necessary, he should call in the attention of his P & I Club, should lodge a Letter of Protest, and notify the Owners.

During the loading, the crew must ensure that all vehicles are lashed, so crew members should be present at the place of loading. If some vehicles are found unsecured or not properly secured, the situation should be brought to the attention of the stevedores, who should then correct the situation. During the voyage, the Master must ensure that the crew is performing regular cargo inspections and that appropriate entries are being made into the logbook. Special attention is to be paid in the case of heavy weather. Damage to vehicles due to the lack of lashings or improper securing might lead to more serious hazards to the ship, such as list, loss of stability, and significant damage to the cargo.

Special attention should be paid during holiday periods when stevedores are sometimes employed for temporary work. Some of the drivers may be intoxicated and if this is the case they should not be allowed to drive. While the ship cannot test the drivers, the crew should observe the drivers for unusual and inappropriate behavior. During the pre-operation meeting this point should be brought to the attention of the stevedore's foreman in order to avoid accidents and damages to the cargo or the ship.

Pilferage by Stevedores

Pilferage is another very frequently seen problem and missing keys, spare parts, etc., are not uncommon these days. The crew must pay special attention to missing keys because this could lead to delays in the discharging port. If keys or other equipment is observed to be missing by the ship's staff, the Chief Officer should advise the foreman and the problem should be resolved. If he encounters any problem or hindrance in resolving the matter, evidence should be taken (pictures and the stevedore's admission to the damage). Finally, the Chief Officer should issue a Damage Report for the missing parts or keys. Pilferage that is found during discharging will make it very hard to defend the Carrier's interest and the Master will not know who is responsible for it.

Missing radios and other equipment are very common problems and should be discovered by ship's crew.

On some occasions, the stevedores at discharging port may require a pilferage report to be signed by the Chief Officer or the Master. Signing of such a report is an acknowledgment of liability. Therefore the Master should sign this report only if authorized by the Owner and only if the following clause is added to the report:

> Acknowledgment of the pilferage reported herein is without prejudice to the contractual and legal defenses of the vessel and/or carrier.

Damage Caused by Driving at High Speeds

As a rule, the speed on board should not exceed 20 km/h (12 mph in USA). The drivers, however, very often exceed this speed and drive carelessly off the ramps. This should also be discussed during the pre-operation meeting with stevedores. If this occurs, the Master should cease cargo operations and advise the foreman of non-compliance with the safety regulations adopted on board. If the drivers continue to drive at higher speeds than allowed, the Master must stop cargo operations and lodge a Letter of Protest.

A video movie would be appropriate evidence to prove excessive speed.

A preventive measure for speeding is the fixing of a driving route by traffic cones inside car decks and especially in the vicinity of the ramps.

Damage Caused by Using Cargo for Towing Purposes as a Service Car

In most well-organized Ro-Ro terminals, the stevedores have at their disposal special service cars for towing and transporting the drivers. However, this is not the case in smaller and infrequently visited ports. It is a bad practice to use cars from the cargo for towing purposes or as taxis. If the ship's crew notices such violations, they should immediately stop cargo operations and inform the supervisor, and the Master should lodge a Letter of Protest. Damages caused by

A stalled car is being towed by forklift. For such a situation, only designated service cars, trucks, or forklifts should be used.

such practice must be accounted for by the Carrier because the Carrier is still responsible for the cargo. Since the cargo is on board, it is still in the Carrier's custody.

Damage Caused by Ship's Crew

The main task of the Carrier, once entrusted the cargo, is to exercise due diligence and deliver the cargo to the receiver in the same condition it was loaded. Apart from damage that can be caused by the stevedores during cargo handling operations, damages caused by the ship's crew are not uncommon. In such cases, it is very difficult for the Carrier to defend himself, especially when the damage has been caused during the voyage and when there are no supporting documents or records from the loading port. In such cases and according to the Hague or Hague-Visby Rules (whichever is applicable), the Carrier will be held responsible for not exercising due diligence. Damage to the cargo by the ship's crew will result in significant claims paid by the Owner. Apart from the costs involved, damage caused by the ship's crew may also affect the Company's image and reputation.

The most serious and unjustifiable damages that can be caused by the crew follow.

Damage Caused by the Crew Due to Vandalism

This is one the strangest and inexplicable damages that can occur. Unfortunately, there are many examples of damage caused by ship's crew on purpose, such as damage caused by paint. This could be considered as criminal offense against the Cargo Owner's interests and, apart from severe compensation to be paid by the Ship Owner to the Cargo Owner, the individual crew member in question will be sued.

In order to avoid such damage the Master must be aware of any movement of the crew inside the cargo decks and restrict such movement to the purpose of safe execution of the voyage and daily routine tasks. Any signs of conditions that may lead to vandalism (problems on board or unpaid wages, for example) should be identified and dealt with in a timely manner.

Pilferage by the Crew

In order to avoid pilferage from cars by the crew, the Master should restrict access to the car decks. In addition, he must ensure that the crew has been familiarized with the Damage Prevention Instructions issued by the Company and/or the Charterers and must keep written records with crew signatures as evidence. It should be kept in mind that such violations will be the personal liability of the person caught pilfering.

It will be very hard to defend the Carrier's interest if the pilferage is found during discharging, as the Master may not know who is responsible for it. In some instances, the stevedores at the discharging port may require a pilferage report to be signed by the Chief Officer or the Master. Signing such a report is an acknowledgment of liability. Therefore the Master should sign this report only when authorized by the Company and only if the following clause is added to the report:

> Acknowledgment of the pilferage reported herein is without prejudice to the contractual and legal defences of the vessel and/or carrier.

Damage Caused to the Cars Due to Maintenance of the Ship

This type of damage is sometimes caused by the painting of the decks, chipping near the ventilation ducts, etc. It is the Master's responsibility to ensure that ship's maintenance is performed during the ballast voyage, as far as it concerns work inside the car decks. Painting of the decks should always be done during the ballast voyage and the time required for drying of the paint must be taken into account when scheduling it.

Unfortunately, there are many examples when tires have been damaged by paint and the Carrier could not reject the claims. Here again we have a clear example of non-compliance with the Hague or Hague-Visby Rules. Under the terms of these rules, the Carrier is obliged to ensure that cargo holds are fit for loading. Freshly painted car decks will be considered unfit and, therefore, the Carrier will bear liability for any damage that occurs. As a preventive measure to avoid such damage, the Master must ensure that all cargo holds are clean, free from fresh paint (all painting operations having been completed well in advance), and with all lashings properly stowed away. In addition, some Charterers request to be informed of any plans for painting of the car decks; such painting can be done after obtaining explicit approval from Charterers. The Master must prove that car decks are properly fit at the beginning of the voyage with relevant records or pictures as evidence.

The presence of rust spots on cars as a result of chipping the deck near ventilation ducts is a problem that is regularly encountered. Such operations should be avoided, but if such operations must be carried out, the Master should ensure that all ventilation ducts are properly closed and that there is no ventilation of the car decks.

Another very common complaint by car terminals is grease damage to vehicles parked in the parking lots. In case of strong wind, the grease used on the wires of the ramps can be blown off and spread onto the parked cars. The claims could be substantial and, therefore, the ship's management should make sure that there is no excessive grease on the wires before arrival at port.

Damage Caused during Inspection of Cargo

This type of damage is also regularly seen. In order to avoid any scratches or other damage to the cargo during cargo and lashing inspections, the Master must ensure that the crew is not wearing anything that can scratch or damage the vehicles, including accessories, watches, rings, soiled clothes, and soiled gloves. As a preventive measure for avoiding such damage, the crew also must be well familiar with the Damage Prevention Measures issued by the respective Cargo Owner. These instructions are to be strictly followed.

Damage Caused by Soot

Soot damage is a clear ground for claims against the Carrier. On new car carriers, the cargo is protected against soot, especially when the ventilation ducts are closed, but in many cases the cargo is damaged while being stowed at the terminal. Precautions should be taken for avoiding any such damage to the cars parked on the pier. The list of these precautions includes, but is not limited to, the following:

- The main engine should not be used excessively when the ship is close to a berth where cars are stowed.
- Special mesh filters should be fitted on the funnel in order to mitigate soot emission and soot deposits on deck during berthing and unberthing.
- The relevant machinery, such as turbo charger, auxiliary blower, inter-cooler, intake valve, exhaust valve, fuel injection valve, fuel injection pump, etc., are to be checked regularly and kept in good order.
- A soot blow should be carried out well before S/B (stand-by: when the vessel is ready for maneuvering) for entering port.
- Soot blowing in port should be prohibited.
- Incineration in port should be prohibited.
- Heating of the waste oil settling tank in port should be stopped.
- The weather deck should be checked before entering the port and cleaned of any soot, as these soot deposits may be blown away by the wind and fall on the wharf after berthing.
- Car deck ventilation fans should be operated in the exhaust mode around the funnel casing in port or stopped with their dampers closed, in order to prevent sudden excess soot from being sucked into the cargo holds.

- Continuous attention should be paid to the conditions of exhaust gas during the port stay, especially when the wind direction is from the ship towards the terminal.

Damage to the Cars by Hydraulic Oil

Considering the presence of many hydraulic oil pipes inside the car decks there is a risk of cars being contaminated by hydraulic oil. In order to avoid leakage of oil and damage to the cargo, the Master must ensure all piping is in good condition. A thorough check of all piping, especially of piping near the ramps, should be carried out during the ballast voyage and all leakages fixed. If leakage is detected during the laden voyage, the Master must ensure that adequate protection is used to protect the cargo.

Damage to the Cars by Throwing the Heaving Line

This damage can happen to cars parked in close proximity of the berth during berthing when the crew throws heaving lines. It can result in broken windows, etc. In order to avoid such damage, the crew should pay out the heaving line but not throw it. In some cases, the heaving line should be thrown into the water in order to be picked up by the lines men. Appropriate attention should be paid to this issue during the pre-mooring meeting and before cargo operations.

Damage to the Cars by Seawater

There are several reasons for car to become contaminated by seawater, including the overflowing of ballast water during ballast operations, sea water coming out from fire hydrants, and sea water leaking from the anchor washing line onto the cars located on the berth.

- **Damage to the cars due to overflow of ballast water during ballast operations:** To avoid such damage, it is essential to keep the ballast system in perfect condition and well maintained as per the Planned Maintenance Schedule. All piping, including those inside ballast tanks, non-return valves, etc., should be thoroughly checked and replaced if necessary. Backflow of ballast water into the cargo hold could lead to a total constructive loss of the cargo. Therefore, it is very important to conduct all ballast operations before commencement of cargo operations. This is not always possible, but if it is necessary to conduct ballast operations during loading or discharging, they should be carried out in accordance with the ballast operation plan. If ballast water damage is caused during the voyage, the Master should notify all parties concerned immediately.
- **Damage to the cargo by water from fire hydrants:** Stowage of cargo should be performed so that all cars are at least 50 cm away from the closest fire hydrant. If for some reason other than an emergency the fire pumps are started, the risk of leakage from hydrants is significant. On the other hand, potential risk exists if PSC officers check the fire pumps during the vessel's stay in port. Therefore, before commencement of cargo operations the Master must ensure that all hydrants are closed in order to avoid leakage. If for some reason, the cars are damaged by leaking from hydrants, the Cargo Owners may claim that the ship was in breach of the Hague-Visby Rules because the holds were not fit for accepting the cargo. In addition, the fire hydrants, including valves, spindles, hoses, and protection caps should be inspected and maintained according to the Planned Maintenance Schedule.
- **Damage to cargo parked on the berth due to leakage of sea water from the anchor washing line:** As the name indicates, the cargo parked on the terminal in close proximity to the ship can be damaged if the ship's crew is negligent about leaving the valves of the anchor wash open. Therefore, the Master must ensure that both valves (or at least the valve supplying water to the hawse pipe on the shore side) are properly closed. **Deck washing in port is absolutely prohibited.** In addition, and especially if it rains, it is recommended to plug the scuppers on the moored side of the ship in order to avoid rain water mixed with soot pouring from the deck onto the cars stowed on the terminal.

Damage to the Cargo Due to Overheating of the Tank Top

If the tank top is overheated, some damage to the tires is to be expected. Such damage can include but is not limited to compression, permanent deformation, or flat spots. Experience shows that such damage can be expected when the cargo is stowed on top of fuel tanks, which require some heating. While this may be caused by a design fault, to avoid such damage the following preventive measures should take place:

- The temperature of the tank top should not exceed 54° C during the voyage. The responsible officer should measure the temperature periodically and make sure that the temperature is not more than 54° C at any time. Having performed some tests with tires at a pressure of 2.3625 kgf/cm^2 for 30 days, it was concluded that permanent defects to the tires would occur if the temperature of deck plate of the tank exceeded 54° C.
- During the summer season the risk of overheating fuel oil tanks exists. Therefore, it is recommended not to heat the tanks unnecessarily. The steam used to heat the tanks should be adjusted to take into account the temperature rise in the tank due to the temperature of the seawater. The condenser, the steam inlet valves, drain traps, and other equipment are to be kept in good order.

Damage to the Cargo Due to the Improper Fixing of Rat Guards

Once the ship is safely moored, the rat guards should be positioned. In most ports, lack of rat guards can lead to serious consequences for the ship if it is inspected by health officers or the PSC. The rat guards can be made of various materials, including wood, plastic, rubber, and metal. In a strong wind, some of the rat guards can drop down onto the pier and damage the cargo stowed at the terminal. In order to avoid such damage, the rat guards should be checked regularly and affixed to the ropes if necessary.

Conclusion

Whatever the damage, the ship's crew should do their best to spot the damage during the loading, gather contemporaneous evidence, try to get stevedore's admission for the damage, and issue a Damage Report. The Master should notify all concerned parties immediately. During the voyage, due diligence should be exercised by the crew to avoid any damage to the cargo. If such damage occurs, the appropriate records should be made and contemporaneous evidence gathered. The parties concerned must be notified without delay.

Most damage caused by human intervention is the result of careless lashing or unlashing work, careless driving, and non-compliance with safety regulations implemented on board. Scattered material, lashings, etc., can be contributory factors in the damage of cars. Some structural elements of the cargo decks, such as pillars, ramps, insufficient height, liftable deck sockets, etc., present a higher potential danger for vehicles. It is advisable that such parts be clearly marked by reflective paint or tape.

Damage to the Cars Due to Inherent Vice

Inherent vice describes the risk of the cargo to "go bad" (in our case "to be damaged by itself"). In this case, the Carrier will not be held responsible, unless he had been told of the risk so that special precautions could be taken. One example of inherent vice regarding vehicles is broken windows of cars due to tension caused by ship's vibration. Some car types are very vulnerable to such damage.

Another type of inherent vice is flat tires. Normally flat tires cannot be considered as damage, but in some occasions they can lead to claims against the Carrier. When such damage is observed during routine checks, appropriate actions should be taken. Evidence should be gathered, the most important being photographs or videos (with date), and relevant entries entered in the logbooks.

Most of the Cargo Owners are aware of such inherent vices. It is a must for the Master to prepare a Damage Report and to notify all parties concerned about the damage. By taking the appropriate steps to prove that due diligence has been exercised during the voyage and that the ship was seaworthy at the beginning of the voyage will almost surely protect the Carrier against any claims (if any) as a result from inherent vice. As a rule cargo claims between the Owners and Charterers are settled in accordance with the Inter-Club New York Produce Exchange Agreement of February 1970, as amended May 1984, or any subsequent modification or replacement.

Damage to the Cargo Due to *Force Majeure* (an Act of God)

In bad weather, the risk of cargo shifting is greater, so special attention should be paid to safe ship handling and cargo inspections. During boisterous weather, the vessel experiences heavy stresses, which are transferred to the cargo via the lashings. If the lashings are insufficient in number or not properly secured, there is a risk that the lashing will break and cargo will shift.

Once the cargo starts shifting it may slide or tip, depending on the friction coefficient between the cargo and the ship deck. Cars will slide rather than tip, but this is not the case for roll trailers. According to R. P. Dalinga in "Safe Securing of Trailers and Deck Cargo," *Proceedings of the International Conference and Exhibition on Marine Transaction Using Roll-on/Roll-off Methods,* the trailer will overturn instead of slide if the static friction is larger than 0.5.

Whether overturning or sliding, the consequences can be disastrous not only for the cargo but for the vessel as well. The ship's stability can be endangered, which should be avoided by all means.

The higher the speed of the ship, the stronger the acceleration forces on the lashings are. As a preventive measure, therefore, the speed should be significantly reduced. The strongest accelerations acting on the cargoes are on the highest car decks, in the fore and aft parts (See chapter. 4), so additional lashings should be placed on the vehicles located in these areas.

The GM (metacentric height) of the vessel should be kept within B/13 (the breadth of the ship divided by 13) in order to mitigate the effect of the accelerations on the lashings.

Damage due to cargo shifting

Contact damage due to cargo shifting in boisterous weather

Cargo on trailers or any static (loose) cargo on deck can easily shift, with all negative consequences, in boisterous weather. Regular cargo inspections before entering, during passage, and upon leaving an area of harsh weather are indispensable preventive measures to avoid such damage.

Damage to the Ship's Equipment Caused by Stevedores

To prevent damage to the ship's equipment, such as ramps, deck lifters, forklifts, deck panels, deck, or even the ship's hull, the Master must restrict access to the movable deck equipment to the ship's personnel only. If, due to lack of attention, stevedores cause damage to the ship's hull or ramps, such damage should be brought to the attention of the foreman as soon as it occurs or is discovered. Contemporaneous evidence, such as eyewitness accounts, pictures, or even videos, should be taken and any broken items should be saved. The Master should prepare a Damage Report and insist this report be signed by the foreman.

The problem here is that the stevedores may deny liability if the damage is not reported immediately. The Master must prove that the stevedores are responsible for the damage and, if possible, get their admission in regard with this. If the foreman refuses to sign the Damage Report for fear of making an admission, he should be requested to sign this report "For receipt only." A Letter of Protest against the Stevedoring Company must be lodged in order to hold them responsible for the damage in question. The Ship Owners, P & I representatives, and all parties concerned should be notified immediately. The Damage Report should be e-mailed to them before the ship departs from the port where the damage occurred.

In the time charter NYPE 93,[6] which is one of the most common charter parties used in car carrier practice, clause 35 states: "the Charterers shall pay for any and all damage to the Vessel caused by stevedores provided the Master has notified the Charterers and/or their Agents in writing as soon as practical but not later than 48 hours after any damage is discovered."

Damage Reports

In the case of any damage to the cargo or the ship, the Master or Chief Officer must issue a Damage Report. As a rule, every Charterer has its own form of Damage Report, which should be used by ship's staff. The Damage Report should be issued immediately after the damage occurred or is discovered. Once the damage has been discovered the Master should advise the foreman and prepare the Damage Report.

There are usually two or three copies of the Damage Report: one is given to the stevedores as an acknowledgment that the latter will be held responsible (if this is the case); one is sent to the Charterers; and one is kept on board as evidence. Nearly all Damage Reports include more or less the same items to be checked and questions to be answered regarding the damage. When making the report the Master should fill out only those spaces applicable to the damage in question. The spaces or questions that are not applicable to the damage should be stroked through as an identification that these questions were not missed or overlooked.

If not caught on spot, the stevedores will often deny responsibility for the damage. It is in the interest of the Master to get the stevedores to admit the damage in question. Even if the stevedores will not admit responsibility they should be requested to sign the Damage Report, without admitting or denying responsibility. Once completed, the Damage Report should be sent to all parties concerned. It should be done, if possible, before the ship departs. If, however, the damage is discovered after leaving port, the report should be e-mailed upon discovering the damage or be sent from the next port. The Master should follow the instructions issued by the Charterers regarding the distribution of copies of the reports. There is a possibility that stevedores will not accept the report. If this is the case, a notation of that fact should be made in the report. In any case, a Letter of Protest against the Stevedoring Company should be lodged.

On some occasions, damage to the cargo may be discovered by the stevedores and not by the crew. In such cases the stevedores can request the Master to sign a Damage Report issued by the Stevedoring Company, forcing the Master to confess liability. The Master shall, in such case, sign the Damage Report adding the comments "For receipt only" and "Cargo discharged as loaded."

As a best defense against any future claims, pictures, drawings, or even videos should be used to support the Damage Report. For this reason, the gathering of contemporaneous evidence is important. Apart from taking pictures of the damage, it is important to make photos of the VIN (Vehicle Identification Number) as well. The VIN consists of 17 figures and letters such as:

The VIN number on the special label

JF1GH3LS58G037316

JF1=Manufacturer's identity number (first three letters)
GH3LS58=special code of vehicle
G037316=production number

The VIN could be taken from the front window or from special labels as shown on the pictures above. These labels are often attached to some of the windows, normally the front and side.

The Damage Report consists of a lot of columns, all of which need to be filled out in a proper manner. In the column "B/L" (Bill of Lading), the Bill of Lading number under which the car is being transported normally should be inserted. However, if the Bill of Lading is not available, the Chassis Number or VIN can be entered. The part where the vehicle is damaged should be detailed, as well as where and when it happened. Details of the various parts of a vehicle are shown in the illustration. Normally the type of the damage is described by letters shown on the back page of the Damage Report form.

It is very important to mention when the damage happened, before loading, during the loading, or while at sea. As a rule, pre-loading damage should be mentioned in the Mate's Receipt, the Bill of Lading, or other cargo documents. It is, however, not always common practice nowadays, and therefore due vigilance by the crew is important.

A-2-3 **The Name of Each Part of Vehicle.**

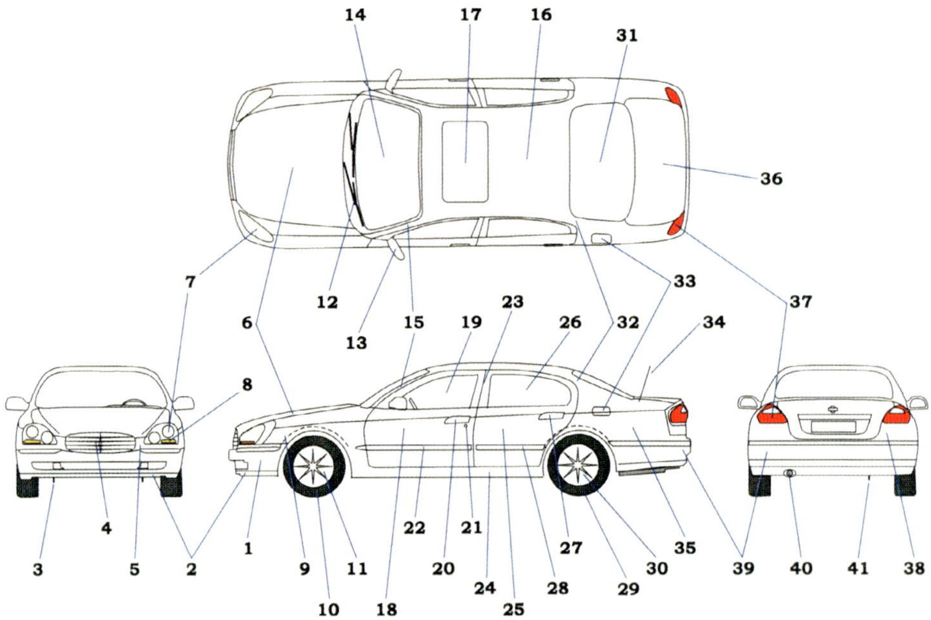

1	FRONT BUMPER	**23**	"B" PILLAR (L/H or R/H)
2	FRONT APRON	**24**	ROCKER PANEL (L/H or R/H)
3	FRONT TIE DOWN HOOK	**25**	REAR DOOR (L/H or R/H)
4	RADIATOR GRILL	**26**	REAR DOOR GLASS (L/H or R/H)
5	FRONT END PANEL	**27**	REAR DOOR OPERATING HANDLE (L/H or R/H)
6	HOOD	**28**	REAR DOOR MOULDINGS (L/H or R/H)
7	HEAD LAMP	**29**	REAR TIRE (L/H or R/H)
8	TURN SIGNAL LAMP	**30**	REAR WHEEL (L/H or R/H)
9	FRONT FENDER (L/H or R/H)	**31**	BACK REAR GLASS
10	FRONT TIRE (L/H or R/H)	**32**	ROOF EXTENSION (L/H or R/H)
11	FRONT WHEEL (L/H or R/H)	**33**	FUEL LID
12	WINDSHIELD WIPER (L/H or R/H)	**34**	RADIO ANTENNA
13	SIDE VIEW MIRROR (L/H or R/H)	**35**	QUARTER PANEL (L/H or R/H)
14	WINDSHIELD GLASS	**36**	REAR COMPARTMENT LID
15	"A" PILLAR (L/H or R/H)	**37**	STOP LAMP
16	ROOF	**38**	REAR END PANEL
17	SUN ROOF GLASS	**39**	REAR BUMPER
18	FRONT DOOR (L/H or R/H)	**40**	EXHAUST PIPE (FINISHER)
19	FRONT DOOR GLASS (L/H or R/H)	**41**	REAR TIE DOWN HOOK
20	FRONT DOOR OPERATING HANDLE (L/H or R/H)		
21	DOOR LOCKING (L/H or R/H)		
22	FRONT DOOR MOULDINGS (L/H or R/H)		

L/H = LEFT-HAND SIDE
R/H = RIGHT-HAND SIDE

A-2-4 **Kind of Damage.**

1. Hairline Scratch	2. Scratch	3. Deep metal, Scratch
4. Gouge	5. Chipped	6. Dent
7. Bent	8. Broken	9. Cut
10. Crack	11. Corrosion	12. Stain
12. Torn	13. Rust	14. Missing

Parts of a car. Courtesy of Eukor.

Cargo Claims

Having been entrusted with the cargo, it is important that the Carrier exercises due diligence and tries to avoid damage to the cargo.

In some cases, the cargo assigned for sea passage is not fit for sea transport and presents a danger for the safety of the ship, the other cargo, and the crew. When this happens, the Master is in position to reject such cargo for shipment.

In the most problematic cases, however, the cargo does not present a risk for the seaworthiness, but **is delivered for loading in such a condition it might be a serious risk for cargo claims against the Carrier/Ship Owner at a later stage.** Some examples of this type of cargo include: vehicles covered by snow; vehicles covered by dust, mud, etc.; and pallets with an unknown quantity of cargo inside.

Whatever the condition, the Master must enter the appropriate remarks in the cargo documents and lodge a Letter of Protest. Clause 8, "Performance of Voyage" of NYPE 93 says that the Master is obliged to supervise all cargo handling. On some revised charter parties (C/P), however, this clause is extended, indicating the Master is not only obliged for the supervision of all cargo handling, but is responsible for cargo handling (loading, stowing, lashing, securing). In that case, any damage sustained by the vehicles will be the Carrier's responsibility and the Master must pay special attention during loading. The most commonly seen problems with condition of the cargoes follow.

Vehicles Covered by Snow

During the winter, cars stowed in the open may be covered by snow. Problems will arise when the snow starts melting during the voyage. It could lead to damage to the cars affected by snow and, in the case of decks that are not gastight or watertight, to those stowed on the lower car deck when the water starts leaking through the lashing holes on deck. Another problem with vehicles being covered with snow is that it is impossible to discover scratches or other damages. These vehicles will not present a risk to the seaworthiness of the ship, so they cannot be rejected for sea passage. It is essential, therefore, that the Master, upon accepting the cargo, make the necessary remarks in Mate's Receipts and lodge a Letter of Protest.

The remark about such a condition of the cargo in the Mate's Receipts should read:

Cars covered by snow

Vehicles Exposed to Seawater

Very often cars are exposed to seawater in port. As a rule, the car terminals are supposed to be protected against seawater sprays, but in case of boisterous weather, typhoons, etc., the cars will be exposed to seawater. When this happens, salt will appear on the surface of the vehicles. In order to be discovered in time to avoid claims issues, several precautions should be taken:

- The weather should be monitored closely and the Master should be aware of any uncommon weather phenomena that took place in the port of loading during the last weeks.
- The ship's crew should be very vigilant to identify cars showing traces of salt water.
- The appropriate remarks should be entered into the Mate's Receipts.

A remark about such condition of the cargo in the Mate's Receipts should read:

Cars affected by sea water

Wiping of droplets from cars and carrying out a silver nitrate test can prove that deposits are from seawater.

Bear in mind that the cars can be washed by seawater that is not part of a weather phenomenon, but due to leakage of seawater from hawse pipes of another ship. Whatever the reason, if some cars are found with salty traces, the respective remarks into Mate's Receipts should be entered.

Vehicles Covered by Dust and Mud

This matter has already been discussed in detail, but it must be made clear that, in cases when he is responsible for cargo handling, the Master must ensure that the appropriate remarks are entered into the Mate's Receipts. Example of such remarks is shown in "Cars covered by dust."

Cars Covered with Bird Droppings

Very often the cars are bespattered with bird droppings, which can give rise for serious claims against the Carrier. The chemical reaction between the excrement and the paint could lead to damage to the paint at a later stage. If such vehicles are loaded, the necessary entries must be made in the Mate's Receipts.

Lack of Cargo Documents

In the Ro-Ro (PCC; PCTC) trade it is not uncommon for cargo to be delivered for sea transportation without cargo documents. Lack of such documents will not allow the Carrier to make appropriate remarks in the shipping documents describing the condition of the cargo at time of loading. When this happens, it is common practice for the Master to issue a Letter of Protest in order to avoid possible claims. It should contain the remarks that would normally be entered into the Mate's Receipts or cargo documents. This letter should be addressed to the Shippers or Charterers. (See chapter 12, Documents, p.188)

Such remarks should look something like:

> **VEHICLES LOADED / STOWED AND COUNTED UNDER CHARTERERS/SHIPPERS INSTRUCTIONS AND SUPERVISION*. CARS STOWED IN THE OPEN BEFORE LOADING. ALL CARS DIRTY COVERED WITH DUST. CONDITION AND CONTENTS OF THE CARGO UNKNOWN.**
>
> ***Note:** "SUPERVISION" can be entered only if the relevant Charter Party (C/P) is amended in clause 8 of NYPE 93 to stipulate that cargo handling is to be conducted under the Master's supervision.

When pallets or other packaged cargo is being loaded, the following remark is to be entered in the Letter of Protest:

> **Said to contain:** Shippers loaded/stowed and counted. Quantity, quality and contents unknown, as not tallied or controlled by Master. **No claims accepted**

In this case, it is advisable to mention in the remark that the cargo is "not tallied or controlled by Master," as far as it concerns the units inside the packages. However, the Master should supervise the number of pallets or packages or he will be responsible for cargo handling of such pallets, etc., depending on the revision of clause 8 of NYPE 93.

When second-hand vehicles are being loaded, the following remark should be inserted in the Letter of Protest:

Used / unpacked / damaged / unprotected second-hand vehicles of unknown condition. Charterers / shippers own, load/count, and stow. Contents and/or accessories unknown to the Master

Normally all these remarks are to be inserted in cargo documents, if they are presented. When, for whatever reason, the Master is not allowed to enter remarks into the cargo documents, he must lodge a Letter of Protest. Moreover, it is the Master's duty to make remarks in the Mate's Receipt. Not doing so is a fraud and falsifying of documents.

When the Carrier Will Not Be Responsible for Cargo Damage

It is not the point of this book to analyze the maritime law. There are a lot of authoritative books on that topic. However, in the context of the responsibilities of the Carrier stipulated in the respective Charter Party C/P and in respective rules (Hague or Hague-Visby), it is fair to point out the rights of the Ship Owner with regard to cargo damage, and especially his immunities.

Article IV, Rule 2 of Hague-Visby Rules shows the excepted perils. They are enumerated by letters (a) to (p) and the Master must be familiar with them.

In every contract, it is implied that a vessel shall proceed on her voyage without departure from her proper course. Hague and Hague-Visby Rules, however, stipulate that deviation in saving or attempting to save life or property at sea would not be deemed to be an infringement or breach of the Rules or of the contract of carriage. In this respect, the Carrier will not be held responsible for any loss or damage to the cargo resulting from that situation. If the justification of such a deviation is called into question, it is the Carrier's burden to prove it.

CHAPTER 9

FIRE PREVENTION

Ro-Ro ships are very vulnerable to the rapid spread of fire for various reasons, including the lack of bulkheads, the concentration of gases inside cargo holds, and other factors. Irrespective of the fact that all cargo decks are fitted with powerful ventilation systems, their misuse can contribute to forming gas spots, which can be easily ignited. Therefore, regular inspection for the concentration of gases inside cargo decks should be performed during the loading and discharging of cargo as well as during the voyage. All fire-fighting systems should be regularly inspected and kept in good working order.

Fire is one of the worst disasters that is faced at sea. Unfortunately, fires happen and, irrespective of the modern fire-fighting equipment on board, they can lead to fatalities, severe damage to the cargo, or the total loss of the ship. Fire on board car carriers and Ro-Ro ships presents a very serious hazard due to the type of cargo carried (vehicles with some quantity of gasoline in their tanks) and the design of the ships. Therefore, ship's personnel must take adequate precautions, including fire patrols and inspections, to ensure that the risk of fire on board is reduced to the minimum.

Notwithstanding the fact that international legislation and conventions have taken into account the seriousness of this problem, fires have occurred in the past, happen today, and will happen in the future. Therefore, it is vitally important that appropriate risk assessments are made and the safety precautions based on them are strictly followed.

Most of the fires occurring on board Ro-Ro ships are fires in enclosures: inside vehicle decks, passenger accommodation, etc. Once started, the fire can develop in different ways depending on the geometry of the space, ventilation, and fuel availability.

The principle convention regulating the requirements for fire-fighting systems on board all ships, including Ro-Ro ships, is SOLAS Ch. II-2. The essential fire-fighting systems and equipment required to be carried on board are listed in this chapter, but the technical requirements for the equipment are mentioned in so-called FSS Code–International Code for Fire Safety Systems. This code has been adopted by Res. MSC 98(73), 2000, which is, at present, compulsory. It should be kept in mind that regulations cited in SOLAS CH. II-2, concerning fire safety on board, are applicable to all ships. Therefore, requirements for fire pumps, fire hydrants, etc., will not be discussed in this chapter. One should always make reference to the respective chapter in SOLAS and relevant resolutions. The purpose of this chapter is not to analyze SOLAS, but to highlight the specific requirements for fire-fighting equipment adopted on board Ro-Ro ships and car carriers.

Considering the vulnerability of gases to explosion, SOLAS Ch. II-2 requires cargo spaces in Ro-Ro ships to be provided with forced ventilation systems capable of providing at least six air changes per hour if the electrical equipment is certified for the entire space and at least ten air changes if the electrical equipment is of a type certified up to a height of 450 mm above the deck. SOLAS requires ventilation on Ro-Ro cargo ships and Ro-Ro passenger ships carrying not more than thirty-six passengers to provide at least six air changes per hour. For Ro-Ro passenger ships carrying more than thirty-six passengers, the ventilation system must provide at least ten air changes per hour.

Drains from vehicle decks may not lead to machinery spaces or other spaces containing sources of ignition. An amendment to Ch. II-2/20, which entered into force on January 1, 2010, addresses the drainage of special category and Ro-Ro spaces to prevent accumulation of water on the vehicle deck of Ro-Ro ships. In this respect, discharge valves for scuppers, fitted with positive means of closing that are operable from a position above the bulkhead deck shall be kept open while the ship is at sea, in accordance with the requirements of the International Convention on Load Lines in force. All operations of valves should be recorded into the log-book. On all ships, closed vehicle spaces, Ro-Ro spaces, and special category spaces, where fixed pressure water-spraying systems are fitted, shall be equipped with the means to prevent the blockage of drainage arrangements, taking into account the guidelines developed by the organization.

The fire-fighting systems adopted on board Ro-Ro ships are CO_2, pressure water spraying system, including hi-fog system, and high-expansion foam system.

CO_2 Systems

CO_2 systems should conform to the requirements of MSC. 1/Circ. 1318, "Guideline for the maintenance and inspections of fixed carbon dioxide fire-extinguishing systems." They should be capable of filling at least 45% of the enclosed space for which they are designed. CO_2 systems can be divided into two main categories, depending on the principle they use:

- Low-pressure CO_2 systems
- High-pressure CO_2 systems

The difference between these systems is in the way they work. Low-pressure CO_2 systems consist of a storage tank containing CO_2 and distribution piping and valves. In contrast, high-pressure CO_2 systems consist of several cylinders filled with CO_2, connected to each other. The starter or pilot cylinder activates the others and the CO_2 is distributed to the area in need.

Low-pressure CO_2 Systems

Low-pressure CO_2 systems are the main fire-fighting system used in cargo spaces on board car carriers. The ship is divided in several zones, marked by numbers or figures. The ship can consist of 4 to 5 zones depending on the number of car decks. The engine room is also included in one of these zones.

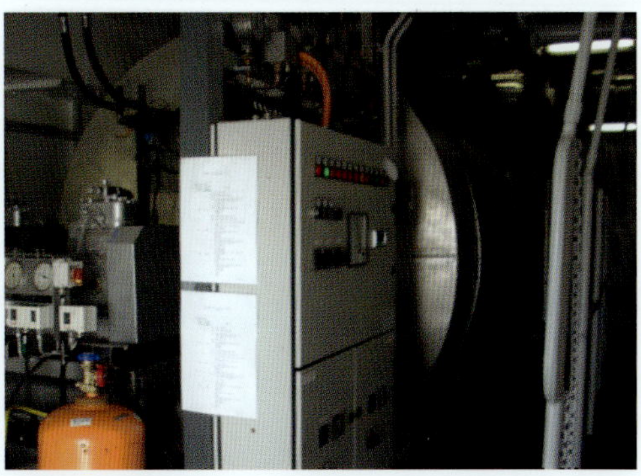

Low pressure CO_2 system

Low-pressure CO_2 systems include a storage tank and piping for delivery of the CO_2. The pressure inside the storage tank is monitored and independent visual and audible alarms are provided for high and low pressure. The high pressure alarms are triggered before the pressure reaches the point where the relief valves are activated. The low pressure alarms are set to activate at not less than 18 bars. Each storage tank is equipped with two gauges, one that provides permanent monitoring of the liquid level and the other to monitor pressure. Each storage tank is to be fitted with two safety relief valves with shut-off valves on their inlet sides.

At least two complete, independent refrigeration plants are to be provided for the CO_2. The containers should be in dedicated rooms, which should be well ventilated. The piping should be steel and on each section of pipe a safety relief device is to be fitted.

Warning signs are to be provided at each access to and within a protected space. Brief operating instructions are to be posted at the release stations.

It is important to remember that the rate of flow in the low-pressure CO_2 system is only enough for extinguishing the fire in one zone at a time. In other words, if there are simultaneous fires in car decks 2 and 3 (in some ships the car decks are marked by letters), which are included in the same zone, and in deck 6, which is part of another zone, the Master must decide which zone to be extinguished by CO_2. It is not possible to start CO_2 in both zones, because it will be ineffective.

CO_2 system can be connected to fire main

Before engaging the CO_2 system, the compartment in question must be evacuated and sealed. Because the CO_2 system extinguishes the fire by smothering, that is robbing the fire of oxygen, the system will be ineffective if the compartment is not sealed.

The system, of course, will smother personnel as well, so should not be engaged until the compartments are evacuated. Audible and visual alarms should be fitted in all compartments and used when the CO_2 system is about to be used. Once a head count of the crew has been completed, the CO_2 can be released.

Because of the danger to personnel, low-pressure CO_2 systems cannot be started automatically. They should be started manually only. The personnel responsible for CO_2 systems must be well trained in operating such systems.

The latest CO_2 systems can be connected to the fire main, thus accelerating the effect with CO_2 and water.

Maintenance of CO_2 systems should be performed according to the Planned Maintenance Schedule and manufacturer's instruction.

High-pressure CO_2 Systems

High-pressure CO_2 systems can be used for extinguishing fires in smaller spaces, such as engine rooms, incinerator rooms, etc. The CO_2 is stored in a bank of smaller cylinders, consisting of a master cylinder and a number of slave cylinders. The cylinders are linked by a manifold and feed into a network of pipes and nozzles to deliver the CO_2. The cylinder bank is housed in a locker. When the locker is accessed, warning alarms are activated for the evacuation of personnel.

The master cylinder can be activated by a remote switch or a time-delayed manual activator, which gives the operator time to get to safety. The system must be capable of being manually operated in case of malfunction. Engaging the master cylinder will cause the main compartment isolating valve and the requisite number of cylinders to open.

CO_2 systems should never be installed inside spaces for human accommodation.

High-pressure CO_2 system

Water Spraying Systems

Pressurized Water Spray Systems

The IMO Res. A. 123 (V) "Recommendations on fixed fire extinguishing systems for special category spaces" sets out the detailed requirements for the design and installation of water spray systems for Ro-Ro decks. Only approved, full-bore nozzles are to be used, and the nozzles should be arranged in such a way that effective, uniform distribution of water is ensured at 3.5 liters/m^2 per minute where the deck height is less than 2.5 meters and 5 liters/m^2 per minute where the deck height is 2.5 meters or more. These figures, however, are not applicable to approved water mist systems when IMO MSC Circ. 914 "Guidelines for the approval of alternative fixed water based fire-fighting systems for special category spaces" applies.

Fire hydrant inside car decks

Fire hose

The room where the distribution valves are located has to be adequately ventilated. Each distribution valve has to be clearly marked, indicating the section it serves. One or more pumps should be provided, the capacity of which should be sufficient to supply the two largest adjoining sections with water simultaneously.

Hydrants should be installed to ensure that water from four nozzles (compare to conventional cargo ships where water from only two nozzles is required) at the prescribed pressure could be simultaneously directed onto any part of the empty cargo space. In Ro-Ro spaces these hydrants should be arranged in the underdeck cargo space. For Ro-Ro spaces, all four nozzles used are to be supplied by a single length of hose.

Requirements for fire pumps, fire hoses, fire hydrants, and nozzles on board Ro-Ro ships are the same as for the other ships. These requirements, which are incorporated into SOLAS CH-II.2 will not be dealt with here. Only special requirements concerning Ro-Ro (car carriers) ships will receive further attention.

Water Mist (Hi-Fog®) Systems

Another water system that is used on board Ro-Ro ships is so-called water mist (Hi-Fog®) system. This system uses water under high pressure. Specially designed spray heads cause the water to enter the space as fine fog (mist) at high speed. This system is used in the machinery spaces, because the high speed of the small water droplets enables the fog to penetrate hot gases and reach the combustion source. The small droplets yield a very large total water surface area, thus providing cooling of the fire and the gases.

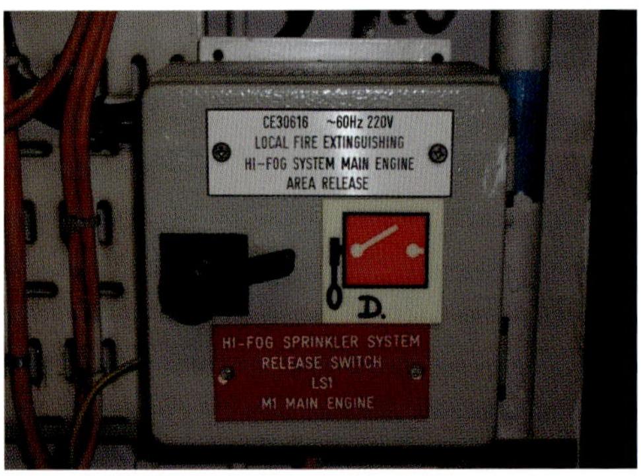

Local release of hi-fog system for the main engine

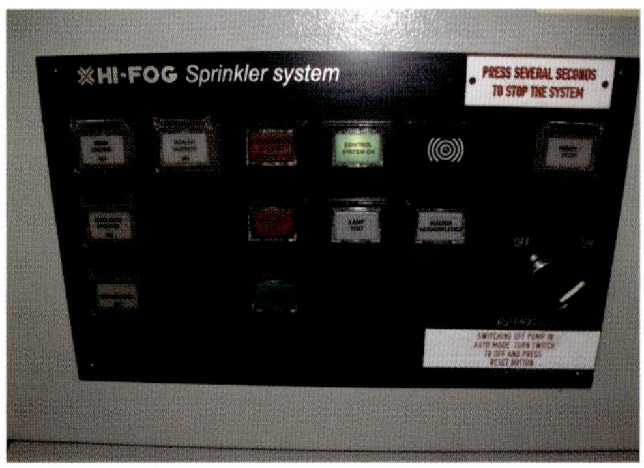

Automatic release of hi-fog system

The system consists of a pump unit, stainless steel piping, an electric control and monitoring system, machinery section valves, spray heads for discharging of fog, filters for the water feeding system, and strainers in the spray heads. The system is connected to the ship's water supply system.

The heads consist of several water mist nozzles, which should comply with the requirements of Resolution A. 800(19), "Revised guidelines for approval of sprinkler systems equivalent to that referred to in SOLAS Regulation II-2/12."

Strainers in the spray heads are intended to protect the nozzles from clogging due to impurities in the water used as fire-extinguishing medium.

The system may be divided into sections, the distribution valves of which should be operated from easily accessible positions outside the spaces to be protected. The pump and its controls also should be installed outside the space being protected.

The system should be kept on standby pressure at all times. If the minimum required pressure drops, the pump supplying the water should start automatically.

The piping used is usually stainless steel with diameter of 12 or 19 mm.

The system is activated automatically; therefore its automatic release mode should be always on. In case of malfunction, the system can be started manually.

High-expansion Foam System

The equipment producing the foam is to be of sufficient capacity to protect the largest space by filling it with foam at a rate of at least 1 meter per minute without allowance for installed machinery and equipment. The supply of foam concentrate should be sufficient for the largest space to be protected. The supply of foam-forming liquid should be enough to produce a volume of foam equal to five times the volume of the largest space. The equipment should be ready for immediate use.

The arrangement of the foam generator for delivery should be such that a fire in the protected space will not affect the foam generating equipment. The foam generators, their sources of power supply, the stored quantities of foam concentrate, foam liquid pumps, and the controls for the systems are to be readily accessible and simple to operate, and are to be grouped in as few locations as practically possible.

Other Fire Protection Equipment

Foam Applicator

On each vehicle deck there should be at least one foam applicator, which consists of a foam nozzle/ branch pipe (either of a self-inducing type or in combination with a separate inductor) capable of being connected to the fire main by a fire hose, together with two portable tanks each containing at least 20 liters of approved foam concentrate (Ref. IMO MSC Circ. 582, "Guidelines for the performance and testing criteria and surveys of low-expansion foam concentrates for fixed fire-extinguishing").

Foam applicator

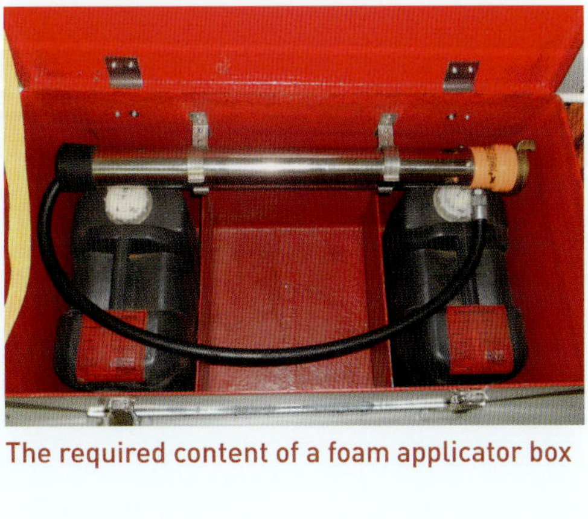

The required content of a foam applicator box

Water Fog Nozzles

At least three water fog nozzles should be supplied on every car deck. The long reach of these nozzles enables them to be used to extinguish fires beneath vehicles.

These nozzles are stowed in a manner that prevents movement. All mechanisms should be slightly greased in such a way that build-up of old grease does not impair the operation of the nozzle.

Water fog nozzle

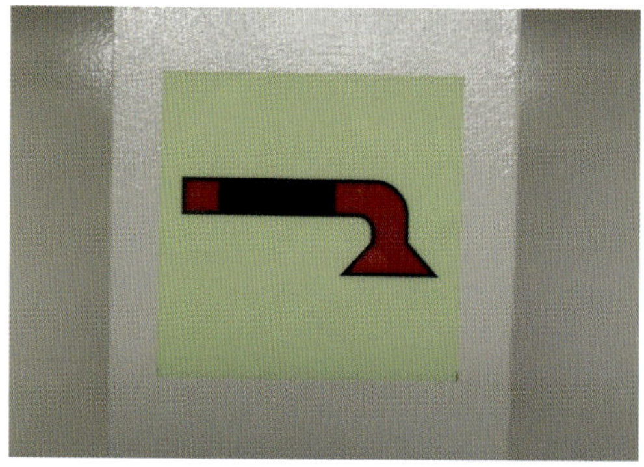

Symbol for water fog nozzle

Fire Extinguishers

Portable fire extinguishers suitable for putting out oil fires should be located on each side of the cargo space, not more than 20 meters apart. One such fire extinguisher is to be located at each entrance to these spaces.

Considering that oil fires are categorized as Class B fires, the most useful fire-extinguishing media are dry powder, foam, and CO_2. The most common type of fire extinguisher in cargo spaces is dry-powder. The inspections of fire extinguishers and their maintenance are to be conducted in compliance with IMO MSC. 1/Circ. 1432, "Revised guidelines for the maintenance and inspection of fire protection systems and appliances" and Res. A. 951(23), "Improved guidelines for marine portable fire extinguishers," and the Planned Maintenance Schedule adopted by the Company.

Portable fire extinguisher

Fixed and Wheeled Extinguishers

These extinguishers may be provided in machinery spaces. They can be of foam, dry-powder, or CO_2 types. The main difference between these extinguishers and the portable ones is the volume of the extinguishing medium. Fixed and wheeled extinguishers have limited portability.

Wheeled fire extinguisher

Fire Doors

As stipulated in SOLAS the fire doors can be divided into three main categories: Class A, B and C. Details for these doors can be found in SOLAS Ch-II.2.

Class A: Constructed of steel or equivalent material, Class A fire doors prevent the passage of smoke or flame for one hour (according to a standard test). Class A bulkheads should be insulated with non-combustible materials so that on the side opposite a fire the average temperature will not rise more than 140° C above the original temperature, nor more than 180° C at any one point.

- Class "A-60" fire doors must prevent the stated temperature rises for at least 60 minutes.
- Class "A-30" fire doors must prevent the stated temperature rises for at least 30 minutes.
- Class "A-15" fire doors must prevent the stated temperature rises for at least 15 minutes.
- Class "A-0" fire doors must prevent the stated temperature rise for at least 0 minutes.

Class B: Fire doors capable of preventing the passage of flame for the first half-hour of the standard test. A Class B fire door must be constructed of approved non-combustible materials, except that combustible materials may be permitted provided they meet certain other requirements. The insulation should be such that on the side opposite to a fire the average temperature will not rise more 140° C above the original temperature, nor more than 225° C at any one point.

- Class "B-15" fire doors must prevent the stated temperature rises for at least 15 minutes.
- Class "B-0" fire doors must prevent the stated temperature rises for at least 0 minutes.

Class C: Divisions are constructed of approved non-combustible materials that do not need to meet the requirements for limiting the passage of smoke and flame nor limitations relative to temperature rise. Combustible veneers are permitted provided they meet other requirements.

Fire resistance of doors and door frames fitted to bulkheads and decks is to be, as far as is practicable, at least equivalent to the bulkhead or deck in which they are fitted. Watertight doors need not be insulated.

SOLAS requires doors to comply with the IMO Fire Test Procedures (FTP) code, effective as on July 1, 1998. The IMO FTP Code requires doors to be fire tested in accordance with IMO Res. A. 754 (18), "Recommendation on fire resistance tests for A, B, and C, class divisions as amended by MSC. 61(67)," by a testing laboratory recognized by the Flag Administration. It also requires factory follow-up inspections by a competent authority accepted by the administration.

It is very important to make sure that all fire doors are closed before departure. Some of the ramps on board Ro-Ro ships are gastight in order to prevent spreading of smoke and gas in case of fire.

An alarm on the bridge will be triggered when these ramps are not closed and secured.

On Ro-Ro passenger ships carrying more than thirty-six passengers, the boundary bulkheads and decks of special category spaces and Ro-Ro spaces shall be insulated to "A-60" class. If there are fuel oil tanks below special category spaces or Ro-Ro spaces, the deck between such spaces may be of "A-0" class.

Fire Dampers

Mushroom type damper

Fire dampers are provided in ventilation ducts and air intakes. This is to ensure that, in the event of a fire, sections may be sealed, thus avoiding the spreading smoke and heat. It is important that these dampers are clearly marked for "open-close" positions and for the spaces served, and are always kept in good working condition. Their maintenance and inspection should be performed as per the Planned Maintenance Schedule adopted by the Company.

The simplest form of a fire damper is a metal plate inside an air duct. Another type of damper is the mushroom type, usually used for accommodation spaces. The dampers must be of such design that they allow for manual operation. However, some dampers can be fitted with automatic closures, consisting of fusible links that are activated at temperatures between 68° C and 70° C. In exhaust ducts serving spaces with high ambient temperatures, such as galleys or drying rooms, the temperature at which the fusible link or other system activates may be increased.

Manual Calling Point

As required by SOLAS Ch. II-2 Reg. 20/4.3.2, manually operated call points shall be spaced so that no part of the space is more than 20 meters away from a manually operated call point. One shall be placed close to each exit from such spaces.

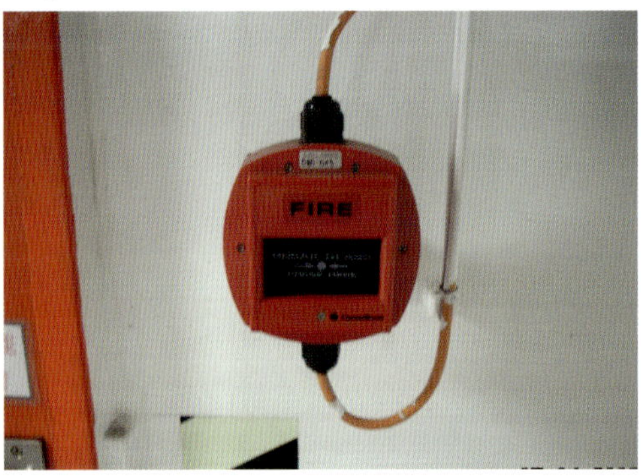

Manual call point

Symbol for manual call point as per IMO MSC Res. 952

Electrical Equipment and Wiring

Lighting shall be of type suitable for use in explosive petrol and air mixtures (SOLAS Ch. II-2 Reg. 20/3.2.1). The lighting should be checked on regular basis and as per the Planned Maintenance Schedule. The lighting inside paint stores should be of an approved type.

Ro-Ro passenger ships have more stringent requirements when it comes to emergency lighting. All public passenger spaces and alleyways shall be provided with supplementary electric lighting able to operate for at least three hours when all other sources of electrical power have failed.

A portable, rechargeable, battery-operated lamp shall be provided in every crew space alleyway, recreational space, and working space.

Fire Detection and Alarm System

Typical smoke detector

Fire detection and alarm systems shall be provided for car decks. The system should be of an approved type. The most common type of smoke detector is the ionization smoke detector, which will react to the invisible smoke particles evolving from a fire. Car decks should be equipped with either this system or with a sample-extraction smoke detection system. This system is designed to give an early warning of fire in cargo holds by providing continuous air sampling from a remote location. As a rule, this system is linked to the CO_2 fire extinguishing system. However, open Ro-Ro spaces are not permitted to be equipped with such a system.

The fixed fire detection system shall be capable of detecting any fire immediately. The type of detectors and spacing shall be to the satisfaction of the Flag Administration. The main type of fire detectors widely used on board Ro-Ro ships and car carriers is a smoke detector. The space between the separate smoke detectors should be as follows:

- Maximum deck area per detector: 74 m^2
- Maximum distance between the centers: 11 m
- Maximum distance from the bulkheads: 5.5 m

The risk of fires on board Ro-Ro ships during loading and unloading operations is increased because the smoke detection system is often disconnected in port to avoid false alarms. This is not in conflict with SOLAS because car decks are manned during on- and off-loading operations. At the same time, the CO_2 system is ineffective (especially a low-pressure system) due to the fact that to close the ramps, which are open, can take 20–30 minutes after a fire is discovered. Most of the reputable companies, with well-established SMS, require special attention during port stays.

When the ship is at sea, more frequent inspections of the cargo and cargo spaces are required for the first 12 hours (every two hours the cargo should be inspected for signs of fire). During the voyage, ventilation of cargo holds must be performed in an appropriate manner in order to avoid accumulation of gases and fumes. If no ventilation is being performed, the ventilators must be closed in order to avoid sparks entering the cargo spaces.

Means of Escape

At least two means of escape should be provided in Ro-Ro spaces. On Ro-Ro passenger ships, the means of escape shall be marked by lighting or photo-luminescent strip indicators placed not more than 300 mm above the deck. They should lead to an assembly station.

Maintenance of Fire-Fighting Equipment

The fire-fighting equipment should be kept in good order and readily available at all times. Maintenance of all fire-fighting equipment should be performed as per the Planned Maintenance Schedule incorporating at least the requirements of IMO MSC. 1 /Circ. 1432 "Revised Guidelines for the Maintenance and Inspection of Fire-Protection Systems and Appliances." The equipment should be inspected on weekly, monthly, quarterly, and annual bases as required, with relevant entries made in the deck logbook.

Fire Control Plans:

Ro-Ro ships should be supplied with fire control plans, which should be permanently exhibited for guidance of ship's officers. They should clearly show the particulars of fire detection systems, fire extinguishing appliances, means of access, ventilating systems, and the location of fire dampers on each deck. The above information may be set out in booklet.

In addition, for Ro-Ro passenger ships carrying more than thirty-six passengers, the fire control plans and booklets should provide information for fire protection, fire detection, and fire extinction.

Fire Precautions on Board Ro-Ro Ships

Fire on board of a Ro-Ro ship can be disastrous. Therefore, all crew must be well aware of the potential sources of fire and take preventive measures in sufficient time to avoid fires. Vigilance for and awareness of shipboard fires is not only the responsibility of the senior staff but of everyone on board! Unfortunately, fires on board Ro-Ro ships can start within minutes and can spread very quickly due to lack of bulkheads.

Correct and efficient action in case of fire can be facilitated through assessing possible causes of fires.

Smoking: One of the principal causes of fire on board is smoking.

- Smoking must be prohibited in cargo decks and only allowed in designated places. Conspicuous warning signs should be displayed in any part of the ship where smoking is forbidden—especially inside car decks.
- Careless disposal of cigarettes can also lead to a fire. At the designated places for smoking, such as in the duty mess, an appropriate number of ashtrays should be provided.
- During cargo operations the duty officer should supervise the stevedores and, if someone is discovered smoking, should stop cargo operations and inform the Chief Officer, who should bring this fact to the attention of the foreman. Good practice is to issue a Letter of Protest, but this will not keep the ship safe. The most important thing during cargo operations is the strict supervision of the stevedores.

Doors and Ramps: It is very important to close and secure gastight doors and ramps upon completion of loading in the car deck. In case of any suspension of cargo operations longer than a few hours, these ramps and doors are to be closed and secured even if the decks have not been fully loaded. Moreover, it is a requirement of SOLAS that all gastight and watertight doors and ramps are closed and secured before departure and that appropriate entries are made in the logbook.

Fire Patrols: Fire patrols are an important part of preventive actions. When the ship is in port and no cargo operations are being carried out, fire rounds should be performed at regular intervals by the duty watchman as well as the duty officer. These intervals can vary depending on the Company instructions, but they cannot exceed two hours. When the ship is at sea, such safety rounds are to be performed every twenty-four hours; in the case of used cars, such rounds should take place every twelve hours. The appropriate entry into the logbook for such rounds and the name of the person in charge should be made.

Training: Training of the crew for fire fighting in car decks represents an essential part of the preventive actions. Appropriate drills should be conducted as required per SOLAS and Company instructions. These drills should be based on real-life scenarios. The appropriate records and guidelines for the drills should be available on board as part of the SMS. Entries into the logbook for such drills have to be made.

Refueling and Charging: Refueling and battery charging on board is strictly prohibited. Special attention should be paid to CFR 49 PART 176, 176.78, and 176.905 "Refueling and battery charging of motor vehicles in the hold of the vessel."

Electrical Equipment: Electrical equipment should be turned off when not in use, especially in the galley and machinery spaces.

Combustible materials: All combustible materials should be taken out of the cargo space while sailing.

Used Cars: The potential risk of fire when transporting used cars should be kept in mind. Refueling and/or battery charging of used cars during loading/unloading should be strictly forbidden.

A study conducted by DNV in 2005 called "Fires on Ro-Ro Decks" attributed most fires on board Ro-Ro ships to short-circuiting, auto-ignition, or shifting of the cargo. In other words, it was not any failure of ship's systems but the cargo itself.

If fire occurs when the ship is in port, the port authorities should be advised immediately, cargo operations should be discontinued, ramps and doors closed, and the appropriate fire-fighting actions initiated. In order to help the shore personnel in fire fighting and assisting the crew, the international shore connections should be in place, complete, and in good order. In addition, SOLAS requires that fire plans with updated crew lists are available in way of every access to the ship—accommodation ladders, ramps, etc. If the fire occurs when in port, the chance for successful fire fighting is greater. However, there are cases where the fire is beyond control and the consequences can be tremendous. *Silver Ray* suffered a total constructive loss in Antwerp in 2002; *Eurasian Dream* suffered total loss of cargo and total constructive loss in 1998, when fire broke out in the port of Sharjah while the stevedores were refueling and jump-starting the cargo before discharging. When the fire occurs while the ship is at sea, the situation could be much more dangerous.

The reasons for fire on board Ro-Ro ships are complex. Apart from auto-ignition, fires can result from shifting of cargo due to bad weather. The danger of fires when the ship is at sea is significant, because the ship might list seriously due to the lack of stability. This is the case when huge amounts of water are being used for extinguishing the fire and the free surface effect becomes greater than initially anticipated. It is essential, therefore, to have a damage stability plan on board to allow the ship's crew to assess the effect of the new free surfaces.

CHAPTER 10

STABILITY

Ro-Ro ships must load and discharge their cargo very quickly, which requires long vehicle decks without subdivisions. Ro-Ro ferries operate in areas with dense traffic where the risk of collision is great. Ro-Ro ships generally have a low freeboard, which is allowed according to ILLC because of the large number of decks that allow for enormous reserve buoyancy when in intact condition. However, in order to facilitate cargo operations the car decks stretch from board to board and from stem to stern without any bulkhead or obstruction. So in case of damage to the hull, the reserve buoyancy will be compromised. With flooded compartments the angle of immersion can become considerably smaller. The lever arm of stability curve (GZ) becomes negative and the ship is likely to capsize.

Intact Stability

The IMO Stability Criteria for Seaworthiness for Ro-Ro Cargo Ships

Stability of Ro-Ro cargo ships, including car carriers, is an important issue because they are very vulnerable to the wind effect. The IMO Code of Intact Stability (the revised code came into force on July 1, 2010) requires that a ship's still water GZ curve meets six minimum stability criteria at all times when the ship is at sea. These requirements are as follows:

1. The area under GZ curve between 0° and 30° must not be less than 0.055 m. rad.
2. The area under GZ curve between 0° and 40°, or Θ_f (angle of flooding), whichever is smaller, must not be less than 0.09 m. rad.
3. The area under GZ curve between 30° and 40°, or Θ_f (angle of flooding), whichever is the smaller, must not be less than 0.03 m. rad.
4. The Θ_h (angle of heel) for the maximum righting lever GZ, must be at least 25° and preferably greater than 30°.
5. If the angle of heel is less than 30°, the GZ value at 30° must not be less than 0.2 m. If angle of heel is more than 30°, the maximum GZ value must not be less than 0.2 m.
6. The minimum upright GM (metacentric height) value must not be less than 0.15 m.

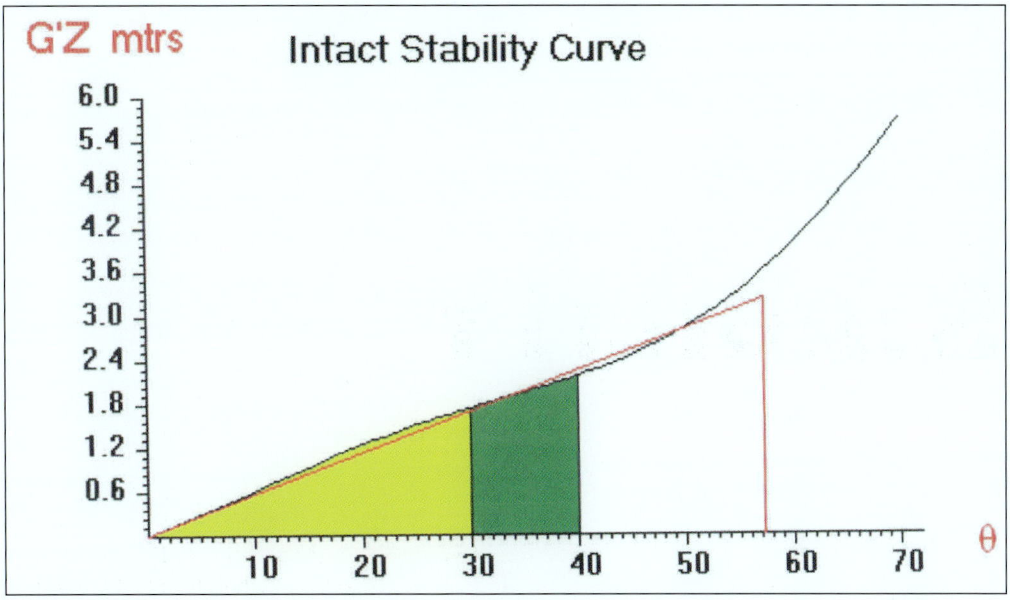

Dynamic stability curve

Irrespective of these requirements, $\mathbf{GM_{CORR}}$ (corrected metacentric height) is very often required to be greater than 0.15 m in order to mitigate and compensate for the harsh influence of the wind. Some classification organizations require GM >0.80 m and some even >1.20 m. When calculating the GM, it should be borne in mind that a large GM (stiff ship) will cause a shorter rolling period and respectively large acceleration forces acting on the lashings, especially on the upper decks. This constitutes a potential risk for cargo damage, as well as affecting the crew comfort, especially in boisterous weather. On the other hand, a small GM (tender ship) will have a negative effect on the ship stability and should be avoided.

So the main issue is: How stable should the ship be? As a rule, the GM should be within the range of 4–6% B, where B is the ship's breadth. Meanwhile, the upper limit of the GM can be obtained by the formula:

$$\mathbf{GM_{UPPER} = B/13} \qquad [1]$$

As was already mentioned, the lower limit of GM_{CORR} should not be less than 0.15 m during the whole passage. From the well known formula

$$\mathbf{GM = \{(0.8 \times B)/\tau\}^2} \qquad [2]$$

The present GM can be easily obtained by only measuring the rolling period τ (sec). However, the coefficient 0.8 is approximate only and for the precision of calculations it should be substituted with C_B-block coefficient obtained by the formula:

$$\mathbf{C_B = \nabla / L \times B \times d} \qquad [3]$$

Where:
∇ = displacement of the ship (m^3)
L = length of the ship, m
B = breadth of the ship, m
d = draft equal to 85% of the least molded depth, m

This formula is given in the International Load Line Convention (ILLC).

In the Stability Information, C_B is given with two values—for loaded and ballast condition. In all cases when using this formula, C_B should be taken depending on the corresponding draft. Using the coefficient C_B as mean value 0.8 may result in inaccuracy. When using C_B with a value of 0.8, it should be stressed that this block coefficient is different for car carriers where C_B ranges between 0.5 in ballast condition and 0.6 in loaded condition.

The IMO Stability Criteria for Seaworthiness of Ro-Ro Passenger Ships

Ro-Ro passenger ships should comply with the requirements mentioned above, but, in addition, these ships should also comply with the following requirements:

- The angle of heel (Θ_h) on account of the crowding of passengers should not exceed 10°.
- The code requires the mass of each passenger to be taken as 75 kg when calculating KG.
- When calculating KG the passengers are to be considered as located 1.0 m above deck level for passengers standing upright. (In the case of seated passengers, the distance could be reduced to 0.3 m)
- The code also requires that the angle of heel on account of turning not exceed 10°. It also gives a formula for calculating the heeling moment:

$$\textbf{Heeling moment} = \frac{0.200 \times V^2 \times W}{L} \times (KG - d/2) \quad [4]$$

Weather Criteria

Ro-Ro ships and, especially, car carriers have particularly large windage areas and are, therefore, exposed to wind influence much more than other ships. To estimate the effect of the wind the IMO Code of Intact Stability Ch. 2 Reg. 2.3 (USCG CFR 46, part 170) detailed so-called weather criteria for all passenger ships and for all cargo ships over 24 m in length. These criteria take into account the effect of steady wind as well as the effect of wind gusts. This influence is expressed by the heeling

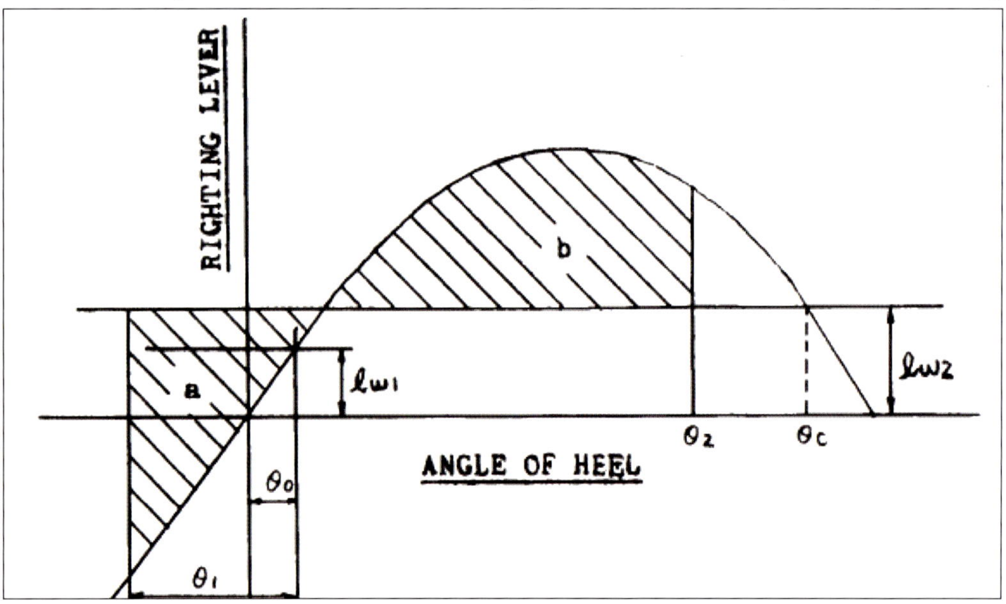

Weather criterion

levers of the respective winds and the corresponding formulas are given for calculating these levers. These criteria are incorporated into the ship's Stability Information and should be calculated as part of the stability calculation before departure.

Applying the weather criteria, the area "b" should be equal to or greater than area "a" on the diagram above.

Where:

- Θ_0 = angle of heel under the action of steady wind
- Θ_1 = angle of loll due to waves
- Θ_2 = angle of downflooding (Θ_f) or 50°, or Θ_c, whichever is lesser
- Θ_f = angle of heel at which openings in the hull, superstructures, or deckhouses that cannot be closed weather-tight are immersed. In applying this criterion, small openings through which progressive flooding cannot take place need not be considered as open.
- Θ_c = angle of second intercept between gust wind heeling lever (l_{w2}) and GZ curves

Steady wind heeling lever:

$$l_{W1} = \frac{P_W \times A \times Z}{1000 \times g \times D} \quad [5]$$

Where:

- l_{W1} = heeling lever caused by steady wind, m
- P_W = lateral wind pressure (504 N/m^2). This pressure corresponds to wind force 10 BF
- **A** = lateral area above waterline, m
- **D** = displacement, t
- **Z** = vertical distance from the center of A to the center of underwater lateral area, m
- **g** = 9.81 m/sec^2

Gust wind heeling lever:

$$l_{W2} = 1.5 \times l_{W1} \quad [6]$$

Where:

l_{W2} = gust wind heeling lever, m

The angle of heel caused by wind:

$$\Theta_R = 109 \times K \times X_1 \times X_2 \times \sqrt{(rS)} \quad [7]$$

Where:

- **K, X_1, X_2** = coefficients taken from tables
- **X_1** depends on ratio B/d and increases when B/d increases; X_1 lies between 0.8 and 1.0
- **K** depends on the roundness of the bilge and whether the ship has bilge keels are fitted or not. K lies between 0.70 and 1.0
- **X_2** depends on C_B and increases when C_B increases. X_2 lies between 0.75 and 1.0
- **r** = coefficient that can be obtained by formula:

  $$r = 0.73 \pm \{0.6 / d(KG - d)\} \quad [8]$$
- **S** is taken from tables depending on the rolling period and reduces as the rolling period increases

It should be kept in mind that wind pressure is based on the assumption that the wind is acting perpendicular to the lateral area of the ship. This will, perhaps, constitute the most serious difficulty to the ship, but if the wind is blowing from an angle to the fore-and-aft direction more complicated calculations should be made to obtain the wind pressure. Based on the above criteria it is possible to calculate the wind pressure acting on the ship depending on the force of the wind and draft of the ship. The lateral area A will depend on the draft as well. There should be a table in the Stability Information, which gives the data for A, Z, and wind lever for various drafts.

Based on the above information, the pressure acting on the lateral area of a car carrier can be calculated as well. The relationship between the wind pressure and wind force can be represented graphically as shown below.

The graph is based on the assumption that the wind is acting perpendicular to the fore-and-aft direction of the ship. If the wind is blowing from an angle to the fore-and-aft direction the pressure it causes will be smaller.

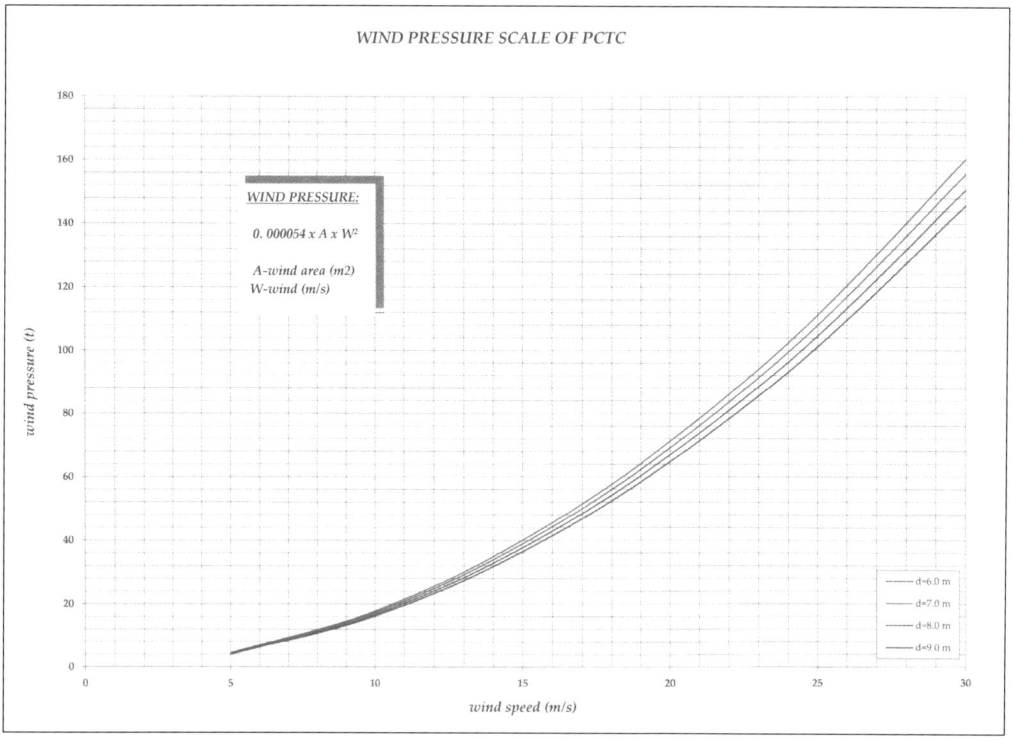

Wind pressure scale of PCTC

Consequences of the Large Windage Area to the Ro-Ro Ship's Stability

It is a fact that Ro-Ro ships and, especially, car carriers are much more vulnerable to the wind effect because of their large windage area. Some of the consequences of enhanced exposure to wind are:

- Strong wind heeling
- Large angle of heel when turning
- Car carriers are more susceptible to yawing and, as such, sailed distance will increase compared to other types of ships
- Difficulties in maneuvering when entering/leaving the port
- Potential for cargo shifting, especially when cargo is stowed on the upper decks

Strong Wind Heeling

As the Ro-Ro ships have an area of several thousand square meters exposed to the wind, it will be appreciated that the pressure caused by the wind will be significant. This pressure will depend on the wind force and draft of the ship. The stronger the wind and/or the smaller the draft, the bigger the pressure will be. Indeed, if the draft is less, the windage area will be larger and the wind pressure will be bigger. It is good practice to calculate the wind pressure, which can be done by creating a table with the wind force and draft. This table should be posted on the bridge for easy reference, especially during maneuvering.

If the wind is blowing for a long time from one side one can expect that the ship will be heeled to a certain angle. The stronger the wind is, the bigger the angle of heel will be. The corresponding angle of heel [7] can be used with the respective values of all coefficients.

Wind pressure (t)

		Wind force (m/s)					
Draft, m	Area A(m2)	5	10	15	20	25	30
5.5	3452.5	4.488	17.953	40.394	71.812	112.206	161.577
6.0	3383.6	4.398	17.594	39.588	70.379	109.967	158.352
6.5	3314.5	4.308	17.234	38.779	68.941	107.721	155.119
7.0	3242.7	4.215	16.862	37.939	67.448	105.387	151.758
7.5	3171.2	4.122	16.490	37.103	65.960	103.064	148.412
8.0	3029.2	3.938	15.751	35.441	63.007	98.449	141.766
9.0	2958.1	3.845	15.382	34.609	61.528	96.138	138.439

Wind pressure calculated by formula:

$$P_W = 0.000052 \times A \times W^2$$

Where:

- P_W = wind pressure in metric tons (tonnes)
- **A** = wind area (m^2) in longitudinal direction
- **W** = wind force in m/s

One of the most useful methods when obtaining the wind force is the method of G. Hughes. The formula used in his calculation is:

$$R_A = 0.5 \times P_A \times C_A \times V_A^2 (A \times \sin\Theta^2 + B \times \cos\Theta^2) \quad [9]$$

Where:

- P_A = specific density of air (kg/m^3). Standard value is considered as 0.124
- C_A = wind force coefficient—1.3 for car carriers
- V_A = relative wind speed
- **B** = projection of above water portion on amidships section (m^2)
- **A** = projection of above water portion on longitudinal section (m^2)
- R_A = wind force (kg)
- Θ = Angle of blowing of the wind

As mentioned, the maximum wind force could be expected when the wind is blowing perpendicular to the ship's side, that is when $\Theta = 90°$, $\sin 90° = 1$, and $\cos 90° = 0$. In this case, the force can be expressed by equation:

$$R_A = 0.5 \times P_A \times C_A \times V_A^2 \times A \quad [10]$$

If the car carrier from the example above has a draft 9.0 m and is proceeding at the most economical speed for the purpose of saving fuel (this speed is within a range of 15–17 kts), then the force will be estimated as:

$R_A = 0.5 \times 0.124 \times 1.3 \times (15)^2 \times 2958.1$
$= 53645.14$ kg
$= 53.645$ t

Large Angle of Heel When Turning

From the theory, it is well known that when a ship is turning a heel will develop. This heel initially will be inward but when the ship has achieved a steady rate of turn the inward heel will be overcome by the effect of the centrifugal force acting outwards through the ship's center of gravity G and an outward heel will be developed. This heel can be represented by the formula:

$$tg\Theta = V^2BG/g \times R \times GM \quad [11]$$

Where:

- **tgΘ** = the tangent of the angle of heel
- **V** = ship's speed
- **BG** = distance between B (center of buoyancy) and G (center of gravity)
- **R** = radius of the turning circle, in meters
- **GM** = metacentric height, in meters

Conclusions

1. **It is clear from [11] that higher the speed is, the larger the angle of heel will be.** Therefore it is strongly recommended not to make a sharp turn at full speed. The effect will be aggregated if the wind is blowing from the opposite of the turning side. If this is the case, the angle of heel caused by the turn will be added to the list caused by the wind. It should be kept in mind that if the rudder is reversed (that means putting the rudder to port during a starboard side turn) the angle of heel will increase significantly.
2. **The angle of heel depends on the GM.** The more stable the ship, the smaller the angle will be.

Ro-Ro Ships Are More Susceptible to Yawing

The deviation of the vessel off the intended track caused by different forces acting on the ship's hull can be adjusted by small alterations of the rudder, but the rudder cannot compensate instantly and completely for the influence of all forces. As a result of these forces, the ship successively deviates off the track and then returns to it. The resultant deviation is a continuous movement called yawing (yaw). The forces causing the yawing can be summarized in three basic groups:

- The effect of the wind and current
- The work of the rudder and the propeller
- The hydrodynamic characteristics of the ship

There are several types of yawing but the most important are:

- **Symmetrical**: when the forces causing the yawing are counteracted by adequate and steady adjustments by the rudder
- **Non-symmetrical:** when the forces causing the yawing are extended and not equal in strength. This kind of yaw is typical for twin-screw vessels.

Irrespective of the type of yawing, it should always be considered as an adverse phenomenon because yawing:

- **Reduces the speed:** The analyses show reductions up to (5–25%)
- **Increases the distance sailed**
- **Increases fuel consumption**

There are formulas for obtaining the difference between the distance to be sailed (S) and the distance actually sailed (S_1). To obtain the difference between the distances S and S1 for a symmetrical yawing:

$$\delta S = S_1 - S = \{S(1 - \cos\gamma)\} / \cos\gamma) \quad [12]$$

Where:
δS = difference between the distance to be sailed and the distance actually sailed
γ = angle of yawing

In case of non-symmetrical yawing considering the above assumptions will have the same result as formula [12].

Conclusions

- **If γ increases, cosγ will decrease and δ S will increase.** If $\gamma = 90°$, the ship will never reach the final destination.
- **To avoid unacceptable values of γ, the auto pilot should be on "Precision" mode during calm weather.**
- **The auto pilot should be on "Economy" mode during heavy weather.**
- **Considering the large area exposed to the wind one could deduce that the main factor affecting yawing of car carriers is the wind.** The above results should be considered when planning the voyage because the increase in distance could be substantial.

Difficulties in Maneuvering When Entering or Leaving Port

Depending on the wind force, Ro-Ro ships and car carriers can encounter certain difficulties when entering or leaving port. In case of very strong winds, some Owners even require the ship to stay outside the port. It is not unusual during port stays for the Master to require one or two tugs standing by in case of strong winds.

Potential for Cargo Shifting, Especially Cargo Stowed on the Upper Decks

The cargo loaded and stowed on the upper decks is much more susceptible to the accelerations caused by the ship's rolling and pitching. The same is applicable for the cargo stowed in way of the forward and aft parts of the car decks. Considering this fact, such cargo requires extra lashing as discussed in chapter 4.

On a stiff ship (large GM), the accelerations and the forces they cause due to the shorter rolling period will be significant, with enhanced risk of cargo shifting as a result. On the other hand, a tender ship (small GM) will not have enough stability, which could lead to serious problems and even loss of the ship. Therefore a reasonable stability, within the range of 4–6% B, should be guaranteed during the whole passage. The upper limit of GM, as it has already been explained, can be obtained by formula $GM_{MAX} = B/13$.

Stability Problems of Ro-Ro Ships

Ro-Ro ships have a special design that allows for quick and smooth cargo operations, including the presence of bow and stern ramps, and the lack of subdivisions on vehicle decks. The specific design of the Ro-Ro ships, including car carriers entails many stability concerns, which are summarized below.

Presence of Bow, Stern, and Side Ramps

The ramps should be watertight to avoid the ingress of water during sea passage. However, the maintenance of the ramps (discussed in detail in chapter 7) will require well-qualified staff and is only possible (in most cases) when the ship is in port.

Of particular concern is the presence of bow ramps (visors) fitted on most Ro-Ro ferries operating in Northern Europe. These visors, their hinges, and locking devices are under constant pressure when the ship is proceeding at high speed. When the ship is traveling in transverse waves and is rolling, the pressure on the bow visor is enormous and might even lead to its failure of the bow visor. The sinking of the *Estonia* in 1994, with the loss of more than 800 lives, was caused by the failure of bow visor, followed by the ingress of water.

The presence of the stern ramp(s) requires a flat transom. This means that the aft part of the ship can experience very heavy slamming, which can result in damage and even failure of the stern ramp(s). (See Slamming below)

Lack of Transverse Bulkheads Inside Car Decks

In order to facilitate the cargo flow, vehicle decks are designed as large open areas without transverse bulkheads. Therefore, any ingress of water will cause a loss of GM due to free surface effects. It will also cause a considerable list if there were no drainage devices on board.

Risk of Cargo Shifting

By their nature, vehicles are very prone to shifting if the ship encounters boisterous weather. This will be a particular concern if the cargo is not properly secured. Apart from causing damage to the cargo stowed in way of the shifted units, cargo shifting can cause hull damage and possible water ingress.

Flooding of Car Decks during Fire-Fighting Operations

As mentioned before, fire on board Ro-Ro ships is a serious risk. This is because most of the vehicles have limited quantities of fuel in their tanks. In case of fire, the quantity of water required for extinguishing the fire could lead to a loss of GM due to the free surface effect. Therefore during fire-fighting operations, the water used for fire fighting either should be drained overboard or into a holding tank in the lower part of the ship. As discussed in chapter 9, Fire Prevention, CO_2 is usually used nowadays as a fire-fighting medium in the vehicle decks.

If the fire hoses must be used for fire fighting, a large volume of water is released into the car decks, accommodations, or the engine room. This can lead to water accumulating on one side of the ship, so the vessel will start heeling and will eventually capsize. To avoid this, the water must be drained overboard or into a holding tank. Portable pumps can be used to facilitate this.

The firemen should monitor the water accumulation as well as the rate at which the water is entering into the area in question. An approximate formula can be used to ascertain the volumetric flow rate of the water from fire hoses.

Capt. I. C. Clark derived such a formula in *Stability, Trim, and Strength for Merchant Ships and Fishing Vessels* (Nautical Institute, 2008, p.280). Based on the potential and kinetic energy of the water:

initial rate of flooding = 180A√h

Where:
A = the area of the hole
h = depth of the hole below the waterline, meters

From this formula, Capt. Clark derived a formula to calculate the flow rate from a hose nozzle, based on hydrant pressure and nozzle size:

Flow Rate (m^3/hr) = **3600 x Nozzle Area x √(2 x P) / ϱ** [13]

Where:
P = static pressure in the nozzle (kN/m^2)
ϱ = water density (t/m^3) The water density can be measured or obtained from reference books or the pilot's advice.

Considering that the pressure in most hydrants is about 3 Bars (300 kN/m^2), with two hoses discharging simultaneously the following outflow rates can be reached:

Rate from 19 mm nozzle: 21.4 m^3/hour
Rate from 16 mm nozzle: 15.2 m^3/hour
Rate from 12 mm nozzle: 8.5 m^3/hour

The results are obtained taking into account a pressure drop of 25% between the hydrant and nozzle.

Effect of the Trim on Stability

When trimmed by the stern in still water, a Ro-Ro ship is supposed to have greater GM (metacentric height) than when on even keel. This is caused by the fact that KB (the distance from the keel [K] to the center of buoyancy [B]) in trimmed condition is bigger. On the other hand, the KB will increase slightly due to the shape of the underwater volume, and the BM (the distance from the center of buoyancy to the metacenter) will be higher. Hence, KM (the distance from the keel to the metacenter) is increased and, respectively, KM and the stability curve (GZ) are increased at small angles for any given value of the center of gravity (KG).

As far as a trim by the stern will increase the stability, the range of such trim should not exceed 1.0 meter where practicable and possible. Considering the form of a car carrier (parallel body), the performance of the engine will be the best at more or less even keel and even when slightly trimmed by the head. Therefore, this fact should be taken into account when calculating the stability and preparing the stow plan. When the Pre-stowage Plan is being prepared by tally companies and sent to the ship, the appropriate ballasting or de-ballasting could facilitate obtaining such a trim.

Meanwhile, when adjusting the trim, the ship should be trimmed in such a way that the propeller is submerged. This will guarantee a good streaming of the propeller and, therefore, better performance, less fuel consumption, and less slip.

Slamming

During pitching the vertical upright movement of the hull can exceed the vessel's draft. If this is the case, then the forward and aft underwater portions of the hull will emerge. Research shows that the most vulnerable parts of the ship that are subject for slamming damage are located 15% to 25% of the ship's length (L) from the bow of the ship. After emerging, these parts will again be submerged at a given speed during consecutive pitching. The impact of the emerged parts onto the water is referred to as slamming. In other words, slamming occurs when the relative water level drops far enough below the forward draft to expose the bottom plates in way of the bow. Slamming could be divided into:

- **Slamming of ship's bottom**
- **Slamming of ship's flare:** car carriers, due to their large bow flare, are vulnerable to such slamming. It can happen in large flared ships with a high relative speed between the water and the flare. The flat transom is also subject to heavy slamming even in moderate seas.
- **Impact of a breaking wave on the bow structure**

Apart from the fact that slamming is not comfortable to the crew, it will cause structural damage to the hull and slow down the ship. Slamming should be avoided. To avoid slamming the draft forward should be at least 2.5% of the ship's length. However it should be kept in mind that slamming will occur only if the following two conditions exist simultaneously:

- The underwater portion of the ship emerges so that the vertical oscillation of the underwater portion of the ship exceeds the draft
- The emerged portion is submerged at a speed exceeding a given critical speed. This threshold speed can be calculated using the equation

  Threshold speed = (0.09–0.12)$\sqrt{gL}$

  Where:
  0.09–0.12 = statistically obtained coefficients
  L = the length of the vessel

If only one of these two conditions exists, the slamming will not take place. In other words, the underwater portion will emerge and submerge without serious impact or damage.

Slamming is likely to occur when the ship is close to resonant pitching in head waves slightly longer than her own length. Immediately after the slamming, high-frequency vibratory stresses, called whipping, will take place elsewhere in the hull, causing damage to the hull.

Parametric Rolling

This phenomenon is most likely to occur in heading or following waves when the encounter period is half the natural roll period. The encounter period can be obtained by the following formula:

$$T_E = 1 / [1/T - 2\pi V\cos\beta/T^2 g] \quad [14]$$

Where:
T_E = encounter period
V = ship's speed (m/s)
β = relative wave direction
T = period of rolling

From this formula, it is obvious that parametric rolling depends on the ship's speed and relative wave direction. To avoid parametric rolling the Master should either reduce the speed to the minimum required for maintaining course in waves and wind or change the course, thus changing relative wave direction.

Effect of the Icing on the Ro-Ro Ship's Stability

A few years ago, it was inconceivable that car carriers would visit frost-bound ports (though Ro-Ro ferries have been trading in such ports in North Europe for many years). The climate, however, has changed drastically and the trade with cars in frost-bound areas, such as the Baltic Sea, has increased significantly. Today, Finnish ports such as Hanko, Hamina, and Kotka are storage areas for thousands of cars awaiting shipment for Russia. Visiting frost-bound ports in winter has given rise to the susceptibility of car carriers to the effect of the ice. More and more car carriers are being built "ice-class," as they are required to visit such ports during harsh wintertimes.

One of the chief problems that affect the ship's stability is icing. The icing buildup should be calculated as either a full-icing or a half-icing allowance.

Full-icing allowance:

- All exposed horizontal / vertical surfaces are carrying an ice weight of 30 kg/m^2.
- All vertical surfaces are carrying an equivalent to 15 kg/m^2 on the lateral area on one side of the ship above the waterline.
- Ice on booms, stays, and rails constitutes 5% of the weight of the vertical surfaces and the vertical moment of this ice is 10% of the moment due to formation on vertical surfaces.

Half-icing allowance:

- Half of the full-icing allowance

In the Code of Intact Stability for all ships, chapter 6 the assumptions are:

- 30 kg/m^2 on exposed weather decks and gangways
- 7.5 kg/m^2 for the projected lateral area of each side of the ship above the waterline

The effect of icing on the ship's stability could be expressed as follows:

- G will rise, which will lead to a reduction of the KG and respectively GM.
- GZ will be reduced.
- Dynamical stability will be reduced.
- Range of stability will be reduced.
- Draft will increase, which could lead to reduced freeboard. Meanwhile the increased draft means reduced Under Keel Clearance (UKC) and potential danger when passing shallow channels with limited draft.
- Asymmetrical icing will lead to undesirable list, which results in an increased draft on the respective side.

Information about the icing should be included in the Stability Information as required by SOLAS Ch. II Reg. 25-8. The calculations given there should take into account the worst scenario, namely icing at deepest draft, when the vessel is fully loaded

The areas where the full or half icing should be calculated are mentioned In the Code of Intact Stability, Chapter 6, 6.3.2.

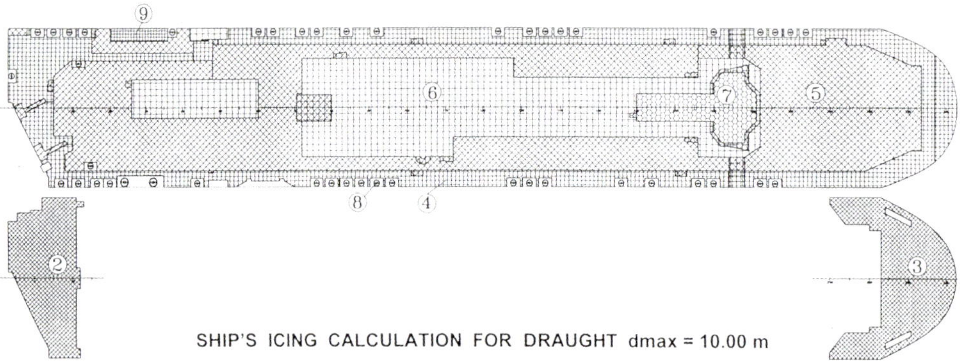

SHIP'S ICING CALCULATION FOR DRAUGHT dmax = 10.00 m

No	SPECIFICATION	AREA	ICE LOAD	ICE MASS	LCM from A.P.	TCM from C.L.	VCM above BL	LONG. MOMENT	TRANS.. MOMENT	VERT. MOMENT
		m^2	t/m^2	t	m	m	m	tm	tm	tm
1.	Lateral area	11084.0	0.0075	83.13	91.61	0.00	24.18	7615.54	0.00	2010.08
2.	Deck No 7 - Aft	358.4	0.0300	10.75	3.03	-1.45	19.99	32.57	-15.59	214.89
3.	Deck No 7 - Fore	448.6	0.0300	13.46	182.41	0.00	19.99	2455.25	0.00	269.07
4.	Deck No 12	1349.1	0.0300	40.47	95.90	-0.55	30.60	3881.07	-22.56	1238.38
5.	Deck No 13	2864.3	0.0300	85.93	95.24	+0.27	35.04	8183.97	23.20	3010.99
6.	Deck No 14	1634.9	0.0300	49.05	89.73	-0.47	37.78	4401.26	-23.05	1853.11
7.	Deck No 15	227.0	0.0300	6.81	143.29	+0.01	40.54	975.80	0.07	276.08
8.	Ventilation	254.5	0.0300	7.64	70.19	+2.28	35.80	536.25	17.42	273.51
9.	Funnel's platform	33.3	0.0300	1.00	22.40	-14.83	42.02	22.40	-14.83	42.02
TOTAL				298.24	-	-	-	28104.11	-35.34	9188.13
Increase of ice mass by 5%				14.91	-	-	-	-	-	-
Increase of vertical moment by 10%				-	-	-	-	-	-	918.81
TOTAL ICING				313.15	89.75	-0.11	32.28	28104.11	-35.34	10106.94

Icing on PCTC

Stability Calculations

Stability calculations should be made well in advance. After receiving the information for the cargo, including the number of units and the weight of each unit, the Chief Officer should make the stability calculations. Sometimes the Charterers do not send the full information about the cargo, but only the total number and models of the cars. If this is the case, the Chief Officer should use his expertise and experience to distribute the cargo properly. The main principle is still valid: the heavier cargoes should be stowed in lower decks and lighter cargoes in upper decks.

Due consideration should also be given to the correct ballast condition, especially if the ship is to pass shallow waters. The draft and stability should be mapped in such a way that the ship is stable at every stage of the voyage. Moreover the GM_{CORR} should not be less than the one, as required by the Charterers (in some instances 1.0–1.2 meters which is several times higher than the minimum required by the Intact Stability Code). Ballast operations should be planned so that a minimum quantity of ballast water has to be exchanged during the voyage. Improperly performed ballast water exchange can have serious consequences when heavy weather is encountered during the voyage. It should be kept in mind that some countries do not allow any ballast water exchange in their territorial waters. The required under keel clearance (UKC) should be maintained during the whole voyage.

Once the Stowage Plan has been prepared, the stability calculations should be made. The results of the calculations should then be compared with the required limits and if the values obtained exceed the allowed criteria, the Stowage Plan should be changed. Apart from verifying the values of GM, GZ, angle of flooding, and dynamical stability, the values of shearing forces and bending moments obtained should be compared with the maximum permissible values given in the Stability Booklet.

The procedure for calculating the stability is the following:

- **The weight of cargo should be determined for each compartment including all cargo holds, ballast water in each tank, as well as the fuel in the respective tanks.** When determining the weight of ballast water the conversion from volume to weight should be adhered to: Ballast Weight = Ballast Volume x Specific Gravity of the ballast water

- **Moments created by the cargo in X, Y and Z axes should be obtained by multiplying the mass of cargo in each compartment by LCM, TCM and VCM.**
  LCM is the horizontal distance from the center of each compartment to the aft perpendicular.
  TCM is the horizontal distance between center of mass in each compartment from center line.
  VCM is the height of the center of mass above the base line.

- **The mass of all ballast water, fuel oil, and diesel oil in each tank should be entered into the respective column and their moments obtained.**

- **The free surface correction should be determined for each partly filled tank.** To do this the following formula is applicable:

  $$FSC = \Sigma M_{FS} / \Delta$$

  Where:
  FSC = free surface correction
  M_{FS} = moments due to free surface
  Δ = displacement

- **Sum up the values in column Mass, moments.** The sum in "mass" means displacement.

- **Calculate the final LCG, TCG and VCG.**
  LCG = MomentX / Displacement (m)
  VCG = MomentV/ Displacement (m)
  TCG = MomentY / Displacement (m)

- **Find the corresponding draft for the displacement using the hydrostatic curves in the Stability Booklet.**

- **Obtain the respective LCB, LCF and MCTC**
  LCB = center of buoyancy
  LCF = center of flotation; the point about which the ship will trim
  MCTC = moment to change the trim by 1 cm

  $$MCTC = \frac{\text{Displacement x } GM_L}{100\ L_{BP}} \quad [15]$$

  Where:
  GM_L = longitudinal metacentric height
  L_{BP} = length between the perpendiculars in meters

- **Calculate the trim (t):**

  $$t = \frac{(LCB - LCG) \text{ x Displacement}}{MCTC} \quad [16]$$

The trim should always be to the stern. The Chief Officer should be aware of the conventions adopted on board when calculating the trim. If the sign of the trim is positive the ship will be down by the head.

- **Calculate the drafts fore and aft.** Compare them with the real situation taken from the draft marks, if possible.
- **Compare VCG with the maximum permissible VCG_{MAX},** given in the Stability Booklet. It can be obtained by using the table or diagram. The input information can either be the draft or displacement. If the value of VCG is within the region of sufficient stability, it means that the distribution of the cargo is acceptable (the ship will be considered stable if it conforms to the other requirements of the Intact Stability Code)

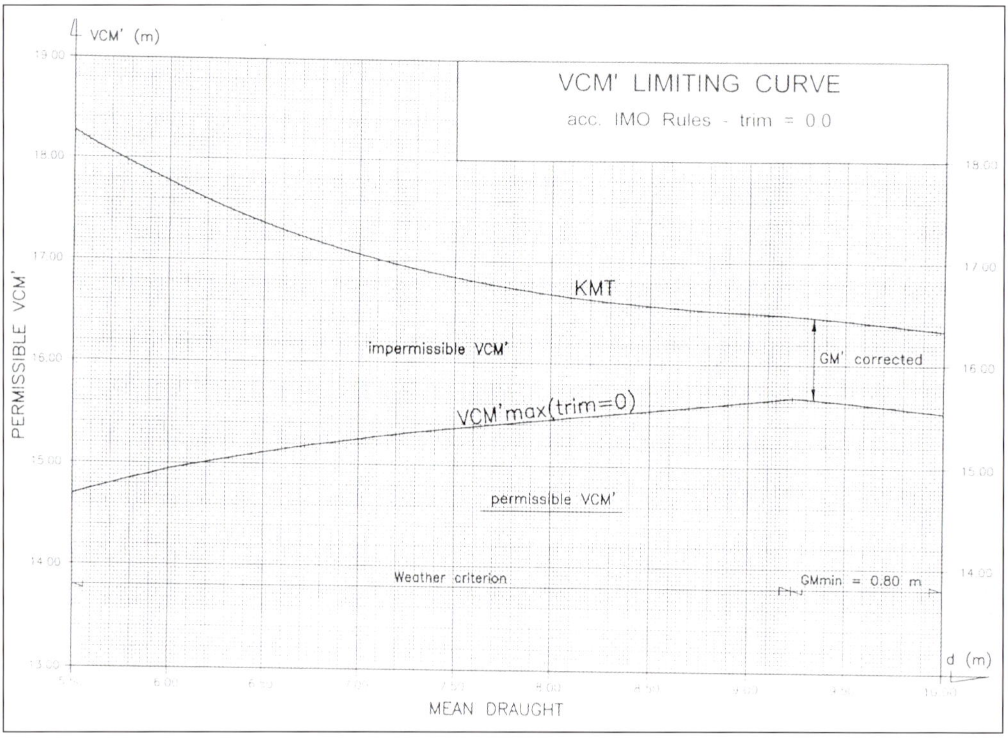

VCM max limit curve

- **Obtain GM = KM – KG**

  Where:
  KM = distance from the keel to the metacenter
  KG = center of gravity

- **Obtain δGM = FSM / Δ**

  Where:
  FSM = the sum moment of all free surfaces in all partly filled tanks
  Δ = displacement of the ship

- **Obtain GM_{CORR} = GM – δGM**

- **Compare GM_{CORR} with the requirements of Code of Intact stability/USCG CFR 46, part 170**

- **Construct the righting lever curve (GZ)**

  GZ = KN – δGM – KG x sinΘ [17]

  Where:

  KN = the horizontal distance between point K (the intersection of the keel and the vessel's centerline, and point N. When a vessel heels, N is point of intersection of a vertical buoyancy force line passing through the new center of buoyancy (B_1) and the horizontal line passing through point K. Data for KN is given in the ship's hydrostatic data, usually as curves known as KN curves or curves of stability.

  δGM = FSM / Δ

  Θ = angle of heel

- **Calculate the area under GZ curve, 0–30°.** Compare it with the required value 0.055 m. rad
- **Calculate the area under GZ curve, 0–40°.** Compare it with the required value 0.09 m. rad
- **Calculate the area under GZ curve 30–40°.** Compare it with the required value of 0.03 m. rad
- **Calculate stability criteria in accordance with the Weather Criterion**
- **Calculate the steady wind-heeling lever using formula [4]**
- **Calculate gust wind heeling lever using formula [5]**
- **Calculate the angle of heel caused by the wind using formula [6]**
- **Obtain angle of deck edge immersion**

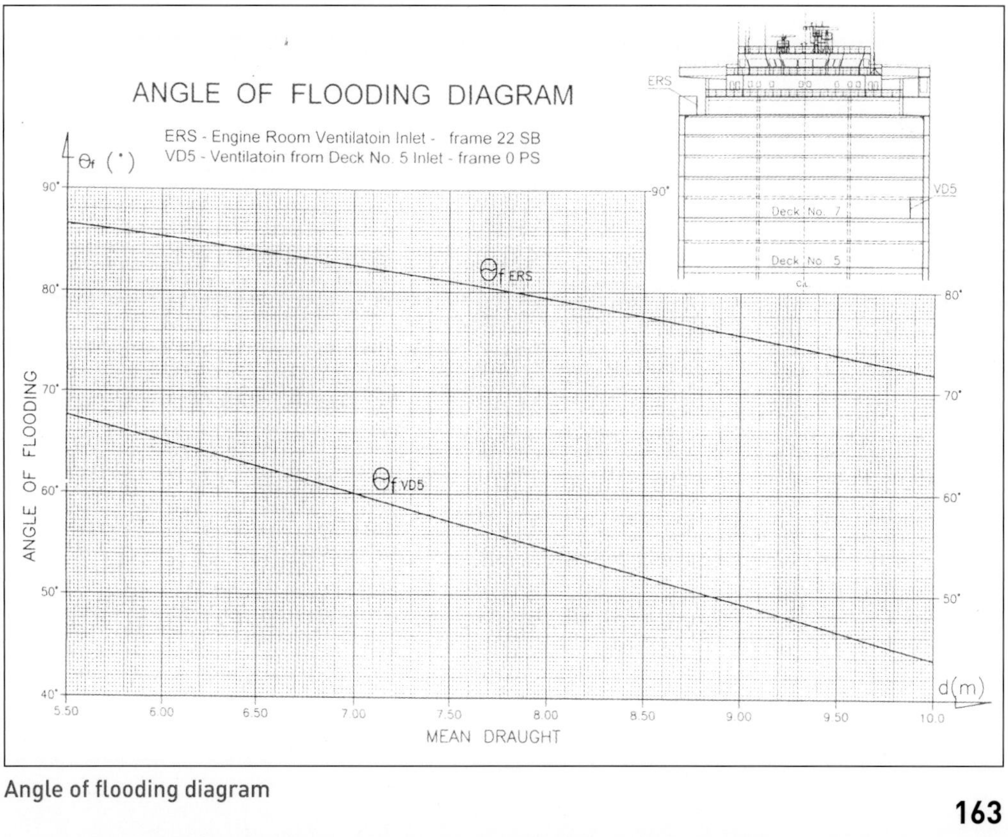

Angle of flooding diagram

- **Obtain the angle of flooding from the table "Angle of Flooding" or from "Angle of Flooding" diagram for the corresponding draft**

Having determined all stability data, the Chief Officer should compare the bending moments and shear forces with the permissible values. The process of calculating bending moments and shear forces is time-consuming and today is performed by stability computers and loading instruments. However, the Chief Officer should be aware of the principles for calculating these moments and shear forces. In the Stability Manual these permissible values are given in diagrams or tables for both harbor and sea conditions.

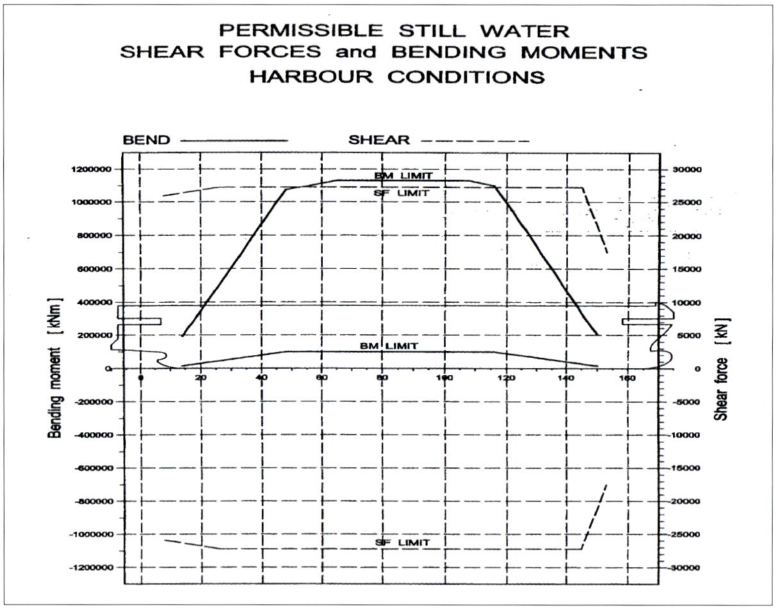

Permissible still water shear forces and bending moments in harbor conditions

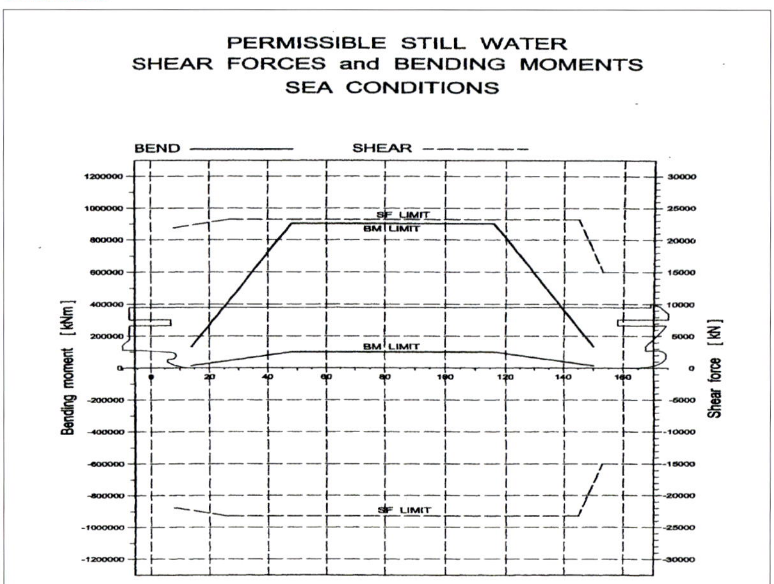

Permissible still water shear forces and bending moments in harbor conditions

Damage Stability

The solution for reducing the risk of capsizing due to flooding is to increase the number of watertight bulkheads thus creating several watertight compartments on each car deck. This will, of course, create problems during loading and discharging, but will enhance the survivability of the ship in case water penetrates the hull.

One very serious issue concerning the safety of Ro-Ro ships is their damage stability. The damage stability of Ro-Ro passenger ships (Ro-Pax) is subject to SOLAS CH. II-1, part B, and Stockholm Agreement (SOLAS Res. A 265). The damage stability of Ro-Ro cargo ships is subject to SOLAS CH. II-1, part B-1 and the latest amendments came into force on January 1, 2009. They were adopted at MSC 194 (80) with the main purpose of enhancing the requirements for the stability of ships being bilged. Compared to the older requirements, the amendments impose more stringent requirements for the damage stability. As the damage stability is based on a probabilistic approach, it is useful to clarify the main idea behind damage stability.

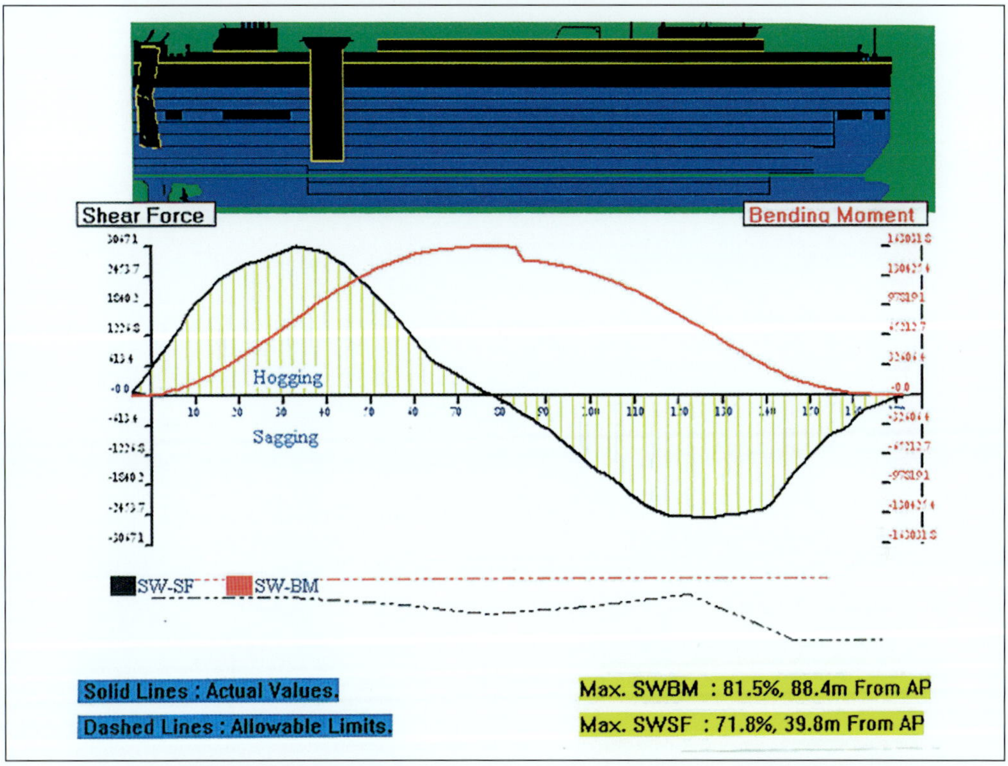

Example of bending moments and shear forces for car carrier calculated with the ship's stability program

The probability of survival of a ship is the sum of the probability for each compartment or group of compartments under consideration that the space might flood, multiplied by the probability that the ship will not capsize or sink with the considered space flooded. This probability is expressed by the so-called Attained Subdivision Index A. This index is compared with Required Subdivision Index (R; provided by SOLAS); if A is greater than R the ship will survive.

"A" is obtained by means of summation that should cover only those cases of flooding that contribute to the value of A.

Attained Subdivision Index A is expressed by the following formula:

$$\mathbf{A = \Sigma\, p_i\, s_i} \quad [18]$$

Where:
i = each compartment or group of compartments under consideration
$\mathbf{p_i}$ = probability that the compartment or compartments under consideration might flood
$\mathbf{s_i}$ = probability of surviving after the compartment or compartments under consideration floods

The new amendments stipulate that the calculations for the minimum attained index should be based on three draughts:

- deepest subdivision draught = d_s
- light service draught = d_l
- partial subdivision draught = d_p

So the new amendments require that A will be determined by the following formula:

$$\mathbf{A = 0.4\, A_s + 0.4\, A_p + 0.2\, A_l} \quad [19]$$

Where:
$\mathbf{A_s, A_p, A_l}$ = indices on the respective draughts d_s, d_p and d_l.

The minimum attained index on each draught should not be less than 0.5 R for Ro-Ro cargo ships:

$$\mathbf{A > 0.5\, R} \quad [20]$$

The minimum attained index on each draught should not be less than 0.9 R for Ro-Ro passenger ships

$$\mathbf{A > 0.9\, R} \quad [21]$$

If the operational trim range of a vessel exceeds ± 0.5% L_S (the entire ship length) then probabilistic damage stability calculations with trim should be supplied.

Other practical peculiarities concerning the damage stability are defined by the following:

Factor " r": Defines the probability that a longitudinal bulkhead will not be breached by the damage. For each longitudinal bulkhead inside the ship's side an "r" value will be calculated.
Factor "p": Factor "r" will be adjusted by factor "p" to obtain a final joint factor "p".
- By default the damage should extend to B/2.
- A limit before B/2 can be set.

Factor "v": Represents the probability that a watertight deck above the waterline remains intact. The maximum vertical extent of damage above a given waterline has changed from 7.0 m to 12.5 m.

Survivability factor "si": The probability of survival after flooding of the zone in question.

For cargo ships, including car carriers, this value is defined by the following:

$S_i = S_{FINAL}$ [22]

Permeability: The amount of space in a compartment that is capable of being filled with water. For a Ro-Ro compartment intended for cargoes, this depends on the draft:

- $d_p = 0.90$
- $d_s = 0.90$
- $d_l = 0.95$

The above information is informative, though it may be beyond the ability of the crew to comprehend in this form. SOLAS requires, however, that understandable damage stability plans be posted on the bridge for quick reference to the officer on the watch. These plans should clearly indicate for each deck and hold:

- the boundaries for watertight compartments
- the openings of such compartments with the means of closure
- the arrangements for correction of any list due to flooding

It is essential that all officers have basic knowledge concerning damage stability.

Damage Stability Regulations

SOLAS established certain requirements concerning the damage stability. The requirements for damage stability for passenger ships, including Ro-Ro ships, built prior to April 20, 1990 are as follows:

- The range of damaged dynamic stability must be at least 15°.
- The area of GZ curves shall be at least 0.015 m. rad, as measured from 7° (for one compartment flooding) or 14° (for two or three compartments flooding) to the angle of downflooding, or 22° (for one compartment flooding) or 27° (for two or three compartments flooding), whichever of these is the lesser. The angle of downflooding (or angle of flooding) is the angle at which flooding can progressively flow into an underdeck space that provides significant reserve buoyancy. For example, the flooding of small lockers is not considered progressive flooding.
- Maximum GZ shall not be less than 0.10 meter.
- The ship must not heel more than 15° at any intermediate stage of flooding, and equalization by cross-flooding must be achieved within 15 minutes.
- At any intermediate stage of flooding, the maximum GZ must be at least 0.05 meters, while the range of dynamic stability must not be less than 7°.
- The equilibrium list should not exceed 7° (for one compartment flooding) or 12° (for two or three compartments flooding).

SOLAS established special requirements for Ro-Ro vessels concerning damage stability.

- All ramps and watertight shell doors should be closed and locked before departure from the port.
- Access to the vehicle decks should be restricted to the ship's crew only.
- The vehicle decks should be closed by watertight doors or ramps.

An amendment to Ch. II-2/20, which entered into force on January 1, 2010, addresses the drainage of special category and Ro-Ro spaces to prevent accumulation of water on the vehicle deck of Ro-Ro ships. In this respect, discharge valves for scuppers, fitted with positive means of closing operable from a position above the bulkhead deck, in accordance with the requirements of the International Convention on Load Lines currently in force, shall be kept open while the ships are at sea. The convention also requires the collision bulkhead and aft peak aft watertight division to extend up into the lower vehicle deck. The position of the inner forward watertight door and bulkhead must be within 5% L + 3m from the forward part of the ship. Where bow doors are fitted and a sloping ramp forms part of the extension of the collision bulkhead deck, the ramp shall be weather tight over its complete length.

SOLAS requires television surveillance (CCTV) and a water leakage detection system to be installed on board Ro-Ro passenger ships. These systems must provide an indication to the navigation bridge and engine room of any leakage of water through inner and outer bow, stern, and side doors that could lead to flooding of special category spaces or Ro-Ro spaces.

Of greater importance for the final condition of flooding is the large heel that may occur during the first 20 to 30 seconds after a side collision due to transient asymmetric flooding, sluggish cross flooding, and, in the worst case, the toppling of trailers. The estimated time of foundering is an important safety feature and SOLAS requires the Ro-Ro passenger ships to be evacuated within thirty minutes of the order to abandon ship.

Considering their lack of watertight bulkheads, the following issues for Ro-Ro ships deserve due consideration in the first minute after a collision (E. Vossnack, H. Bonstra, "Integration of damage stability improvements in the design of Ro-Ro vessels," TU Delft):

- Rapidly increasing list.
- Cross-flooding may be sluggish and is effective only in case the ship has a positive righting moment.
- The car deck will be immersed if listing continues and entering water will spread out over the continuous deck.
- The sequence of events may lead to capsizing if downflooding of water is too sluggish.

If a ship is being bilged, the ingress of water will cause an inclining moment. This inclining moment is caused by the weight of the water present in the flooded compartment. It is very difficult to calculate precisely where the center of gravity of the water in the compartment is. The inclining moment caused by the flooded water can be expressed by the following formula:

Inclining moment due to water flooding = $\rho g \nabla \times (y\cos\Theta + z\sin\Theta)$ [23]

Where:
ρ = density of flooded water
g = gravity
∇ = volume of water in the compartment in question
y = transverse distance between center of gravity and center line parallel with the ship's fore-and-aft direction
z = vertical distance between center of gravity and base line
Θ = angle of heel

The total inclining moment equals the sum of the moments of each flooded compartment.

The Stockholm Agreement (SA) was produced by several northwest European countries in respect to Ro-Ro passenger ships' safety. The SA requires these ships to survive a prescribed amount of free-flowing water on any vehicle deck that is also a bulkhead deck.

As per the SA, the total probability of survival depends on the probability that a compartment is being flooded and the probability that the vessel will survive flooding of that compartment. MSC/Circ. 574, "The calculation procedure to assess the survivability characteristics of existing Ro-Ro passenger ships when using a simplified method based upon resolution A.265(VIII)," outlines the simplified procedure to assess the survivability of Ro-Ro ships. The SA requires that Ro-Ro passenger ships comply with SOLAS 90 standards of damage stability in sea conditions normal to the ship's trading areas, but with significant wave heights no greater than 4 meters.

The SA also requires the calculation of an A/A_{MAX} value, where A is the attained subdivision index and A_{MAX} is the maximum value of survivability for the ship.

The SA requires that the effect of the hypothetical amount of water that is assumed to have accumulated on the first deck above the designed waterline be taken into account (SA, Annex 1, para 1.1).

The SA also restricts trading routes to seasons and sea areas where the significant wave height does not exceed 1.5 meters.

Furthermore, the SA requires the ship to retain a minimum damaged freeboard of at least 2 meters in any of the damage scenarios considered by SOLAS 90, thus allowing the Ro-Ro deck to remain above the level of the wave crest with a significant height of 4 meters.

The SA also requires the ship to retain a minimum damage freeboard of at least 1 meter and that the ship's sides enclosing the Ro-Ro deck are fitted with freeing ports. The freeing ports should be evenly distributed along the sides of the compartment and their size should not be less than 0.3 l, where the l equals the length of the compartment in meters. These freeing ports should be located within 0.6 meters above the damaged Ro-Ro deck, and the lower edge of the ports should be 2 cm above the damaged Ro-Ro deck.

The SA calculations are based on damage located close to amidships. The amount of the assumed accumulated seawater is calculated based on a water surface having a fixed height of 0.5 meters. Therefore, the SA is sometimes referred to as "SOLAS 90+50."

Finally, the SA also assumes that the equilibrium depth of floodwater at the damage location remains constant at any angle of heel.

Load Line Requirements

Ro-Ro ships are classed as type "B" as per International Convention on load lines, 1966 as modified in 1998.

During the design, the freeboard deck must be decided upon first. Modern Ro-Ro ships, having a lot of vehicle decks, allow for choosing which deck is to be considered as the freeboard deck. In case of Ro-Ro ships with a lower vehicle deck and an open upper deck, when the lower deck is chosen as freeboard deck, the freeboard will be small, because the sheer and superstructure freeboard deductions will be considerable. This freeboard will be measured from the lower vehicle deck.

If, however, the upper open deck is chosen as freeboard deck, the summer freeboard will be considerable. In this case, there are no deductions for superstructure.

Car carriers, on the other hand, may have up to thirteen car decks. In this case, as a rule, the freeboard deck is generally the deck where the ramps and shell watertight doors are mounted.

It should be noted that "Conditions of Freeboard Assignment" should be taken into account. The ship design may be such that it protects the lower vehicle deck from flooding and result in an additional freeboard being assigned to the vessel.

The assigned freeboard is measured from the deck line. This freeboard should be recorded in the Load Line certificate.

Load Line Marks are marked on both sides of all ships and therefore also on the Ro-Ro ships. The standard Load Line Marks are subject of many books and it is not the intention of this book to detail them here.

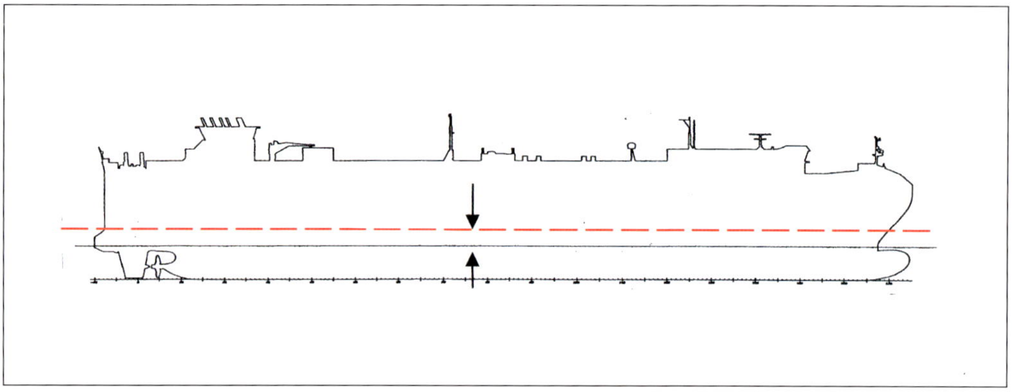

In this case, the main deck is chosen as freeboard deck-small freeboard.

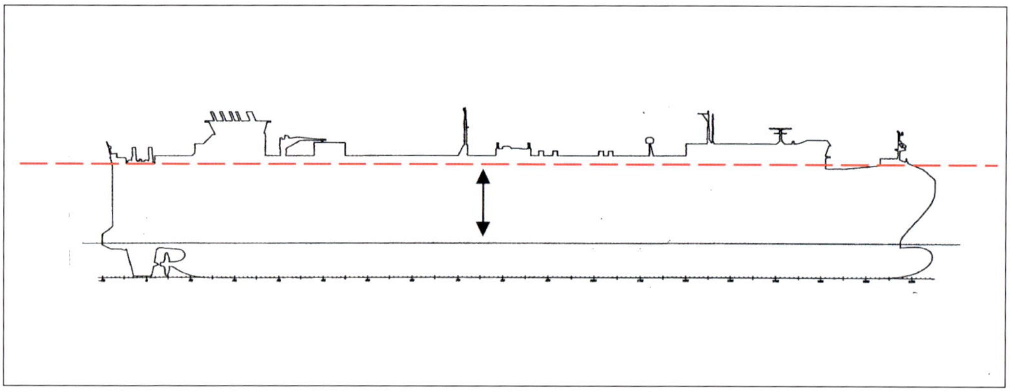

In this case, the upper deck is chosen as freeboard deck-large freeboard.

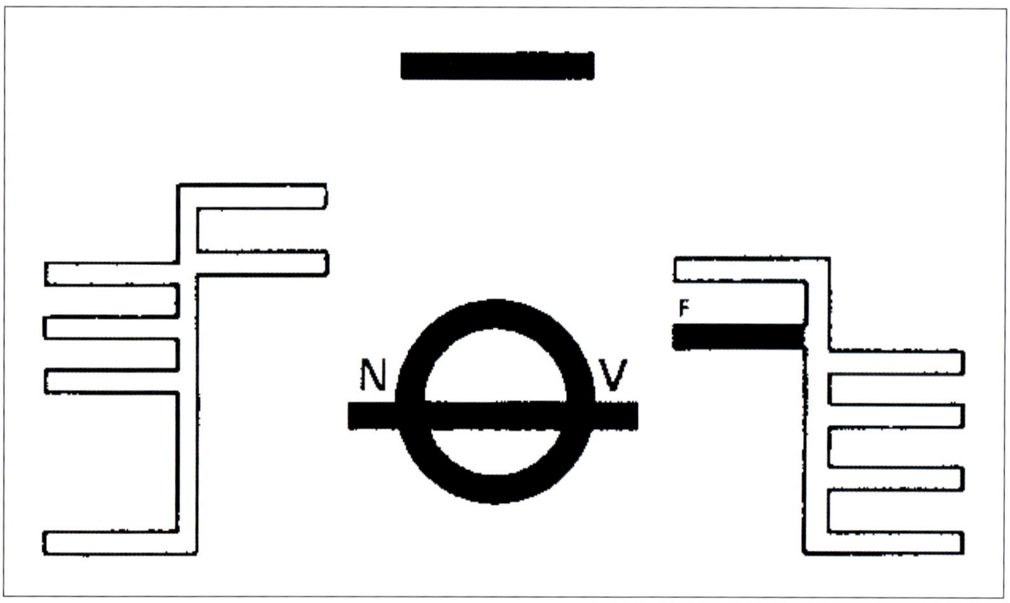

Seasonal load line mark

Regulation 6(6) of the ILCC allows a ship to be assigned a "greater than minimum freeboard." If this is the case, the "All seasons" load line will be marked on both sides. This is only possible if the resulting freeboard is not less than the largest minimum freeboard that would otherwise be assigned to the ship.

SOLAS Chapter II-1, Part B-3, Regulation 18, requires that all passenger ships, including Ro-Ro ferries, have a load line corresponding to the approved subdivision draught assigned and marked on the ship's sides. Such subdivision load line will be recorded into the Passenger Ship Safety Certificate. This load line will be distinguished by the notation P1 for the principal passenger service, and P2, P3, etc., for the alternative configurations. In this respect the principal passenger service will be taken as the mode of operation in which the required subdivision index R has the highest value.

Improvement of Ro-Ro Stability

Improving Ro-Ro stability in order to meet the SA requirements may be (and has proved to be) expensive for many ferry operators.

Improving Ro-Ro stability can be done by structural modifications such as:

- **Fitting the vehicle deck with transverse bulkheads that are kept open during cargo operations, but are kept closed during the sea voyage.** Such bulkheads will improve the stability, but will affect the cargo flow.
- **Building camber into the vehicle deck.** The increased height along the centerline will reduce the weight of floodwater that can accumulate on the vehicle deck.
- **Fitting longitudinal bulkheads with transverse portions below the vehicle deck in order to limit the extent of flooding under the waterline.** Needless to say that such spaces will require extra cross-flooding arrangements to reduce the list in case the vessel is bilged.
- **Fitting side sponsons to increase the width of the vessel's waterline compared to the width of vehicle deck.**

Ballast Operations

Ballast operations constitute a very important part of the procedure for ensuring adequate stability, not only on Ro-Ro ships but on board all ships. Therefore, a good understanding of ballast-related issues is crucial.

The concept of ballast operations is that seawater will be pumped out of or into ballast tanks in order to ensure adequate stability, trim, and list during all stages of a voyage. When ballast operations are performed, they should follow a premeditated ballast plan. It should be always kept in mind that when ballast operations are underway, there may be loss or reduction of stability, and if a strong wind is blowing or the ship is encountering boisterous weather, any improperly considered ballast operations can lead to severe consequences, such as structural damage to the ballast system, the ship's hull, and equipment, and even the total loss of the ship. In order to avoid any stability problems as a result of ballast operations, ballasting should be completed before departure, having considered all "pitfalls" during the voyage such as limiting drafts, consumption of fuel, etc.

Ballast is actually "dead cargo"—the Owner is not paying for carrying tons of ballast. In addition, extra ballast will increase the draft and the water resistance of the hull, fuel consumption, and operational costs. Therefore, it is important that an optimum quantity of ballast is taken—just enough to ensure adequate stability of the ship in the worst possible scenario during the voyage and to reach the required draft.

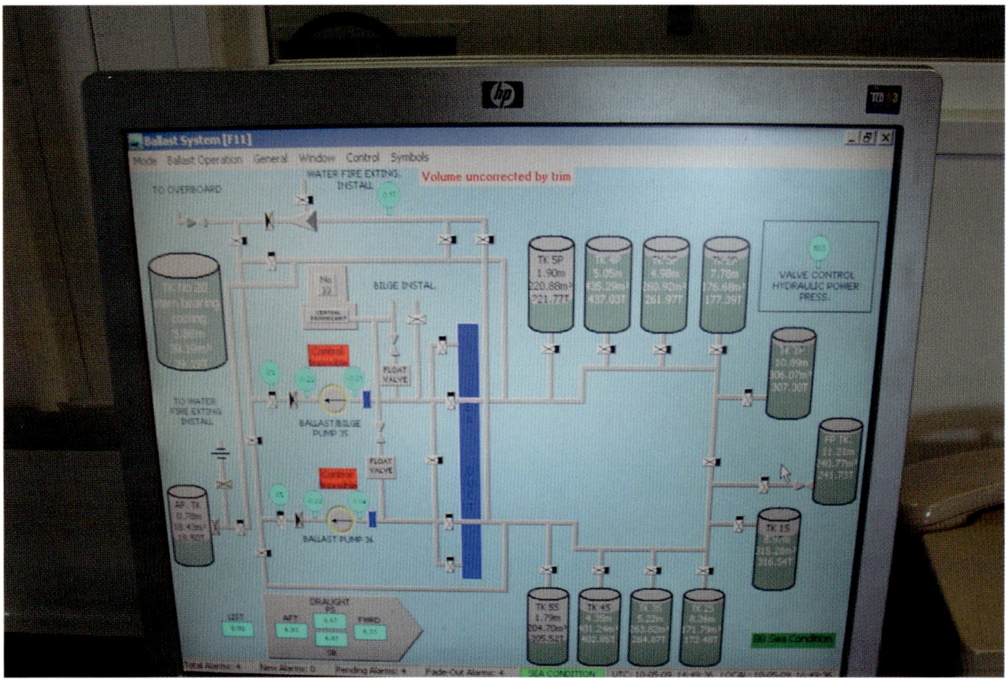

Centralized ballast system control

The ballast plan should be prepared well in advance of ballast operations, normally when information on the cargo has been received, and this plan should be strictly adhered to. The ballast system on Ro-Ro ships can be either centralized or local. With a centralized console, all ballast operations are performed by a ballast computer. Today, most new ships are equipped with such a centralized system, which shows the positions of all valves and gauges indicating the performance of each pump. All ballast tanks are shown as well, together with all piping connecting the tanks. Remote gauges show the quantity of water in each tank, though this should not be considered a substitute for manual sounding of ballast tanks. On older ships, the ballast system can be local, meaning that part of the operation is conducted by the duty engineer and part by the duty officer or Chief Officer. Even in centralized ballast systems, there is the option for manual operation of the valves of the tanks, if necessary.

The pumps used for ballast operations on board a car carrier are normally centrifugal. Usually there are two separate pumps that can be used together or separately. The capacity of these pumps can be taken from the Tank Capacity Plan.

Filling or emptying tanks should be done simultaneously on both sides, using a pair of tanks, one on starboard and one on port. This is very important; if not done a list will develop that may lead to capsizing, even when the ship is alongside!

Before commencing any ballast operation the Chief Officer should make sure that the following items of ballast system are checked:

- **No leakages from the pipes**, which can damage vehicles already stowed in car decks.
- **No leakages from the manholes;** these must be tight and properly battened down.
- **Air pipes in good working condition.** The best way to do this is to check the air coming out when pumping in the ballast. Otherwise, a visual check before commencement of ballast operations is a must and can be done by checking the non-return float by hand.

- **Pumps working properly**
- **Sounding pipes of tanks are not blocked.** The normal way of checking if the sounding pipe is blocked is to read the figure on the sounding line when the bob just touches the striking plate. This reading should be checked with the reading from the sounding tables; any difference most probably indicates a blockage of the pipe, which will require future inspection and corrective action.

Precautions and Tips When Ballasting

When all preparations for ballast operations have been taken, the tanks have been chosen, and the respective valves of the tanks and the discharge valve of the pump opened to about 20%–30%, the pump can be started. When the pump starts working, the valve should be opened gradually until the recommended pressure is reached.

Ballasting in ice conditions should be avoided. If, however, it is necessary, it is strongly recommended to use the bottom sea chest instead of the side one. This is the only way to avoid sucking any ice remnants into the ballast piping system. The pre-heating of ballast tanks is necessary in ice conditions.

Avoid over-pressurizing the tanks. Over-pressurizing of the tanks can lead to structural damage to the tank if the latter is being filled too fast.

Avoid filling the tank to 100% (full capacity), as this will cause water to leak from the air pipe, which may cause damage to the cars, personnel injury if someone slips on the wet deck, or other complications. A relevant risk assessment always should be conducted and personnel safety should get priority even during ballast operations.

The forepeak tank is fitted with a manual valve on the deck where the pipeline penetrates the collision bulkhead. This valve should only be opened during filling or emptying. When ballast operations are completed, this valve should be closed and kept closed during the sea passage.

Maintenance of Ballast System

Maintenance of the ballast system should be performed as per the Planned Maintenance Schedule. See chapter 1 for further details.

CHAPTER 11

SAFETY ON RO-RO SHIPS

Safety hazards related to loading, discharging, and transportation of vehicles should be identified and rectified. To assure that this is done, the Ship Owner needs to establish procedures for safe handling of cargo operations. At the same time, procedures for identifying and assessing all risks should be established. The majority of accidents are caused by human error and operational faults. To guarantee the safety of the ship and crew, attention should be paid to both technical and operational issues ashore as well as on board the ship.

Introduction

In this chapter we will focus attention on technical aspects, maintenance standards, and shipboard management as regards risk. How can we predict risk and what should we do to avoid it? Risk exists everywhere, but the point is to assess the acceptable level of risk. Appropriate risk assessment is the core of mitigating potential accidents. The total risk is the product of probability (p) and severity (s). In reality, the acceptable risk level can be presented graphically as a border between the acceptable and unacceptable risk area. When the risk spreads into the unacceptable risk area it must be reduced. This can be achieved either by reducing the probability (i.e., by adopting good operational procedures and practices) or by reducing the severity. Severity can be reduced by:

- **Good design of the ship with reserve strength and integrity, and enough life-saving appliances or fire-fighting equipment.** As this is beyond the control of ship's crew, shore management will play an important role in this.
- **Good emergency preparedness of the crew.** This includes conducting regular and realistic drills and trainings, and maintaining life saving appliances and fire fighting equipment to ensure that it is readily available.

To be prepared means that all potential risks must be taken into consideration. Before any operation the Master must perform the appropriate risk assessment in order to reduce all potential risks. The crew must strictly follow the safety procedures adopted on board. During monthly safety committee meetings, all near misses and accidents should be analyzed and preventive measures adopted. During pre-operation meetings with the crew all aspects of the forthcoming cargo operations should be detailed and preventive measures considered.

General Safety Procedures

Although the Company's procedures for safe cargo operations can vary, the following precautions are generally to be observed:

Basic safety precautions during cargo handling operations for avoiding personnel injury and damage to the cargo:

- The crew must be properly dressed and safety helmets are to be worn.
- Crew working inside cargo decks where cargo-handling operations are being conducted should wear reflective vests.
- The crew should wear safety shoes.
- Vehicles should be directed and parked by a cargo guide who is properly trained and dressed for this purpose.
- The speed inside cargo holds and car decks should not exceed 20 km/h (12 mph for USA).
- Only personnel involved in cargo operations should stand on or near the ramps.
- Only authorized and well-trained personnel are to operate the ramps.
- Ramps are to be kept clear of any obstacles.
- All pillars inside car decks should be clearly marked by black and yellow tiger reflective tape in order to avoid any damage to the cargo.
- Safety routes should be established inside cargo holds using safety cones in order to facilitate cargo operations and to reduce the risk of damage or injury.
- Ramp slopes should be adjusted in such way (using buttress cylinders) that safe passing of vehicles is ensured. Ramp slopes can be measured by slant rulers or by special indicators mounted on the ramps.
- There should be a safe pedestrian passageway on the ramps.
- The cargo passing over the ramps should not exceed the SWL of the ramps. The SWL should be properly marked in close proximity to the ramp.
- Rubber mats should be affixed to the ramp's flaps in order to avoid damage if the nose of the cargo hits.
- The lashing gangs should be properly dressed and wear reflective clothes; they should work in teams in sight of each other. They need to use standardized hand signals and whistles for stopping the cars. The lashing crew should be trained in lashing procedures. However, if the ship's crews are in doubt about the proper execution of lashing related duties, they must advise the foreman. In no case shall the ship sail without all cargo being properly secured.
- The ventilation should be working continuously from the beginning of cargo operations. In some cases the stevedores can refuse to work if ventilation is not in order. In addition, the ventilation must be in order to avoid accumulation of gases in cargo decks. In this respect the number of vehicles with engines running simultaneously should be minimized. If the ventilation is out of order the ship will be considered unseaworthy.
- Crew trained in vehicle management should supervise cargo operations. Such supervision is necessary due to a myriad of problems, including the necessity to take contemporaneous evidence related to ship's and cargo damage, to give advice to the stevedores for proper execution of cargo handling operation, etc.
- As a rule the cargo assigned for transportation by sea should be in satisfactory condition for this purpose. Therefore the crew involved in cargo operations should be alert to and check the cargo presented for shipment in a thorough way.
- No operations with deck panels are to be performed during cargo handling operations. If the situation arises where this cannot be avoided, the panels should be handled with utmost attention and all precautions should be taken.

- All openings and open ramps should be clearly marked with safety signs and cones. No vehicles should pass over ramps when opening and closing operations are in progress.
- Smoking should be strictly forbidden inside cargo holds. Conspicuous "No Smoking / No Naked Lights" signs should be displayed.
- All decks and ramps should be kept clean and free of oil, grease, or any other liquid that might cause a person to slip or which might act as a lubricant to a shifting load.
- Cargo holds should be clean, tidy and all lashings should be well arranged. Otherwise the ship could be considered to be in breach of Hague (Hague-Visby) Rules due to the fact that cargo holds are not suitably fit to receive the cargo.
- The ship's mobile handling equipment should be properly secured in its stowage position.
- The cargo should be checked for any damage as stipulated in chapter 8.
- All watertight ramps and doors should be properly closed and locked before departure.

Clean holds are an obligation to be fulfilled by the Carrier.

- All gastight openings should be closed upon completion of loading or discharging of a certain cargo compartment.
- Fire detection system should be off during cargo operations and on when cargo operations are stopped or completed. Fire detection should be on when at sea!
- Sawdust should be prepared in the vicinity of the ramps as well as inside cargo holds in order to treat any oil spills.
- Upon leaving every discharging port, the stowage area from which cargo has been discharged should be checked because some remaining cargo might have been unlashed by mistake.

Basic safety precautions during the voyage. During the voyage, the risk of fire and damage to the cargo should not be underestimated. The Carrier should exercise due diligence regarding the cargo as required by applicable Hague (Hague-Visby) Rules. In this respect, regular inspection of cargo holds should be performed as per Company's instructions.

- The fire detection system should be on all the time. Respective entries should be made in the ship's logbook. In addition, all smoke detectors should be checked for malfunction and, if necessary, replaced as per adopted Planned Maintenance Schedule.
- All watertight and gastight doors should be kept closed and locked during the voyage. If for some reason their opening is requested, an appropriate entry into the ship's logbook should be made.
- Lashings should be inspected at regular intervals as required by the Ship Owners or Charterers. All loose lashings should be retightened. In addition, such inspections should be performed in case of boisterous weather or after experiencing rough seas.
- Any liquids should be cleaned on the spot or drained if necessary.

On a laden voyage, the following should be checked on a daily basis:

- Any abnormal noise or smell
- Leakage of ballast water from pipes or valves
- Sounding of ballast should be conducted at least once per day and the respective soundings must be entered into the Ballast Record Book
- During the voyage the ventilation should be used as prescribed in chapter 3 for dispelling of gases, if any. It is a good practice to keep the ventilation open if weather permits, but it should be kept closed in case of bad weather conditions.

Safety Equipment On Board Ro-Ro Ships

Ro-Ro ships, as all ships, should comply with the regulations concerning safety equipment as stipulated in SOLAS and the International Life-Saving Appliances Code (LSA Code). LSA equipment as well as fire fighting equipment should be kept readily available and in order for immediate use during port stays and during the voyage.

Lifeboats

Ro-Ro ships can be fitted with different types of lifeboats: the open type and the totally enclosed type or free-fall. On board older car carriers, the most common type of lifeboat is open type, while the most common type on board newer Ro-Ro cargo ships is the free-fall lifeboat.

The estimation time of foundering and sinking is an important safety consideration and SOLAS, therefore, requires the Ro-Ro passenger ships to be evacuated within 30 minutes of the abandon ship order.

Ro-Ro passenger ships have more complicated requirements concerning lifeboats. SOLAS divides the voyages into international and short international voyages.

Ro-Ro passenger ships engaged on international voyages should carry partially or totally enclosed lifeboats. On each side, these boats should have such capacity to accommodate not less than 50% of persons on board. SOLAS allows these lifeboats to be replaced with life rafts of an equivalent total capacity under certain conditions. The Flag Administration has the authority to approve this.

Ro-Ro passenger ships engaged in international voyages should, in addition, carry inflatable or rigid life rafts with sufficient capacity to accommodate at least 25% of the total number of persons on board. These life-rafts should comply with the requirement of the respective section of LSA Code.

Ro-Ro passenger ships engaged on short international voyages should carry partially or totally enclosed lifeboats with the capacity to accommodate at least 30% of the total number of persons on board. Additionally, these ships should carry inflatable or rigid life rafts of such capacity that, together with the lifeboat capacity, they can accommodate the total number of persons on board, plus 25%, for a total capacity of 125%.

SOLAS also stipulates the requirements for passenger ships of less than 500 gross tonnage with the total number of persons less than 200. Such ships are frequently Ro-Ro ferries. These ships are not required to carry lifeboats, but inflatable or rigid life rafts with a total capacity that is sufficient to accommodate all persons on board.

Ro-Ro cargo ships, including car carriers must carry one or more totally enclosed lifeboats on each side of such capacity that they can accommodate the total number of persons on board. This is dictated by the fact that, in case of failure of the lifeboat on either side, all the crew could escape on the other side. In addition, these ships have to carry one or more inflatable or rigid life rafts with capacity enough to accommodate the total persons on board. These life rafts are required to have a mass of less than 185 kg and to be stowed in such a way to allow easy side-to-side transfer on a single open deck without obstructions. If these requirements are not fulfilled, then the total capacity of the life rafts on each side should be enough to accommodate the total numbers of persons on board.

Ro-Ro cargo ships, including car carriers can be fitted with free-fall lifeboats, capable of being launched from the stern of the ship with the capacity to accommodate the total number of persons on board. This type of lifeboat, however, has some shortcomings when installed on car carriers:

- Due to the height at which these lifeboats are mounted (about 20–25 meters,) they are potentially dangerous when used in the free-fall method.
- If the car carrier has two stern ramps, such boats cannot practically be installed on board the ship.

- The slip for free fall lifeboat reduces cargo space due to its location, thus reducing the profits that can be achieved.

Today, more car carriers are being fitted with totally enclosed lifeboats.

Irrespective of the fact that in recent years more car carriers are being extended in length in order to mitigate the negative effect, this type of lifeboat turned out to be inappropriate for car carriers. Most new car carriers are fitted with totally enclosed lifeboats on both sides of the ship.

All personnel involved in the operation of lifeboats should be well aware of the procedure for lowering and heaving up of the lifeboats. Needless to say, the person in charge of LSA should maintain them as per Planned Maintenance Schedule. MSC 1./Circ. 1206, "Measures to prevent accidents with lifeboats," should be referenced, as well, regarding the testing of totally enclosed lifeboats. The crew should be trained in the use of all LSA equipment as required by SOLAS Ch. III and included in the ship's manager drill and training schedule.

The "abandon ship" drill should be carried out as realistically as possible. The appropriate entries should be made into the logbook as evidence for the required drills. All the crew should be very familiar with the rest of the LSA equipment such as life rafts, rescue boats, etc.

Rescue Boats

It is a requirement of SOLAS that Ro-Ro passenger ships of 500 gross tonnage and more shall carry at least one rescue boat on each side and that one of the rescue boats shall be a fast rescue boat complying with the respective section of LSA Code.

Ro-Ro cargo ships, including car carriers, are not required to have such fast rescue boat, though they must carry at least one rescue boat complying with the respective section of the LSA Code.

Rescue boat

Fire Equipment

See chapter 8, Fire Prevention

Helicopter Areas

All Ro-Ro passenger ships should be provided with a helicopter pick-up area. The helicopter landing area is designed for emergency and other occasional landings of a helicopter. The heli-deck should be provided with main and emergency escapes. SOLAS Ch. II-2, Part G: "Special requirements," stipulates the required fire-fighting equipment that should be located in close proximity of the helicopter area. This equipment should include the following:

- At least two dry-powder extinguishers having a total capacity of not less than 45 kg;
- Carbon dioxide extinguishers of a total capacity of not less than 18 kg or equivalent;
- A suitable foam application system consisting of monitors or foam-making branch pipes capable of delivering foam to all parts of the helicopter landing area;
- At least two nozzles of an approved dual-purpose type (jet/spray) and hoses of sufficient length to reach any part of the helicopter landing area;
- Two sets of fireman's outfits

In addition, at least the following equipment should be readily available in the helicopter area:

- An adjustable wrench
- A blanket (fire-resistant)
- Cutters, bolt 60 cm
- A hook, grab or salving
- A hacksaw, heavy duty, complete with 6 spare blades ladder
- A life line, 5 mm diameter x 15 m in length
- Pliers, side cutting
- A set of assorted screwdrivers
- A harness knife complete with sheath

Winch only area

On most car carriers, the helicopter area is winch only. This means that the helicopter cannot land there, as the local strength of the deck is insufficient for landing. In this case evacuation or landing of personnel can be done by hoists only.

Noise Level on Car Decks

Another safety issue is the noise levels on car decks. During loading and discharging the crew working inside car decks probably will be exposed to noise level more than 80 Db, as legally allowed by Code on Noise Levels on board ships, 2014. Even so, the use of ear protecting devices is not recommended, as the people wearing ear protectors will not hear the approaching vehicles. If the task involves a prolonged stay inside the car decks, wearing ear muffs or ear plugs can be justified, provided the crew involved is wearing high visibility clothing, as required for working inside car decks. Another solution is to institute time limits for exposure, so that the crew is not exposed to noise levels more than 80 Db for a 24-hour period. For exposures of less than 8 hours, the crew working inside car decks without ear protectors should not be exposed to noise levels exceeding 85 Db.

Moreover, the Code (Chapter 2, Reg 2.3.3) requires that the noise level during cargo operations to be measured.

As an additional measure, the appropriate signage should be posted to the doors leading to the car decks.

Sailing in Ice Conditions

As the vehicle trade has developed, car carriers visit cold weather ports that have never been visited by them before, such as those on the Baltic Sea in Finland, Russia, and Estonia, as well as those in Canada. There is nothing special about these ports at first sight; nothing apart from the fact that they are ice-bound in winter. Sailing into such areas and ports puts an extra burden on the Master.

Precautions that are to be taken when a Ro-Ro vessel or car carrier sails in such a harsh environment are listed below. The list is not exhaustive and merely indicates the most important items.

The first thing that the Master should do when receiving the order to proceed to an ice-bound port is to verify with the C/P if the port and berth is considered "safe." If he has serious grounds to believe that the port or berth is not "safe," as per the terms of C/P, he is in a position to refuse to call at the port in question.

Having accepted the port as "safe," the ship should be prepared in all respects for sailing in ice-bound waters and arctic conditions:

- Water ballast tanks should be heated (if possible) which requires good maintenance and preliminary check of pre-heating system of the tanks.
- Trim, draft, and stability should be kept within reasonable limits to ensure that the propeller is submerged to avoid any structural damage. This is of particular importance for car carriers without ice class. Drafts should be kept within the ice class range. The trim and draft should be so adjusted to be within "ice belt" limits; the belt is an area over which the shell plating is required to be reinforced for ice navigation.
- The fire mains and fresh water should be drained well in advance.
- All windlasses, mooring ropes and other critical equipment should be protected against possible icing and properly greased as required.
- All hydraulic pumps for the ramps should be turned on well in advance for good preheating of hydraulic oil in the system. The manufacturer's preheating instructions should be carefully read.
- All wires of the ramps, davits, etc., as well as all open gears and bearings, should be well greased as a preventive measure against icing.
- During port stays the use of ventilation should be reduced to its minimum, though, considering the importance of ventilation on board car carriers, there should be several vents working continuously. The ventilation should be set in the "at sea" mode and the Chief Officer should select a number of suitable vent ducts. In case the air temperature drops to -15° C, extra caution should be exercised.
- During cargo operations all precautions should be taken to avoid any damage to the cargo and de-icing salt or sand should be littered over the ramps that are exposed to weather conditions; the vehicles should be driven on and off at slow speeds in order to avoid sliding.
- Extra anti-slip sand should be ordered and used.
- All deck equipment, such as deck lifters, sweeping machines, and forklifts, should be started in due time in order to warm up. If any difficulties are encountered during the starting of the machines, the quick-start aerosol should be used (the quick-start aerosol should be readily available for such cases). If any such machinery will not be used, its battery should be dismantled and kept in a warm and dry storage place.
- Antifreeze additives in lifeboat motors should be checked well in advance.
- When the ramps are open, antifreeze should be applied on the rubber gaskets and salt should be sprinkled on the compression bars.
- The windows on the bridge should be heated all the time using the window heaters. Fresh water for washing the bridge windows should be drained well in advance.

- Navigation lights should be kept at all times while the ship is in port to prevent them from freezing.
- It is good practice to keep the radar scanners running in order to avoid their freezing.

Berthing and unberthing in such hostile sea conditions can be a serious problem for car carriers, especially if strong wind is experienced. Sometimes the ship cannot be safely moored. This might lead to difficulties when opening and positioning the ramps. The ramps, as already mentioned, can be used in case of trim up to ± 2° and list up to ± 3°. The maximum distance "off berth" in which the ramp can be used is about 1.5–2.0 meters. If the ship cannot be brought alongside due to heavy ice, the ramp cannot be lowered. Even when the ship is safely moored and the ramp lowered, the ship can be taken off the berth by strong tidal currents, which can bring along some heavy pack ice. In such a case, the ship should be shifted to a safer berth that is well protected from such tidal streams.

Additional mooring ropes will not help against the effect of the currents mixed with such heavy ice and the only option is to shift the vessel. In ports where such conditions can be expected (mainly in Canada), the Pilot's advice is indispensable and it should be obtained well in advance.

CHAPTER 12

DOCUMENTS IN RO-RO TRADE

The documents generally used in Ro-Ro practice are more or less the same as those used in traditional shipping. In this chapter we will focus on some peculiarities related to the Ro-Ro trade. Charter Party (C/P), Bill of Lading (B/L), Sea Waybills have already been analyzed and a lot of information on these subject is available. However, for the clarity it is worthy to pinpoint some practical aspects of such documents adopted in car carriers' and Ro-Ro practice.

Charter Party (C/P)

A Charter Party (C/P) is the formal contract between the Owner and a Charterer for the services of a ship. It includes all the expectations that are upon both parties There are various common types of Charter Party.

A **time charter** is a contract between the Owner and the Charterer (usually the manufacturer of the vehicles) for a specified period of time. The Owner manages the vessel but the Charterer selects the ports for loading and discharging, is responsible for all the cost for fuel, port stay, etc., and pays a daily hire to the Owner. The most common type of Charter Party for this type of charter is the New York Produce Exchange (NYPE 93).

A **voyage charter** is the hiring of a vessel and crew for a voyage between a load port and a discharge port. The Charterer pays the vessel Owner on a per-ton or lump-sum basis. The Owner pays the port costs (excluding stevedoring), fuel costs, and crew costs. The payment for the use of the vessel is known as freight. A voyage charter specifies a period, known as "laytime," for loading and unloading the cargo. If the laytime is exceeded, the Charterer must pay demurrage. If laytime is saved, the Charter Party may require the Owner to pay despatch to the Charterer.

A **contract of affreightment** is a contract similar to a voyage charter, but Ship Owner undertakes to carry a number of cargoes within a specified period of time on a specified route. The agreed upon frequency of cargoes may require more than one ship. This type of Charter Party is frequently used in car carrier's practice.

Ro/Pax Time Charter Party

Work is ongoing to develop a standard time Charter Party to be used in the Roll-on/Roll-off Passenger Vessel (Ro/Pax) sector. The new form will be loosely based on GENTIME, but with specific and detailed provisions designed for the Ro/Pax trade dealing with trade specific issues.

Bill of Lading

A Bill of Lading is a document fulfilling the following three functions:

- To act as a receipt for cargo actually received on board
- To act as a document of title for the person who can claim for the cargo at the discharging port
- To act as a contract of carriage

On car carriers it is uncommon that a Master will ever sign or issue a Bill of Lading (B/L). However, as general and project cargoes are being shipped at sea by Ro-Ro vessels and car carriers, it could be of some interest to point out several issues concerning the B/L.

Types of B/L

- **Through B/L:** Issued when transportation will involve both sea and other means of transport and different carriers will be engaged. The sea carrier issues this type of B/L, but he will only accept liability for the sea passage.
- **Direct B/L:** When direct transportation between two ports will take place
- **Long-form B/L:** Has numerous boxes on its front for entering details. The conditions of carriage are printed on backside of the B/L.
- **Short-form B/L:** Contains a few standard terms printed on it. For this reason it can be completed before being presented to the Master for signature.

Peculiarities of B/L

It is a Master's duty to sign a B/L or to authorize the Agent to sign the B/L. Normally the B/L is presented to the Master, who will sign it upon receipt, but the Master can and will only sign the B/L if it contains true and correct data. On car carriers, the Master is occasionally given a B/L "as presented" and he has to sign or refuse to sign it.

Very often the Master is required to sign a B/L without being able to check the cargo. In such cases, the Master has the right to include the relevant remarks in the B/L, which makes the B/L "claused" or "unclean." These remarks are based on the remarks entered into the Mate's Receipts (the latter being issued from the ship to the Shipper). Therefore it is of utmost importance that the Chief Officer and the crew pay attention when loading vehicles or general cargoes. Lack of attention during the loading can lead to the failure to detect damaged cargo and to enter the appropriate remarks in the Mate's Receipts (or loading documents). If this happens, the Master may sign a "clean" B/L when the cargo is actually damaged. Normally the Shipper will require a "clean" B/L because it will facilitate the bank payment.

The cargo can be paid in cash, but the most frequent payment procedure involves the seller's bank. The seller's bank keeps the key documents concerning the cargo in its possession, and releases them when the payment has been received from the buyer or when some credit arrangement has been made. In a credit arrangement, the receiver of the cargo guarantees by a letter of credit to the seller that the bank will pay against the receipt of the shipping documents, normally the Bill of Lading (B/L). For smooth arrangements, the so-called Uniform Customs and Practice for Documentary Credits (UCP) was adopted. At present UCP 500 is in force, clause 23 of which specifies the information that should be included in the B/L in order to pass through the banking system. The 2007 revision of UCP 600 was published in July 2007. It contained significant changes to the previous rules, including a reduction in the number of articles from 49 to 39, new articles on definitions, and interpretations providing more clarity and precision in the rules, etc.

Remarks in the B/L

The most frequent remarks that can be entered in the B/L are:

- **"Shipper's figures" / "Said by the Shipper" / "Shipper's load, stow and count":** This remark is applicable when the cargo cannot be checked by the ship.
- **"Said to be" / "Said to contain":** Although widely used, these remarks cannot be considered as very powerful for the purposes of protecting the interest of the ship if not used in connection with some other remarks.
- **"Weight, measure, quantity, condition, contents, and value unknown":** This is one of the most valuable and powerful remarks that can be entered in the B/L. It is applicable when general cargoes, or project cargoes, or parcels are being shipped. The Master should try to put this remark in the B/L if it is not already mentioned there.

Reasons not to Sign the B/L

- **Predated or post-dated B/L:** The Master should never sign a B/L that is predated or post-dated. The B/L should be signed only if it is dated with the actual date. A predated or post-dated B/L is misleading and incorrect.
- **Blank or partially filled in B/L:** The Master should never sign a B/L that is incomplete. If for some reason the Master is forced to sign such a B/L, he must first ask for advice of his P&I Club.
- **B/L in a foreign language:** If the B/L is written in a language that is incomprehensible to the Master, he should insist on a translation. If this is not possible the Master should issue his own B/L or refuse to sign such a B/L.

Mate's Receipt

The Mate's Receipt is issued and signed by the Chief Officer, or the Agent on his behalf, for the cargo received on board. This is not a document of title. It contains information on which the details entered in the B/L will be based. Normally, a Mate's Receipt should contain remarks concerning the apparent condition and quantity of the cargo. The Mate's Receipt is a Ship Owner's form and is issued in a triplicate form; the original is given to the Shipper, a copy should be given to the Agent, and the second copy should be retained on board.

If the ship's management cannot check and/or count all the vehicles, the appropriate remarks should be entered by hand or endorsed in the Mate's Receipt or loading documents presented to the ship. The following remarks are the most common in the car carrier trade:

In the case of loading of used vehicles:

- Used / unpacked / damaged / unprotected used vehicles.
- Charterers / shipper's own load / count and stow.
- Contents, condition and / or accessories unknown to the Master.

In the case of loading of cargo in pallets or packages:

- Said to contain / Shippers load / Stow and count.
- Weight, measure, quantity, contents, and value unknown.

In this case it is practical to mention in the remark that the cargo is "not tallied or controlled by Master," as far as it concerns the units inside the packages. However, the Master should supervise the number of pallets or packages, as he will be responsible for cargo handling of such pallets, depending upon the revision of clause 8 of NYPE 93.

MATE'S RECEIPT

Shipper
TIGER SHORING CO.LTD.
194-52 OKRYUN-DONG, YEONSU-GU,
INCHEON,KOREA
TEL:011-9740-3031 , FAX: 032-833-1710

B/L No.
EUKOKRGA1027950

Consignee
ANTHONEY OWUSU MENSAH
P.O.BOX SE 214 KUMAS GHANA
TEL:0243-056726

Notify Party
SAME AS CONSIGNEE

Vessel	**Voyage**
MORNING CROWN	060
Port of Loading	**Port of Discharge**
PYUNGTAEK, KOREA	TEMA, GHANA

PARTICULARS FURNISHED BY SHIPPER

Mark & Numbers	No.& Kind of packages	Description of Goods	Gross Weight	Measurement
	1 UNIT		925 M/T	10.167 CBM
N/M		1 UNIT OF USED CAR		
		RIO 2000 KNADC2412YS115475		
GHANA AGENT				
HULL BLYTH GHANA				
SEATEC HOUSE,AKOSOMB				
ROAD, TEMA, GHANA.				
TEL:+233 22 300894/5				
MR.CAROLINE BALDWIN				
		** SELF-PROPELLED VEHICLES **		
		"FREIGHT PREPAID"		
		SAY : ONE(1) UNIT ONLY.		

Remarks

EL NO. ______________________________

EL Date ______________________________

This Receipt is fiven subject to all the conditions of our principal Bill of lading
RECEIVED ON BOARD.

By ______________________________

NO & Kind of packages ______________________________

Stowed in hatch No. ______________________________

Date of Print : **By** ______________________________

Mate's Receipt

In case of loading new vehicles:

- Shippers load / stow and count under Charterer's / shipper's instructions and supervision.
- Cargo wet before shipment / dirty / covered with dust and excrement

Supervision, here, can be entered only in the case that it is stipulated in the relevant C/P that cargo handling are to be conducted *under the Master's supervision*. If the C/P states that the Charterer will load and discharge the cargo *under the Master's supervision,* the Charterer remains responsible for the stowage of the cargo and any loss or damage of the cargo due to bad stowage. If the C/P states that the Charterer will load the cargo *under the Master's supervision and responsibility,* the Ship Owner is responsible for the planning of cargo operations and conducting loading, stowing, and discharging of the cargo. The Ship Owner can only avoid such responsibility if he is in position to prove that the Charterers have intervened or interfered with the operation.

Since it is not practical to check all vehicles for any external and internal damage, it is worth entering a remark into the Mate's Receipt that "most of the vehicles have external scratches and minor damage."

In case of vehicles being exposed to abnormal weather conditions such as snow:

- Vehicles covered with snow

Shipping Note

Very often the Shipper may decide to issue a Shipping Note instead of the Mate's Receipt; this is very widely used in the UK liner trade. This Shipping Note contains all the details that a Mate's Receipt should normally contain:

- Name of the Shipper
- Name of the ship
- Port of departure and destination
- Description of the cargo

The Shipping Note should be checked and signed by the Master when vehicles are loaded.

Sea Waybill

The Sea Waybill is a receipt for goods shipped on board. It identifies the person to whom delivery of the goods is to be made. In contrast to a B/L, the Sea Waybill always bears the consignee's name. It:

- is not negotiable
- is not a document of title. Possession of Sea Waybill does not give a right to possession of the goods
- may contain the full conditions of carriage
- is issued by the Carrier

The Sea Waybill is carried on board, which means that it will arrive at the discharging port together with the cargo. Because they are not documents of title, they are less likely to be used fraudulently.

Letter of Protest

When the Master is dissatisfied with the way that cargo operations are performed or if they are not being performed as per the safety standards implemented on board, the Master is obliged to issue a Letter of Protest, because it may be very helpful in rejecting a claim filed against the ship.

The Letter of Protest should be properly made. It can be hand-written or typed. The original letter and one copy should be sent to the appropriate party (normally the Stevedoring Company, when the Letter of Protest is being issued for cargo loading and discharging or related matters) who should be asked to sign and return a copy to the Master. Copies of this Letter of Protest should be sent to the Company and the Agent. A Letter of Protest can be issued in the following cases:

- **When cargo operations on board are not being performed as per safety standards adopted on board**
- **When the stevedores are driving very fast.** See chapter 7, Damage

LETTER OF PROTEST

PCTC:
Date: Port of:
Voyage: Loading / ~~Discharging~~
To: *Name of Stevedoring Company

DEAR SIRS,

I, the undersigned Master of m/v .... hold You fully responsible for any damage to the cars and all consequent damage arising out of over speeding contrary to our verbal and written agreed instructions that max driving speed is 20 km/hr.

Protest lodged by: Received and signed:

MASTER: .... STEVEDORES / AGENT: ....

Letter of Protest addressed to the stevedoring company for driving cars above the speed limit

- **When the cargo is being used for service car or as taxi.** See chapter 7, Damage.

LETTER OF PROTEST

PCTC:
Date: Port of :
Voyage: ~~Loading~~ / Discharging

To: *Name of Stevedoring Company
CC: Charterer's agents

DEAR SIRS,

I, the undersigned Master of m/v ……… remind You that cargo must not be used for transportation of drivers and I will hold You fully responsible for any damage to the cars and all consequent damage(s) arising out of not observing these instructions.

Protest lodged by: Received and signed:

Letter of Protest addressed to the stevedoring company for using cargo vehicles to transport/ taxi for stevedores or as a service car

- **When cargo documents are not presented.** Very often the Master is not provided with the appropriate cargo documents, such as the B/L, Cargo Manifest, etc. This could result in a claim against the ship at a later stage. Lack of such documents will prevent the Master from entering proper remarks in the relevant B/L (if such are presented to him for signature). Moreover, lack of information about the cargo could cause some technical problems when having to calculate stability or when delivering the cargo at the discharging port.

LETTER OF PROTEST

PCTC:
Date: Port of :
Voyage: ~~Loading~~ / Discharging

TO: shippers / charterers
CC: charterer's agents

Dear Sirs.

Due to lack of cargo documents presentation, such as tally receipts, etc. for the cargo of …………………… loaded at the port of ………………………… on ……………………………… , please find here below relevant cargo remarks which must be mentioned in the mate's receipts and are valid for the above said cargo, in conformity with the (*relevant clause of C/P) of the governing charter party.

Protest lodged by: Received and signed:

MASTER: ……………… STEVEDORES / AGENT: ………………

Letter of Protest for failure to present cargo documents addressed to the shippers or charterers

- **When the stowage of the cars or vehicles is very tight or very loose.** As mentioned in chapter 4, Cargo, there are requirements imposed by the manufacturer or Cargo Owners concerning the stowage. If the stevedores do not strictly abide by these requirements and the vehicles are being stowed very close together, the Master should lodge a Letter of Protest. Tight stowage, apart from being in contradiction to good stowage practice, could endanger the safety of the ship, especially in case of bad weather.

  There is also a spacing problem if the space between the vehicles is more than required. The cargo space will not be used to its maximum, which could lead to increased broken stowage and claims against the Carrier, especially if the cargo assigned for carriage cannot be loaded due to lack of space. Therefore the Master should order the stoppage of such loading and stowing operations and lodge a Letter of Protest against the stevedores. There is usually a distance of 40 cm between the cars when stowed. However, if the cargo is in a quantity that can be loaded without a problem, this distance can be wider. For example, if the car capacity is 5,000 cars, but only 4,000 cars are being loaded, the space can be wider.
- **When the cargo is improperly lashed.** It is a requirement under SOLAS Ch. VI that all cargo should be properly secured before the ship leaves the berth. The securing of the cargo is normally performed by the stevedores. However the Chief Officer should supervise them and make sure that securing is performed as per the requirements of the Cargo Securing Manual. If this is not the case, the Master should lodge a Letter of Protest against stevedores for improper lashing.

LETTER OF PROTEST

PCTC:

Date: Port of :
Voyage: ~~Loading~~ / Discharging

TO: shippers / charterers
CC: charterer's agents

Dear Sirs,

I, the undersigned Master of m/v .... will hold You fully responsible for any damage to the cars and ship's lashing materials and all consequent damages / injuries arising out of improper lashings of numerous cars, stowed on deck ..., destined for ....
The abovementioned cars are lashed in contravention of Cargo Securing Manual; Pure Car Truck Operation Manual and Guide to Damage Prevention & Cargo Handling.
The vessel will not accept any responsibility for whatever damages occurred to the vessel and / or her cargo as a result of this wrong practice.

Protest lodged by: Received and signed:

MASTER: .... STEVEDORES / AGENT: ....

Letter of Protest against the stevedores for improper lashing

- **When berth or fendering is inadequate or the berth or port is not considered as "safe"**
- **When passing vessels cause ranging when the ship is being loaded or discharged.** It is very important that the duty officer or duty watchman is vigilant for passing ships, especially when the ramp is down. Ranging or surging of the ship can cause structural damage to the ramp and therefore it is vital that a Letter of Protest is lodged against the passing ship. In this case, a Letter of Protest against the passing vessel should be lodged through the Agent or should be sent to the Ship Management Company of the passing vessel.
- **When damage to the vessel is caused by other ship, port equipment, etc.**

The Master can also be issued a Letter of Protest if it is believed that his ship caused damage. If he receives such a letter, the Master should confirm acceptance by including the remark "For receipt only," in order to avoid any implication that he accepts any liability. In any case, before signing any letter, he should contact his Owner or P&I Club for further instructions.

Cargo Manifest

This document gives detailed information about the cargo on board. The Cargo Manifest is issued by the Shippers or their Agents at the port of loading and its content is based on the information contained in the B/L. The number of units, their respective weight, and some peculiarities of the cargo are included in the information detailed in the Cargo Manifest. The Shipper is obliged to supply the Carrier with cargo information well in advance of loading under the regulations of SOLAS Ch. VI.

The accuracy of the information is very important because the stability calculations are based on the data taken from the manifest. Still, it is not uncommon for the information in the manifest to deviate from the reality. Here the experience and expertise of the Chief Officer and Master gleaned from previous loadings can be helpful. It is important that the Master has several copies of the manifest at hand, because sometimes the port authorities of transit ports can request such manifest.

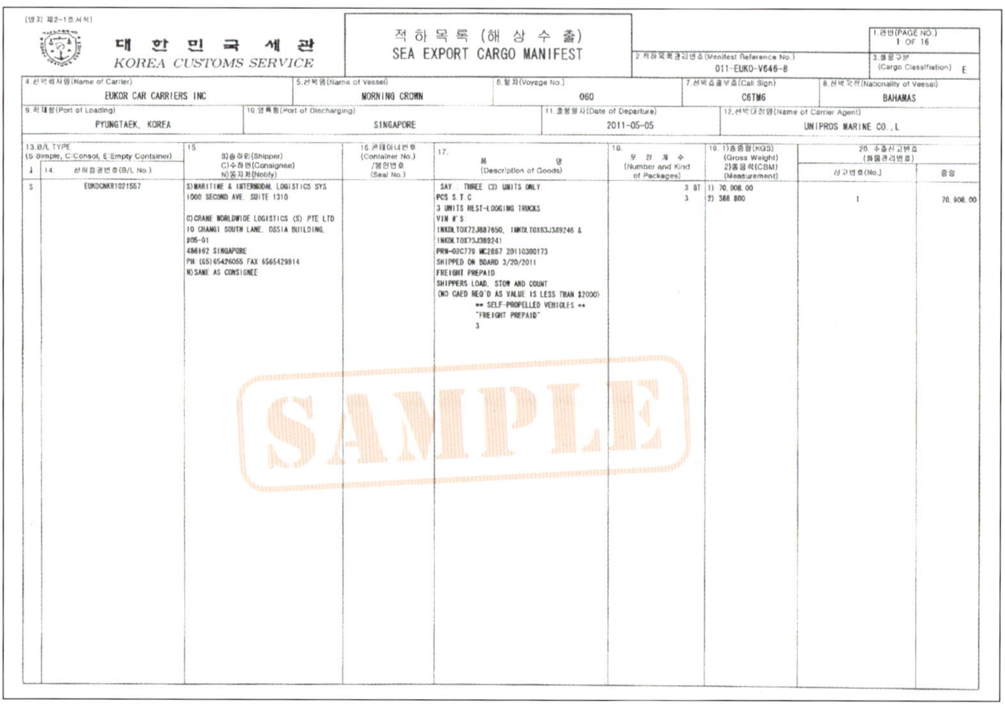
대한민국 세관
KOREA CUSTOMS SERVICE

적하목록 (해상수출)
SEA EXPORT CARGO MANIFEST

1. (PAGE NO.) 1 OF 16
2. (Manifest Reference No.) 011-EUKO-V646-8
3. (Cargo Classifiation) E

4. (Name of Carrier)	5. (Name of Vessel)	6. (Voyage No.)	7. (Call Sign)	8. (Nationality of Vessel)
EUKOR CAR CARRIERS INC	MORNING CROWN	060	C6TM6	BAHAMAS

9. (Port of Loading)	10. (Port of Discharging)	11. (Date of Departure)	12. (Name of Carrier Agent)
PYUNGTAEK, KOREA	SINGAPORE	2011-05-05	UNIPROS MARINE CO.,L

13. B/L TYPE (S:Simple, C:Consol, E:Empty Container)	14. (B/L No.)	15. S)(Shipper) C)(Consignee) N)(Notify)	16. (Container No.) /(Seal No.)	17. (Description of Goods)	18. (Number and Kind of Packages)	19. 1)(KGS) (Gross Weight) 2)(CBM) (Measurement)	20. (No.)	
S	EUKOCNKR1021557	S)MARITIME & INTERMODAL LOGISTICS SYS 1000 SECOND AVE. SUITE 1310 C)CRANE WORLDWIDE LOGISTICS (S) PTE LTD 10 CHANGI SOUTH LANE, OSSIA BUILDING, #05-01 486162 SINGAPORE PH: (65)65426055 FAX: 6565429914 N)SAME AS CONSIGNEE		SAY : THREE (3) UNITS ONLY. PCS S.T.C 3 UNITS WEST-LOGGING TRUCKS VIN #'S: 1NKDLT0X72J887650, 1NKDLT0X83J389246 & 1NKDLT0X73J389241 PRN-02C779 MC2867 20110300173 SHIPPED ON BOARD 3/20/2011 FREIGHT PREPAID SHIPPERS LOAD, STOW AND COUNT (NO CAED REQ'D AS VALUE IS LESS THAN $2000) ** SELF-PROPELLED VEHICLES ** "FREIGHT PREPAID" 3	3 GT 3	1) 70,908.00 2) 388.800	1	70,908.00

SAMPLE

Cargo Manifest

Stevedores' Time Sheet

This document records the times worked by the stevedores chronologically. When presented to the Master or Chief Officer for signature the usual remark "For receipt only" should be entered. The Master should be very vigilant about signing the time sheet. He should read the information contained in the time sheet and check the times against those recorded by the duty officers on board. Special attention should be paid for any remark concerning the overtime claimed by the stevedores and especially for the lashing and unlashing work performed. It is important to carefully check these details because there is a chance that claims will be lodged against the Carrier for extra payment to the stevedores if the information in the time sheet justifies overtime.

August Sundmäker Stauerei GmbH
Bremen **Tel. 0421 – 52 19 70**
Bremerhaven **Tel. 0471 – 95210-0**

xxx Loading

TIME - SHEET

DATE: 05/07/09.01.09 VESSEL: Nordic Ace SHED: NH/KH
DATUM: SCHIFF: SCHUPPEN:

SHIFTS / SCHICHTEN **2** NUMBER OF GANGS / ANZAHL DER GÄNGE **4** WINCHMEN / WINDENLEUTE LIFT-TRUCK / STAPLER

	ASHORE	O'SIDE	FLOATING CRANE
1st	**06:00**	**14:00**	**(loading Cars)**
2nd	**14:30**	**15:30**	**(loading Cars)**
3rd	**14:30**	**22:30**	**(loading Cars)**

SAMPLE

OVERTIME: ......Men each ....hrs End of loading: ....
ÜBERSTUNDEN: ....Men work during overtime hour break. End of lashing:.................

SPECIAL WORK
EXTRA-ARBEITEN: At 07.01.09 from 14:30-15:30 o'clock loading 46 Cars, then gangs change to "Prestige Ace" to unlashing Cars.

WAITING-TIME:
WARTEZEITEN: NIL

MATERIAL: NIL

SIGNATURE FOR THE VESSEL : TOTAL TONNAGE:

All work performed as well as lashing and securing has been carried out to the satisfaction of ship's command.

Stevedore's Time Sheet

Satisfaction Note for Lashing and Securing

This note is issued by lashing personnel upon completion of lashing / securing operations.

Statement of Facts

This is a chronological list of all events concerning the stay of the ship in port. Again all precautions that apply to time sheets are valid here.

Mitsui O.S.K. Bulk Shipping (Europe) Ltd.
Time Sheet & Statement of Facts

Vessel Name: NORDIC ACE
Voyage Number: 040/A
Port: LIVORNO(ITALY)
Trade: EUROPE/MEDITERRANEAN SEA/EUROPE

ARRIVAL

End of Sea Passage	09.46	Hrs	13-02-2009	Bunkers on Arrival		
Anchored		Hrs		MDO	85.00	MTONS
Raised Anchor		Hrs		IFO	739.24	MTONS
Pilot on board	10.15	Hrs	13-02-2009			
Entered lock		Hrs		Draft on Arrival		
Exited lock		Hrs		Forward	6.90	M
All Fast	11.15	Hrs	13-02-2009	Aft	7.30	M
Ramp down	11.30	Hrs	13-02-2009			

WORKING

Commenced discharge	13.37	Hrs	13-02-2009
Completed discharge		Hrs	13-02-2009
Commenced loading		Hrs	13-02-2009
Completed loading		Hrs	13-02-2009
Ramp Up		Hrs	13-02-2009

Date	Shift(e.g.for morning)	Started	Finished	Amount Discharged	Amount Loaded	Stoppages
13-02-2009		13.30	19.30	158 UNITS	2 UNITS	

Remarks: e.g. if extra labour or tugs ordered reason why
NONE: SEE POR LOG.

Master's Signature

C. I. L. P.
Terminal L. Da Vinci
Stevedore's Signature
Responsabile Operativo
Casarola Sergio

Agent's Signature
RENZO CONTI s.r.l.

SAILING

Left Berth		Hrs	13-02-2009	Bunkers on Sailing		
Entered Lock		Hrs		MDO		MTONS
Exited Lock		Hrs		IFO		MTONS
Drop off Pilot		Hrs	13-02-2009			
				Draft on Sailing		
				Forward		M
				Aft		M

Agent's Signature
RENZO CONTI s.r.l.

Statement of Facts

Loading List

The Loading List contains information about cargo that is about to be loaded. This list is prepared before completion of loading, so there is sometimes some deviation between the cargo assigned for loading and the cargo actually loaded. As a rule the cargo specified in this list should be loaded, but, because this is not always the case, the Chief Officer should be very careful and vigilant for any deviations from the loading list.

Cargo Summary

The cargo summary is the list of the cargo actually loaded on board. It can be issued by the stevedores on completion of loading, but if this is not the case it should be prepared by the Chief Officer on basis of data contained in the Cargo Manifest. When receiving a Cargo Summary from the stevedores, the Chief Officer should make sure that the information inside the summary corresponds with his own observations and the figures he has counted in the course of loading. If any discrepancy is found, the appropriate remarks should be entered.

Hermann Runge GmbH

Tallying — S U M M A R Y of Total Load — (MOL0113) — Page 1

M/V: NORDIC ACE — Voy:36 — dep:16.12.08

Agent MITSUI OSK LINES — from

Port	Status	20'	40'	oth.	packg	gross-wgt	net-weight	cont-tara	cbm
HAMINA	SUZUKI-CARS				1.090	1.314.996	1.314.996		12.350,795
					1.090	1.314.996	1.314.996		12.350,795
KOTKA	MAZDA				600	816.000	816.000		7.023,297
					600	816.000	816.000		7.023,297
Grand Total	MAZDA				600	816.000	816.000		7.023,297
	SUZUKI-CARS				1.090	1.314.996	1.314.996		12.350,795
Total Load					1.690	2.130.996	2.130.996		19.374,092

Cargo Summary

Flow-Stow Chart

The Flow-Stow Chart shows the cargo flow pattern of all cargo on board. It is useful when the stevedores in the discharging port have to check the discharging sequence or have to shift some cargo that is on drift.

Damage Report

A Damage Report is issued on behalf of the ship in case of any damage to the cargo and/or the ship's equipment. The situations for which a Damage Report is to be issued are broadly discussed in chapter 8. The form of Damage Report may vary, but basic information is the same in all the formats, including the type and location of damage, the extent of the damage, and when and where it happened. If the Master is presented a Damage Report on behalf of the stevedores he should sign it with remark: "For receipt only."

Pre-stowage and Stowage Plan

The cargo plan has been discussed in chapter 5. The Stowage Plan shows the stow position of every unit on board. Normally the Chief Officer will receive the Pre-stowage Plan well in advance from the Charterers. Having received the plan the Chief Officer should check the stability, rotation, and panel positions. Every Pre-stowage Plan contains the number of units, the weight of the vehicles in every hold, the model of vehicles, and the ports of loading and discharging (normally expressed by codes). However this plan is only preliminary. On completion of cargo operation, the Chief Officer should prepare the final Stowage Plan showing the deviation of the Pre-Stowage Plan if any. The principles for preparing the Stowage Plan are detailed in chapter 5. The cargo for different ports should be marked in different colors in order to avoid any confusion and to facilitate the stevedores' work. In addition the Stowage Plan should be sent or given to the stevedores well in advance.

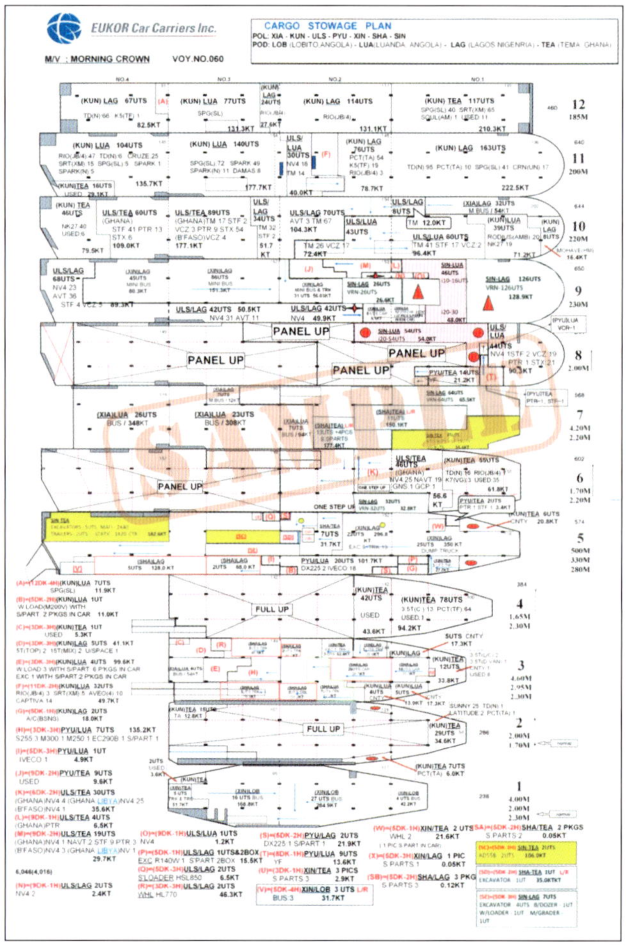

Pre-stowage Plan

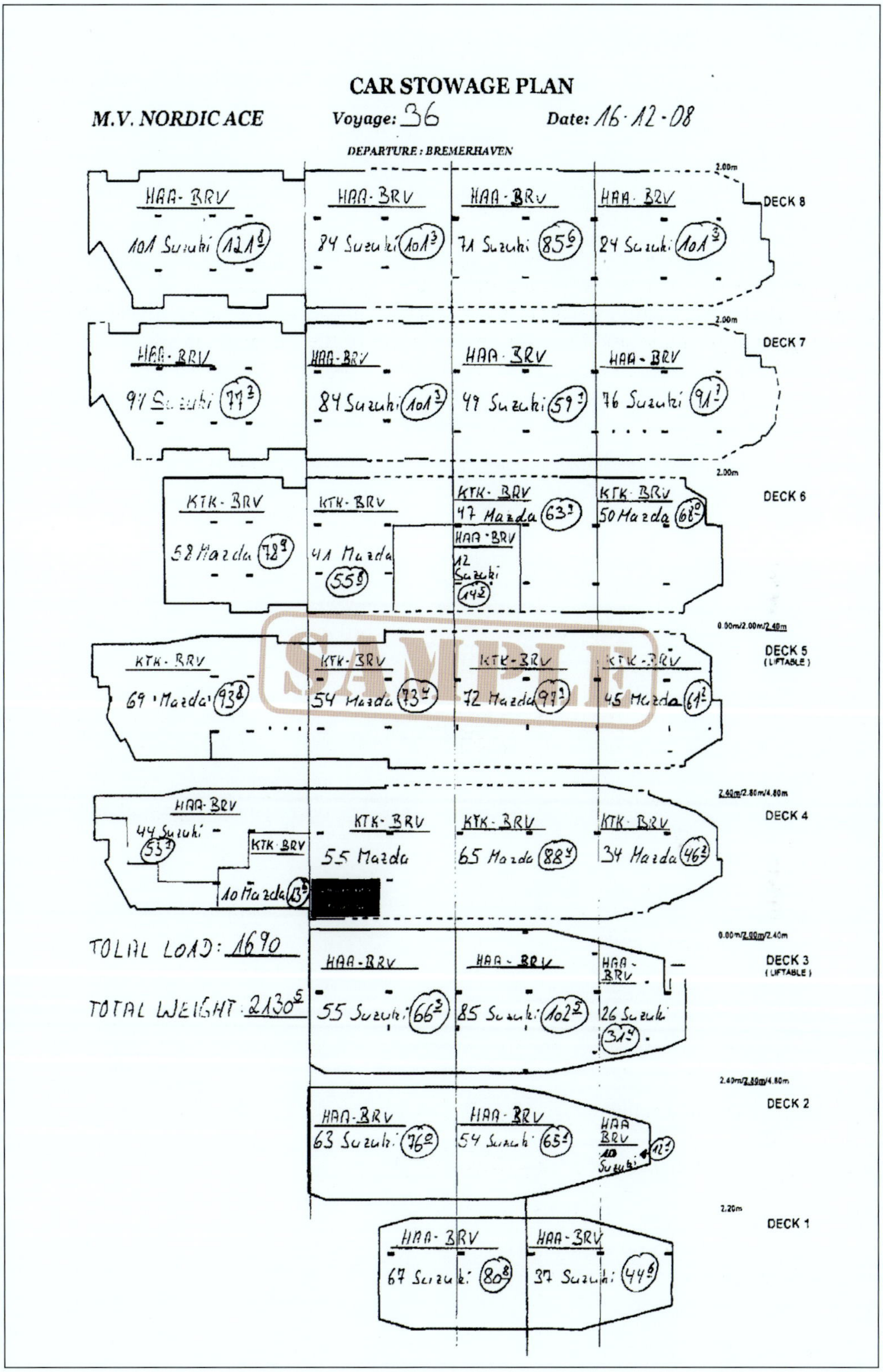

Stowage Plan

Stability Report

On completion of the cargo operations the Chief Officer should prepare his Stability Report showing that the ship will be stable on departure and during the voyage. This report should be prepared by using the required by SOLAS loading computers. They have to be approved by the Flag Administration. The Master, having checked and approved the stability calculation should sign this report. The procedure for preparing the stability calculations and Stability Report is discussed in chapter 10.

Cargo Condition List

Very often the stevedores supply the Chief Officer with a so-called "Cargo Condition List," stating the general condition of the cargo. This is where the Chief Officer should enter any remarks concerning the condition of the cargo.

Postfach 120453
27518 Bremerhaven
Telefon (0471) 413769
Telefax (0471) 42070
e-mail: runge.tally@nord-com.net

HANSE-TALLY KONTOR HERMANN RUNGE
Bremen-Bremerhaven-Nordenham-Brake-Hamburg

CARGO-CONDITION-LIST
(pre-loading)

Schiff
Ship NORDIC ACE nach/to FINLAND Shed TERMINAL C

POS. NO.	Märke & Nummern Marks & Numbers	Inhalt Contents	Beschädigungen / Besonderheiten Remarks, Damages, Exceptions
			NIL

Cargo Condition List

Cargo Exception List

This list contains the information of damage sustained by the cargo. This is where remarks can be made from the ship's perspective concerning the condition of the cargo. Very often the ship is not supplied with a B/L or other cargo documents. Even if the ship is supplied with such documents, it is unlikely that the Master will be allowed to enter remarks concerning the condition of the cargo into them, so the Cargo Exception List should be used.

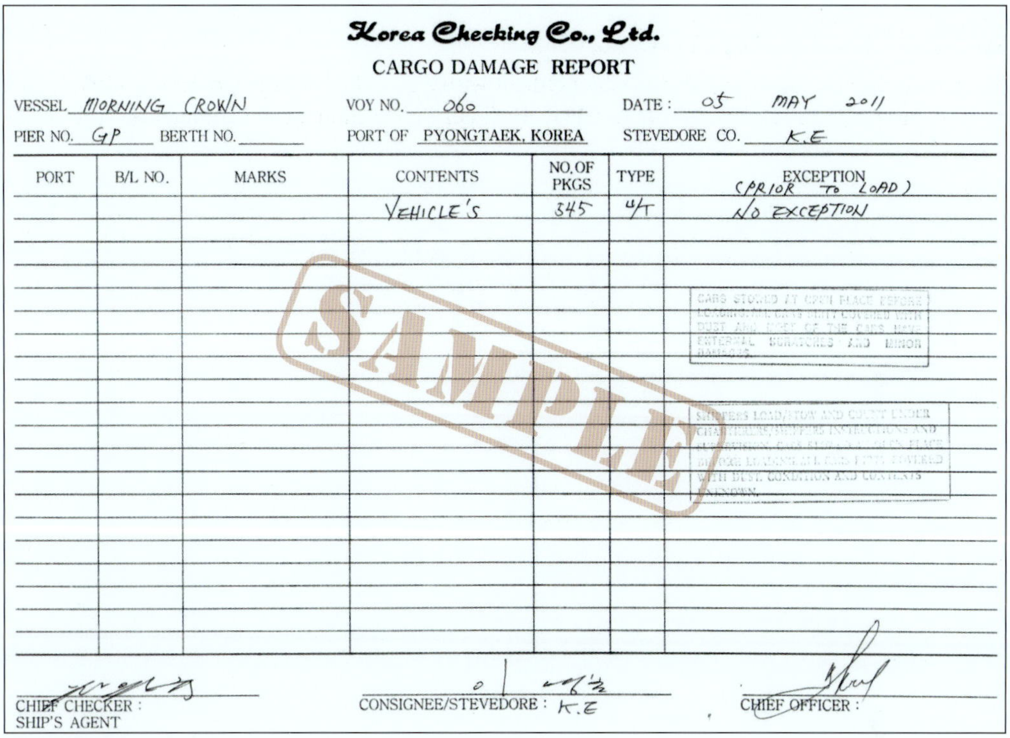

Korea Checking Co., Ltd.

CARGO DAMAGE REPORT

VESSEL MORNING CROWN — VOY NO. 060 — DATE: 05 MAY 2011

PIER NO. GP — BERTH NO. — PORT OF PYONGTAEK, KOREA — STEVEDORE CO. K.E

PORT	B/L NO.	MARKS	CONTENTS	NO. OF PKGS	TYPE	EXCEPTION (PRIOR TO LOAD)
			VEHICLE'S	345	U/T	NO EXCEPTION

CARS STOWED AT OPEN PLACE BEFORE LOADING. ALL CARS DIRTY COVERED WITH DUST AND MOST OF THE CARS HAVE EXTERNAL SCRATCHES AND MINOR DAMAGES.

SHIPPERS LOAD/STOW AND COUNT UNDER CHARTERERS/SHIPPERS INSTRUCTIONS AND [illegible] BEFORE LOADING. ALL CARS [illegible] COVERED WITH DUST. CONDITION AND CONTENTS UNKNOWN.

SAMPLE

CHIEF CHECKER : SHIP'S AGENT

CONSIGNEE/STEVEDORE : K.E

CHIEF OFFICER :

Cargo Exception List

Short- or Over-Landed Cargo Checklist

This is a checklist for ship's use, prepared by the Chief Officer to verify that no cargo has been short- or over-landed in the discharging port. Upon completion of discharging of each compartment, the duty officer should check that compartment and confirm that all cargo for the particular discharging port has been discharged. At the same time, he should check the integrity of separation tape of the remaining cargo. If some discrepancy is found, he must advise the Chief Officer at once. The form of this checklist varies.

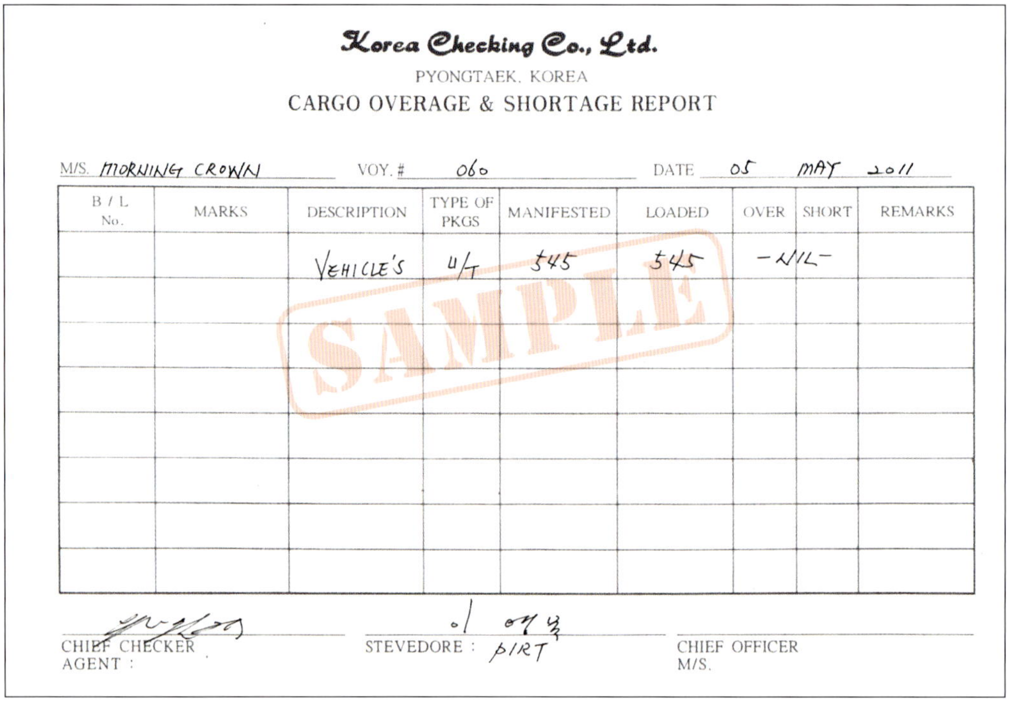

Korea Checking Co., Ltd.

PYONGTAEK, KOREA

CARGO OVERAGE & SHORTAGE REPORT

M/S. MORNING CROWN VOY. # 060 DATE 05 MAY 2011

B / L No.	MARKS	DESCRIPTION	TYPE OF PKGS	MANIFESTED	LOADED	OVER	SHORT	REMARKS
		VEHICLE'S	U/T	545	545	-NIL-		

CHIEF CHECKER
AGENT :

STEVEDORE : PIRT

CHIEF OFFICER
M/S.

SAMPLE

Short- or Over-landed Cargo List

Lashing Report

In the loading and discharging ports, the Master or Chief Officer can be presented with a Lashing Report stating the number of vehicles lashed and unlashed. Special attention should be paid to the figures recorded in this report; they must be checked against the cargo actually loaded or discharged. The Master should bear in mind that in most cases the Charterers are obliged to pay for the stevedoring services and that any discrepancy in the report and the number of vehicles actually handled could put the Master in a difficult posit

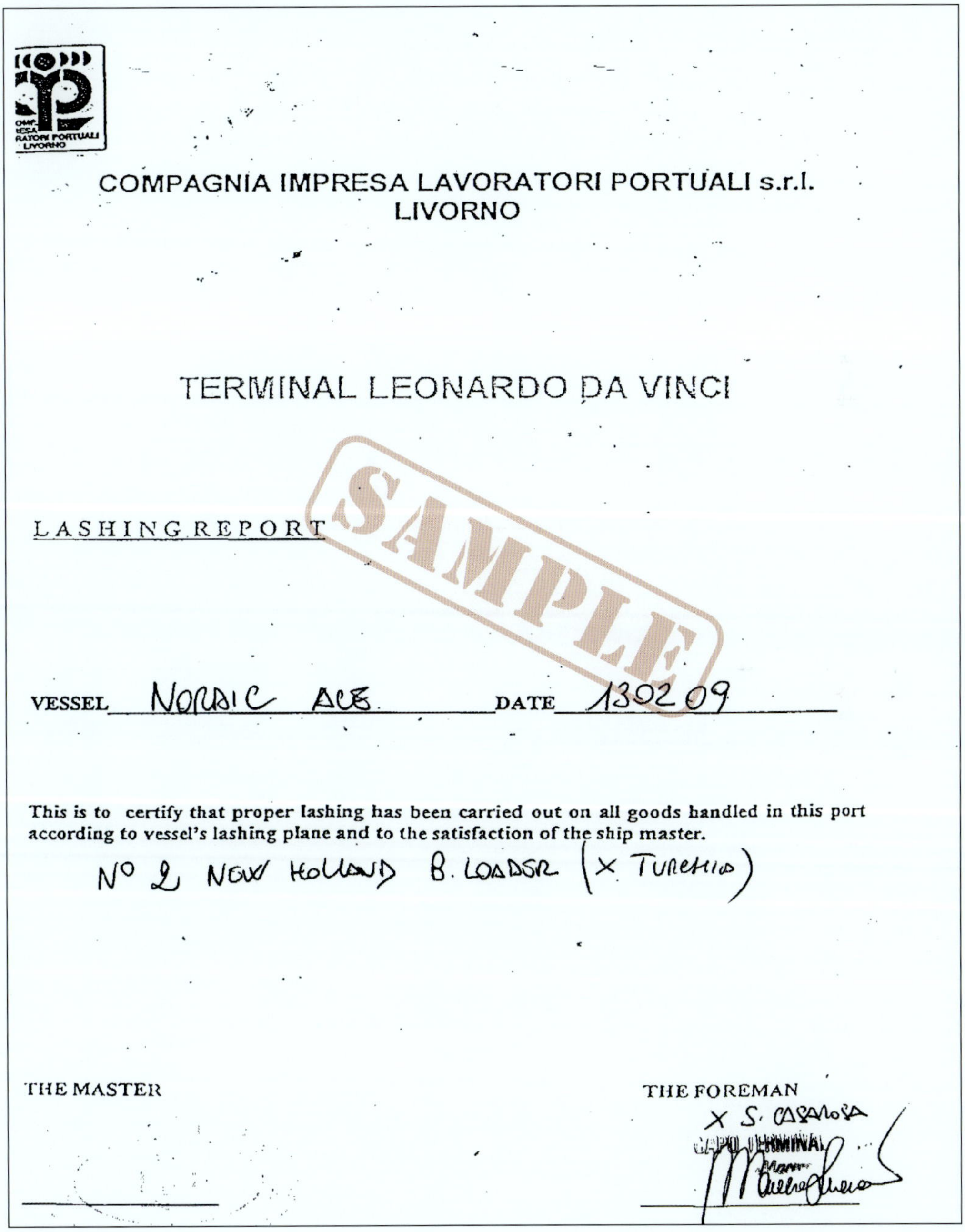

COMPAGNIA IMPRESA LAVORATORI PORTUALI s.r.l.
LIVORNO

TERMINAL LEONARDO DA VINCI

LASHING REPORT

VESSEL NORDIC ACE DATE 130209

This is to certify that proper lashing has been carried out on all goods handled in this port according to vessel's lashing plane and to the satisfaction of the ship master.

Nº 2 NEW HOLLAND B. LOADER (X TURCHIA)

THE MASTER

THE FOREMAN
X S. CASAROSA
CAPO TERMINAL

Lashing Report

Outturn Report

When the cargo is discharged, the Outturn Report should be issued by the Chief Officer as evidence that all cargo has been discharged as loaded and that no injuries have occurred during cargo operations. The Chief Officer should endeavor to obtain the stevedore's signature. Although this Outturn Report will be of little use in defending the Owner's interest in case of any claims for short- or over-landed cargo, the presence of a stevedore's signature will definitely mitigate the extent of such a claim.

Vehicle Packing Certificate

This certificate is required when dangerous goods are packed in vehicles. Those responsible for packing, shippers or agents at the loading port, should provide such certificate specifying the VIN of the vehicle and certifying that the operation has been conducted in accordance with relevant regulations. This certificate is required under SOLAS Ch. VII , Reg. 43 and should confirm that the vehicle is in all respects ready for loading dangerous cargoes. If this certificate is not issued by the Shippers, MSC/Circ. 506/Rev. 1 of January 10, 1990, "Container packing certificates / vehicle packing declarations," recommends the Master to refuse the cargo.

Dangerous Cargo Manifest (IMO FAL Form 7)

This manifest is issued by the Shippers at the loading port. It states the quantity of dangerous goods and certifies that these goods are properly named, packed, and in proper condition for sea transport. This document is presented for signing to the Master and, before he signs, the Master should satisfy himself that the stated quantities of dangerous cargoes loaded are correct. The Master and the Shipper will each keep one copy, and copies may be requested by the authorities in discharging ports and/or transit ports.

Gas Free Certificate

If an empty portable tank or road tank is to be shipped, it should be delivered with a Gas Free Certificate, showing that the vehicle is no longer considered as dangerous cargo. In Europe, this document is known as the European Cleaning Document (ECD). Details about the document can be found on http://www.eftco.org.

CHAPTER 13

HANDLING RO-RO SHIPS

Maneuvering abilities of Ro-Ro ships are subject to the influence of wind much more than other ships. The large windage area and the accommodation located forward make these ships very difficult to handle when entering and leaving port, especially when strong winds are encountered. Ro-Ro ships, and especially car carriers, are also very susceptible to the wind effect while at anchor, and the risk of dragging anchors should be assessed in due time. In this chapter we will focus on the maneuvering and anchoring characteristics for Ro-Ro ships and car carriers.

Handling of car carriers during periods of strong winds can be very difficult. The main issue is their large windage area, which makes car carriers much more vulnerable to the influence of the wind compared to other types of ships. This requires that the Master have a profound knowledge about the behavior of the ship he is commanding. The large windage area and the superstructure, which is located forward, will affect the main points concerning the ship's handling-pivot point (P) and the point of the effect of the wind (W).

Another issue to be considered when it comes to the handling of Ro-Ro ships and car carriers is the use of tugs. Some Owners require the Master to order at least one tug (normally it will be located aft) irrespective of weather conditions. However, it is always the Master who should decide how many tugs will be ordered, depending on the weather conditions during berthing and unberthing. Needless to say, the appropriate assessment of the situation should be done well in advance, using all appropriate measures. These include but are not limited to obtaining weather facsimiles, NAVTEX information, local forecasts, and pilot information.

While at anchor, the Master should take all necessary precautions to avoid dragging of the anchor, especially if the anchorage is close to the shoreline. A lot of authoritative books have been written about ship handling. Therefore it is not the purpose of the author to work out the details of ship handling, but to point out only the particulars of ship handling issues for Ro-Ro ships.

Location of Pivot Point (P) and the Point of Effect of the Wind (W)

From theory it is well known that the point over which the ship is turning—the pivot point (P)—is located somewhere in the underwater portion of the ship. When the ship is stopped this point will almost coincide with the center of gravity of the ship. When the ship starts moving, however, this point will automatically shift forward to a distance of about one-third of its length (⅓L) from the bow (some sources cite a distance of ¼L). When the ship gets a sternway, the position of P shifts forward to a distance of ⅓ L from the stern. So, in both cases, when the ship is underway the distance between W and P will define a turning lever that will affect the behavior of the ship in a certain way. In the following paragraphs we will analyze the behavior of car carriers when stopped, when moving ahead, and when moving astern. These three situations will be analyzed when the ship is at even keel or has a trim to the stern.

At Even Keel

Vessel stopped

Due to the fact that the superstructure is located forward, the location of W will be in front of P; it has already been said that P is approximately the center of gravity (P~G). As a result of the disposition of these points the bow will fall off the wind, regardless of how small the turning lever created between W and P is.

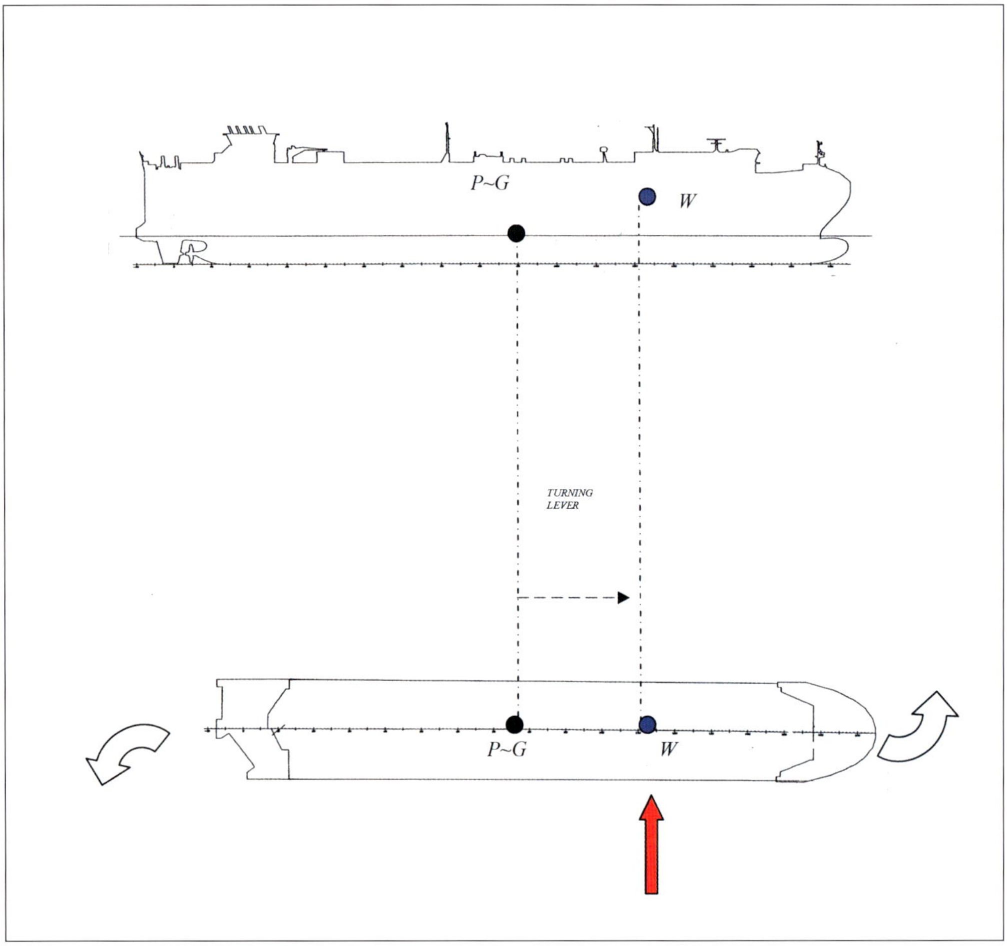

Vessel stopped at even keel (P~G)

Vessel moving ahead

When the ship starts moving ahead, P shifts to new location P_1 at a distance ⅓L from the stem. At the same time, W keeps the same position, as far as the lateral area exposed to wind is the same. The turning lever created between P_1 and W will be small and consequently the ship will be quite stable on the course (depending on the speed). A small deviation of the bow towards the wind occur and the stern will fall off the wind.

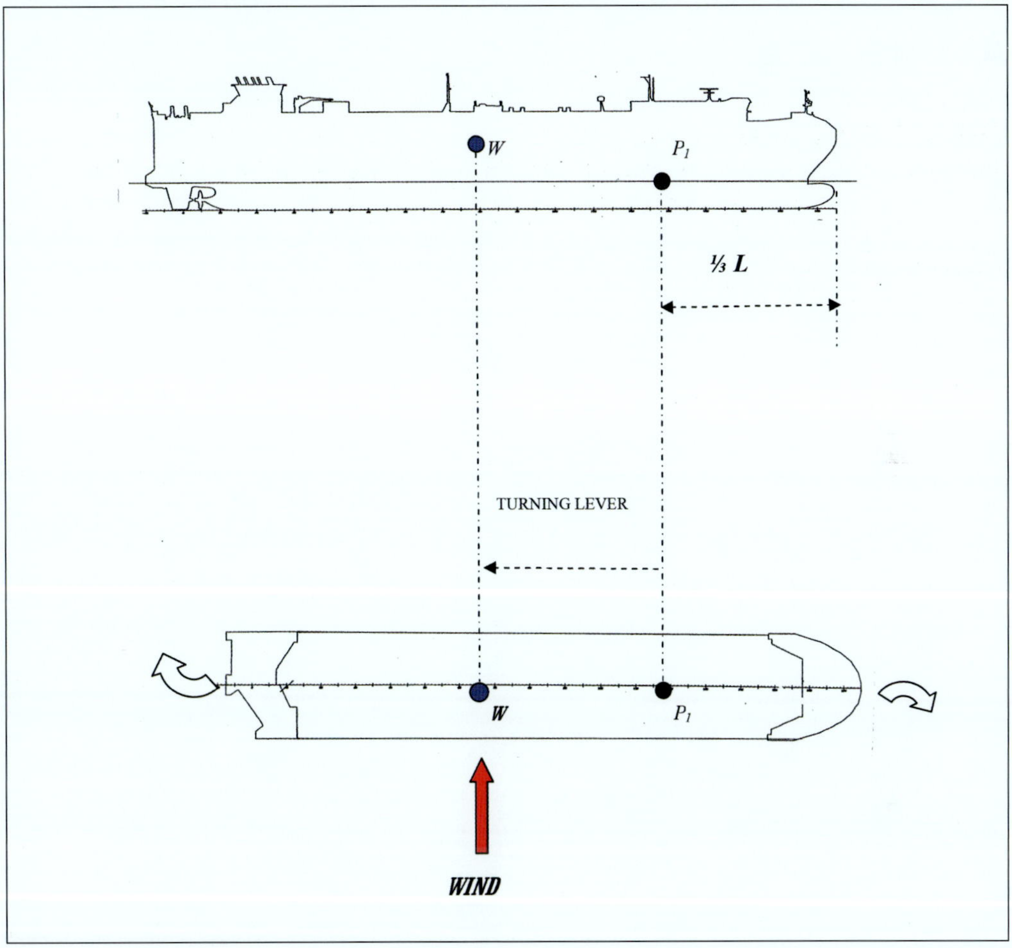

Vessel moving ahead

Vessel moving astern

When the ship is moving astern P is shifting to P_2 at a distance about ⅓L from the stern. The point W will be at the same position and therefore the turning lever created between W and P_2 will be considerably larger compared to what is created between W and P_1 when the ship is moving ahead. The stern will swing towards the wind and the bow will fall off the wind. This effect can be compensated by using the bow thrusters, as they are very effective for controlling the stern in a sternway. Needless to say, thrusters can be used if the speed is up to 4 to 5 knots. (See the "Use of bow/stern thrusters" below)

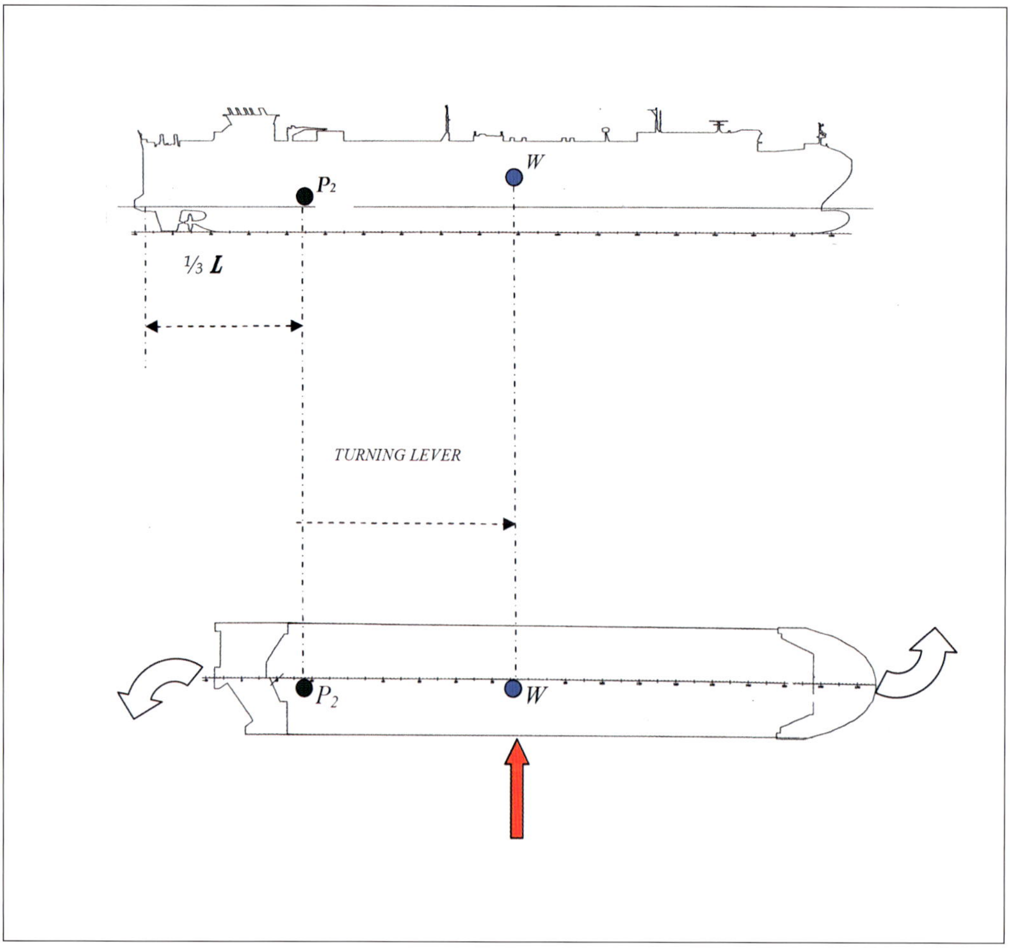

Vessel moving astern

Trimmed by the Stern

The effect of the trim (as it has already been stated the trim should be within the range of 1.0 meter) is that the forward part of the ship will be more exposed to the influence of the wind. This will, indisputably, move W to W_1 and therefore all conclusions valid for even keel will be applicable here, with the only difference being that the rate of turn will be stronger.

Vessel stopped

The bow will fall off the wind with a higher rate of turn than when the vessel would be at even keel. This is due to the fact that the turning lever created between W1 and P is bigger.

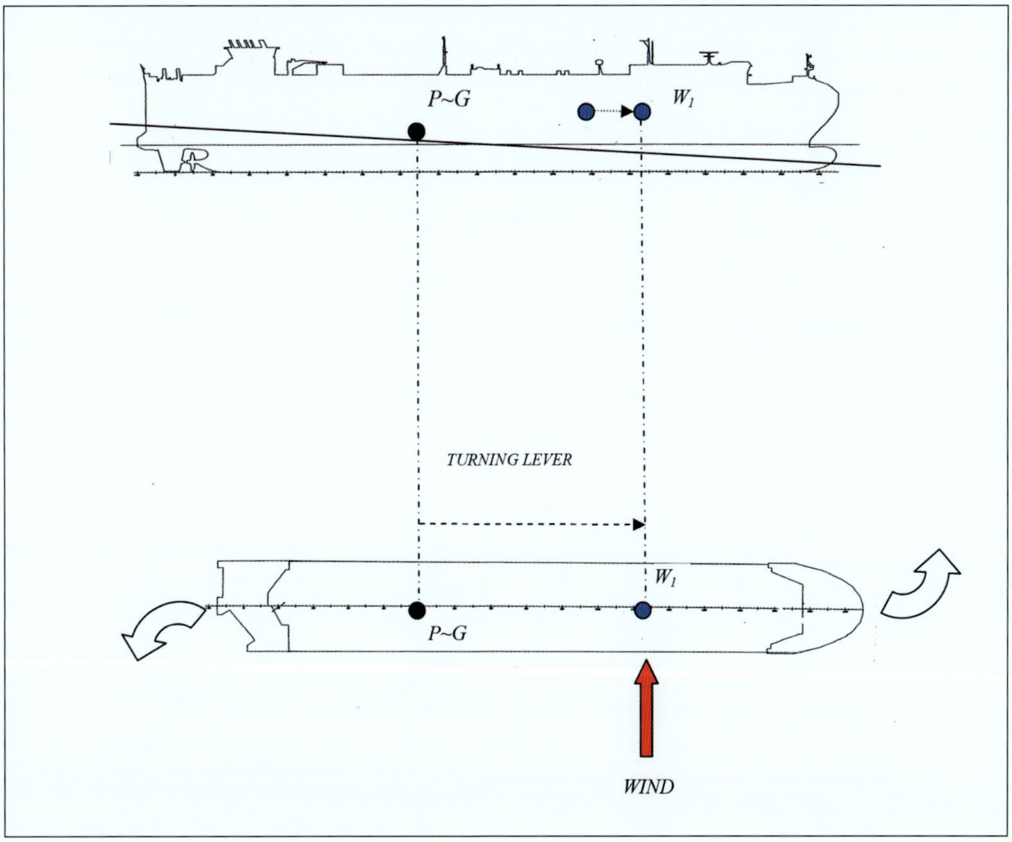

Vessel stopped, trimmed by the stern

Vessel moving ahead

In this case pivot point P is moving ahead to P_3 at a distance ⅓L from the bow. The turning lever created between W_1 and P_3 will be smaller than the lever when the ship is at even keel. Therefore the effect of the wind will be insignificant as far as it concerns the swinging of the bow and the stern—the bow will swing towards the wind but insignificantly.

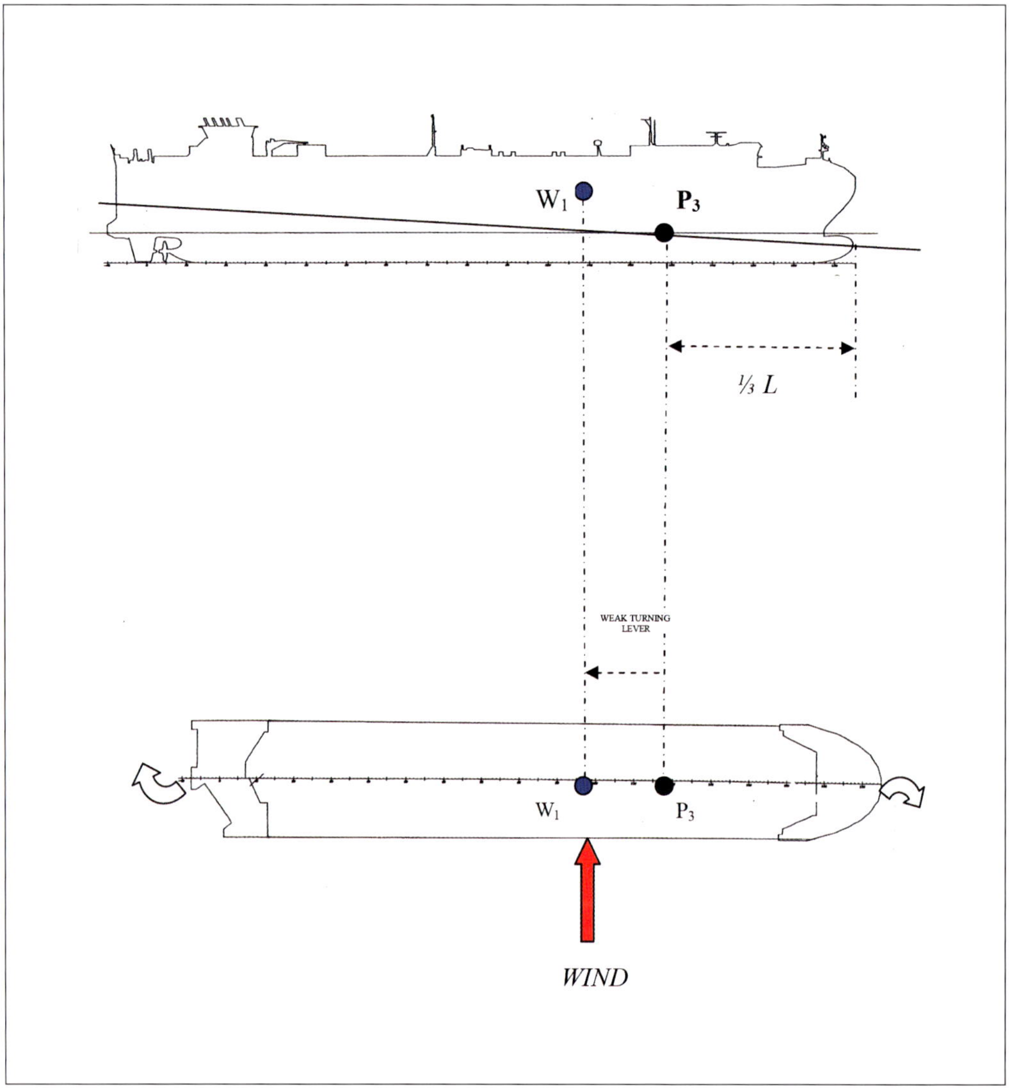

Vessel moving ahead

Vessel is moving astern

This is the situation when the ship will be affected the most. The pivot point will be shifted to P_4 at a distance about ⅓L from the stern. Meanwhile, W will be shifted to W_1. The turning lever created between W_1 and P_4 will be significant and, therefore, the bow will fall off the wind sharply and the stern will swing towards the wind rapidly.

All the above-mentioned conclusions are based on the assumptions that the wind is blowing from either side. If there is a tidal stream in the area, the behavior of the ship will be more complex, especially if the wind and the current are acting from opposite directions. Also the effect of the wind will be stronger when the ship is at lower speeds. This means that the effect of the wind will be strongest during berthing and unmooring operations. The stronger the wind is, the stronger its effect will be.

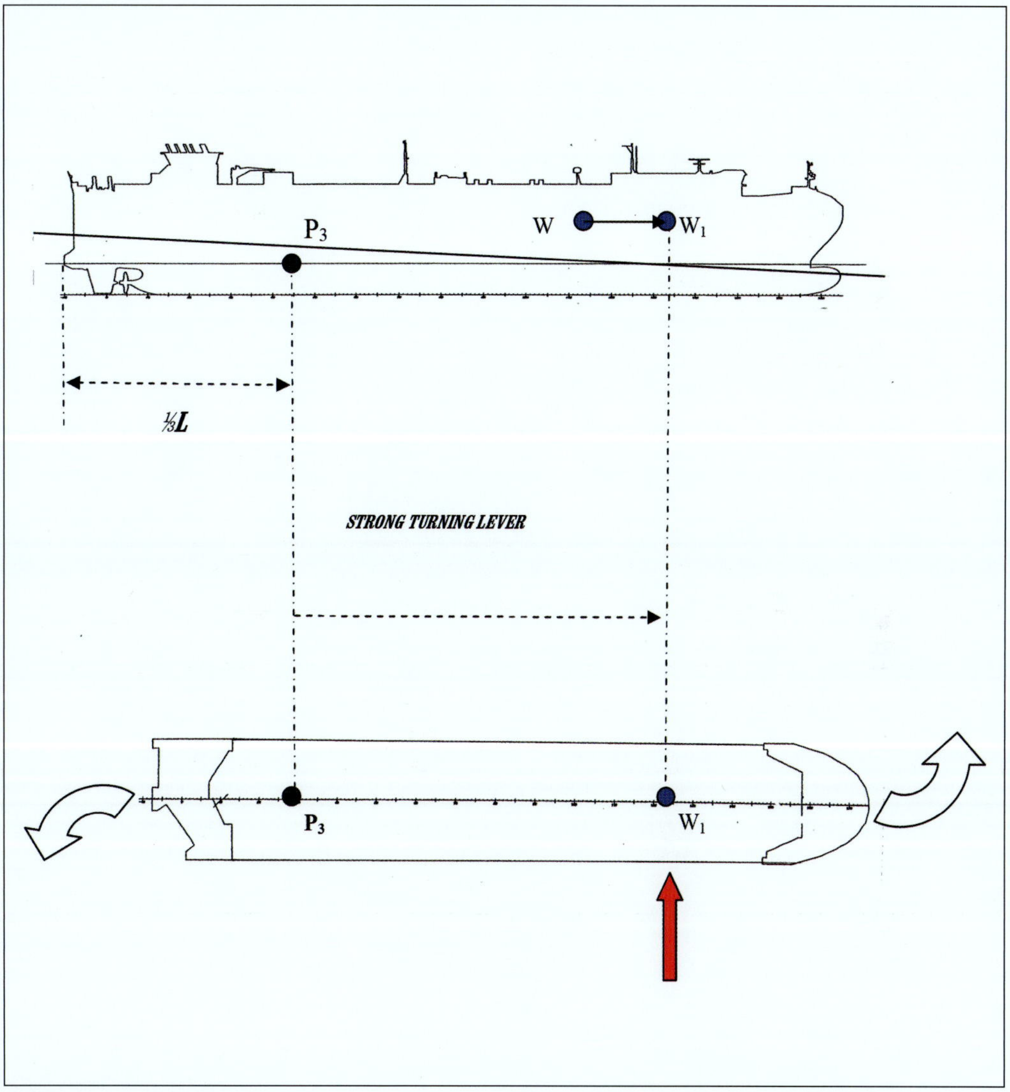

Vessel is moving astern

Calculating Wind Force

Several formulas exist for calculating the wind force.

Formula of G. Hughes
$R_A = 0.5 \times \rho_A \times C_a \times V_A^2 (A_H \times \cos\Theta^2 + B_A \times \sin\Theta^2)$ [1]

Where:
R_A = wind force (kg)
ρ_A = specific density of air (kg/m^3). The standard value is considered as 0.124
C_A = wind force coefficient; 1.3 for car carriers
V_A = relative wind speed to the ship
A_A = projection of above water portion on amidships section (m^2)
B_A = projection of above water portion on longitudinal section (m^2)
Θ = angle of the wind

Simple Formula

For practical calculations of wind force the following simplistic formula can be used (*The Shiphandler's Guide*, Captain R. W. Rowe, FNI, 1998):

$R_A = V^2/18$ [2]

Where:
V = wind speed (m/s)
R_A = wind force (in tonnes) per 1000 m^2

From the above formulas, it is clear that wind force depends on the wind speed: increase of wind speed will increase the force by its square.

The wind resistance coefficients should be given in the ship's documentations. However, if this is not the case the approximate coefficients proposed by Force Technology of Lyngby can be used as follows: 0.52 for longitudinal coefficient and 0.39 for transverse coefficient. Therefore:

Athwart wind force can be obtained by the following:

$R_W = 0.52 \times 10^{-4} \times A \times V_W^2$

Where:
0.52 = longitudinal coefficient
A = wind area (m$^{2)}$
V_W = wind speed athwart (m/s)

Frontal wind force can be obtained by the following:

$R_F = 0.39 \times 10^{-4} \times A \times V_F^2$

Where:
0.39 = transverse coefficient
A = wind area (m$^{2)}$
V_F = frontal wind speed (m/s)

There is a graphical solution of the above formula giving the relation between the wind speed and wind force. This graphical solution is shown here and it is good practice have such a diagram on the bridge of any Ro-Ro vessel for easy and quick reference.

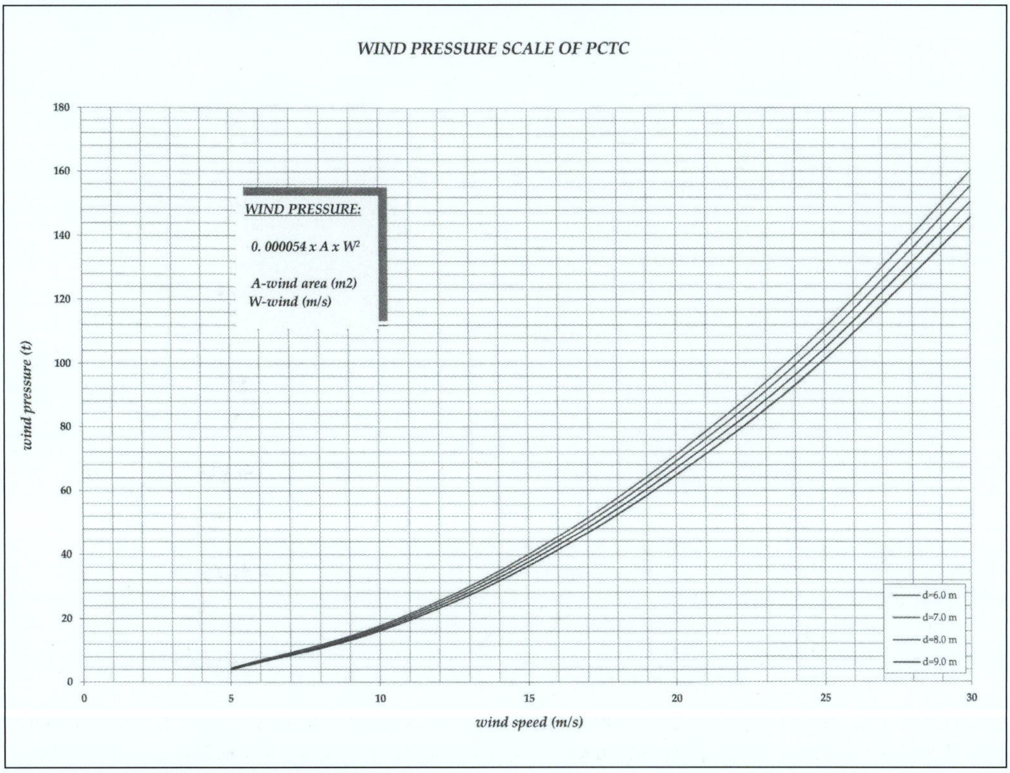

Graphical relation wind speed~wind force

Some research has shown that, in strong winds, car carriers can keep their course when proceeding at reduced speed if the ratio of wind speed to ship speed is 3.0 or more.

The required rudder angle to keep the course will depend on the direction of the wind and the "wind speed / ship speed ratio. A pure car carrier (PCC) will be uncontrollable if the wind is blowing between 75° and 150° off the bow with speed about 30 knots and rudder declination of 15°.

Kick Ahead

The undesirable effect of wind while entering and leaving a port can be mitigated by means of kicks of the engine or the bow or stern thrusters. With this technique, control can be achieved by positioning the rudder full to the side and using short thrusts of the engine. If the bow is falling off the wind, hard to starboard rudder and a short thrust of the engine ahead should be given and vice versa. The duration of the kick ahead for the movement should be limited to the time needed to reach the engine revolutions ordered. For example, if an order for a kick ahead to dead slow is given, power should be taken off when the respective RPM for dead slow are reached.

In all cases the rudder should be deflected to the side before the engine thrust is initiated.

Using Bow or Stern Thrusters

Newly built car carriers are fitted with bow thrusters of different power. Some, especially smaller car carriers, are fitted with stern thrusters as well. The use of thrusters is justified and effective up to speeds of 4 or 5 knots. At speeds more than 5 knots the bow thrusters lose more than 40% of their power, and at speeds of 7 knots and higher the bow thrusters are completely ineffective. The reason for this is that turbulence will develop inside the thruster tunnel when moving ahead, thus impairing propeller performance. More important, however, is the position of pivot point when the vessel is making headway. As described earlier, the pivot point will be positioned about ⅓L from the bow, meaning that the thruster will have a very short turning lever with a very small turning moment.

Critical Wind Force for Using Bow or Stern Thrusters

When using the thrusters on Ro-Ro ships (including car carriers), it is most important to keep in mind the critical wind force for safe berthing when using thrusters. Different research has used various methods for calculating the critical wind force. Critical wind speed is expressed by a graph explaining the relationship between wind to ship speed and relative wind angle. L. L. Martin in "Ship Maneuvering and Control in Wind," *SNAME Transactions*, Vol. 88, 1980, stated that the ratio of ship drift speed to wind speed is approximately proportional to the square root of the rudder angle and of the ratio of effective rudder area to above-water lateral area. However a ship's motion in port is very unsteady and speed is almost zero. To keep a car carrier in an almost fixed position in windy conditions is a really difficult job. Therefore, when considering the critical wind velocity, the reduced effect of the ship's speed and effect of the rudder in such reduced speed situations should be taken into account. As the ship's motion is relatively slow in port the influence of wind and current is significant. This is actuated by the fact that at slow speed the pivot point shifts even farther forward. Isherwood in "Wind resistance of merchant ships," *RINA*, Vol. 115, 1973, created a model of the wind affecting ships. In Isherwood's model, assuming that the wind is steady, the hydrodynamic forces, acting on the ship due to the wind will be:

$$\mathbf{X_W = 0.5C_X \; x \; \rho \; x \; V_R^2 \; x \; A_T}$$
$$\mathbf{Y_W = 0.5C_Y \; x \; \rho \; x \; V_R^2 \; x \; A_L}$$
$$\mathbf{N_W = 0.5C_N \; x \; \rho \; x \; V_R^2 \; x \; A_L \; x \; L}$$

Where:
$\mathbf{X_W}$ = coefficient of wind forces, acting in fore-and-aft direction
$\mathbf{Y_W}$ = coefficient of wind forces, acting in lateral direction
$\mathbf{N_W}$ = wind induced moment
$\mathbf{V_R}$ = wind speed relative to the ship (m/s)
ρ = air density: 0.124 kg/m^3
$\mathbf{C_X}$, $\mathbf{C_Y}$ = coefficients for wind force
$\mathbf{C_N}$ = coefficient for wind induced yawing moment
$\mathbf{A_T}$ = transverse projected area (m^2)
$\mathbf{A_L}$ = lateral projected area (m^2)
L = length overall (m)

The moment of the thrusters can be obtained from the following formulas:

$$P_{BT} \times D_{BT} = M_{BT}$$
$$P_{ST} \times D_{ST} = M_{ST}$$

Where :
P_{BT} = output of bow thruster (max about 1400 Kw~1900 Hp)
P_{ST} = output of stern thruster
D_{BT} = distance between the bow thruster and center of the ship
D_{ST} = distance between the stern thruster and center of the ship

To obtain critical wind velocity below which the ship can keep its position on a fixed point we can use the following equations:

In case of bow thruster only:
$$P_{BT} = Y_W \quad [3]$$
$$M_{BT} + M_W = 0$$

Where:
Y_W = hydrodynamic force of the wind
M_W = turning moment due to the wind
M_{BT} = turning moment created by the bow thruster

In case of bow and stern thrusters:
$$P_{BT} + P_{ST} = Y_W$$
$$M_T + M_W = 0 \quad [4]$$

Where:
M_T = turning moment due to effect of the thrusters

If the wind side force and wind moment are given (or more precisely, if we can calculate them) then we can calculate the thrusters' output. The critical wind velocity will be reached when the thrusters' output reaches its maximum.

In practice, it would mean that for a bow thruster of average power 1400 Kw the critical wind speed is about 15 kts (Force 4).

How do we derive this practical conclusion?

The power of thrusters is expressed in kilowatts, which can be very frustrating indeed. This power can be converted into shaft horse power (shp) or tonnes (t) force, using the following:

1 shp = 0.74 Kw
1 t = 100 shp

Thus the most common types of thrusters fitted on board car carriers will have the following power:

1000 Kw = 1351 shp = 13.5 t
1400 Kw = 1892 shp = 18.9 t

Then for a thruster of 1400 Kw (19 t) the critical wind should not exceed 19 t.

Assuming a standard car carrier with length of 200 meters and freeboard 30 meters, this will give us a pretty good windage area of about 6000 square meters (200 x 30).

Total wind force should not exceed 19 t = 6 x wind force per m^2.

The wind force per square meter, then is:

$$19 / 6 = 3.2 \text{ t} / \text{m}^2$$

From formula [2] we can derive that wind speed that corresponds to wind force of about 3 t is about 7.5 m/s or 15 kts (Force 4).

It should be kept in mind that gust winds will worsen the situation and, practically, the thrusters may not be able to overcome the wind effect. It is particularly important with strong onshore wind gusts when the vessel is close to the berth.

Using Bow Thruster When the Vessel Is Stopped

This is the best situation for using the bow thruster, because once the thruster is activated it will work on a pivot point that is positioned well aft. Thus the turning lever and the respective turning moment are great and the effect of the thruster is the largest.

Using Bow Thruster When the Vessel Makes Headway

This is probably the worst scenario for using the bow thruster. On a modern carrier it is not uncommon for dead slow ahead to give a good speed of about 9.0 kts. This speed, as it was already explained, will make the thruster ineffective. Taking into account the critical wind force, if the speed is less than 5.0 kts, the thruster will be effective. When the vessel is making headway, the pivot point will be shifted forward at a distance from the bow of about ⅓L, which will coincide, more or less, with the location of the thruster. This will result in very short turning lever and a respectively small turning moment.

Using Bow Thruster When the Vessel Is Making Sternway

The thruster can be very useful when the vessel is making sternway, because the pivot point will shift aft at a distance of about ⅓L from the stern. This will result in very long turning lever and respectively in large turning moment.

Precautions When Berthing and Unmooring

When Ro-Ro ships are involved in berthing or unmooring operations, special attention should be paid not to hit fenders on the berth.

The contact with the berth is due to huge flares of these ships fore and aft. The range of critical positioning is determined by the face line of the berth and the angular deviation of the ship's heading and the berth. The range of permissible overhang is a function of the angular deviation from the wharf.

Parallel Berthing

Parallel berthing is the most common way of berthing for large car carriers. Depending on the weather conditions, one or two tugs will be used to bring the vessel alongside. Once the vessel takes her way off, the tugs positioned forward and aft will start pushing at a speed of about 0.3 kts until the vessel gets alongside.

It is highly recommended that tugs are made fast to the ship, either on deck or on sunken bitts. In case of failure of bow or stern thrusters the tugs can easily control the swinging of bow or stern.

If only one tug is used and the stern is brought to a position for safe ramp lowering but the bow is off the quay, the use of the thruster could very easily check in the situation. Perhaps the conclusions valid for critical wind force should be taken into account, but no prudent Master of a large car carrier will allow himself to be trapped in with only one tug in fresh wind conditions.

It should be kept in mind that if the vessel is stopped, the use of the thruster will be very effective and will bring the bow to the pier, but the stern will drop off the berth. This can be easily rectified by the tug gently pushing on the respective quarter to the berth.

Mediterranean Mooring

Mediterranean mooring is a mooring method whereby the ship gets alongside with the stern and the swinging of the bow is controlled by both anchors. While this kind of mooring is very frequently used by Ro-Ro ships and ferries, it is usually not used for large car carriers. The reason for this is that these ships are designed to get alongside starboard or port side, depending on the location of the ramp. Due to the very large area exposed to the wind, car carriers are very susceptible for yawing, which could result in damage to the ramp and the ship itself in the case of a sudden wind gust.

The berthing procedure will depend on the type the Ro-Ro ship in question, but generally the following sequence is to be followed:

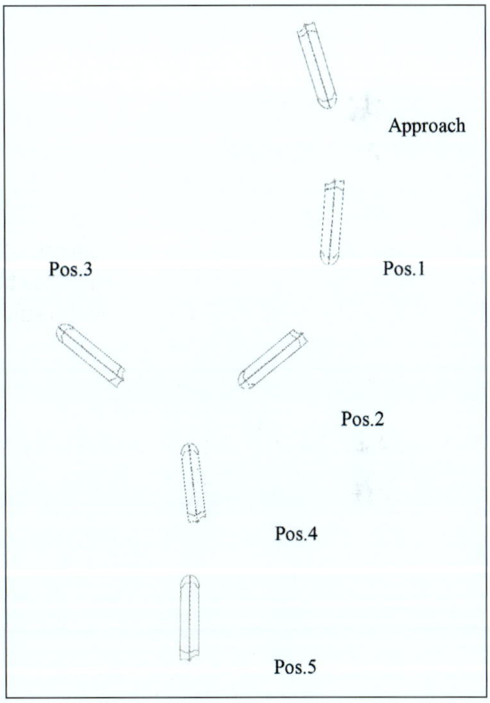

Mediterranean mooring

- **Position 1:** Engine stopped; speed less than 1.0 knot. Bow thruster full to starboard; rudder hard to starboard
- **Position 2:** Let go starboard anchor and keep the brake open
- **Position 3:** Hold the brake of starboard anchor and let go port anchor. Short kick astern. Tugs will start swinging the stern to port.
- **Position 4:** Ship is moving slowly astern. When possible let go one stern line from each side in order to stop swinging of the stern. Once these long ropes are made fast, let go two short stern lines in order to move the ship astern.
- **Position 5:** When the stern is about 12 to 15 meters off the berth hold the brakes of the anchors and make fast all stern ropes (usually 3 / 3 stern lines)

Mediterranean mooring

Vessel Alongside

Once the vessel is alongside, she should be properly moored. The number and disposition of the ropes depends entirely on the size of the vessel and prevailing / expected weather conditions.

Large car carriers use the most common pattern for mooring: four (4) headlines, two (2) spring lines forward and four (4) stern lines, two (2) spring lines aft.

Headlines and stern lines are used to control surge, sway, and yaw of the vessel and spring lines control drift of the vessel.

The ropes should be as long as possible, considering the fact that in case of strong wind (or another weather factor) the lines will break one by one, starting from the shortest one.

Every rope has a mooring force, which is the horizontal component, needed to withstand the motion of the ship, exerted by an external force on the ship's hull. The sum of all mooring forces is the resultant mooring force.

Unusual berthing for car carrier—port side alongside to. The angle between mooring lines and pier is very large due to the high location of the mooring stations.

Standard mooring of car carrier

The resultant mooring force will depend on the ropes' condition (more specifically their strength). So, we can define critical mooring force, which is the force needed to counteract all external forces acting to the hull when the vessel is moored. This critical mooring force should be within the range:

External force on the hull ≤ 0.6 Minimum Breaking Load (MBL) of the rope

Or

External force on the hull ≤ Breaking power of mooring winch

For car carriers, the breaking power of the winch is about 30 to 40 metric tons (tonnes).

It should be kept in mind that, due to the high positioning of the fairleads, the angle between the mooring lines and the pier is usually very large. This will weaken the effectiveness of the ropes.

The number of the ropes will be affected by various factors such as weather conditions, especially prevailing wind, presence of swell and tidal streams inside the port, location of the ramps, etc.

When the vessel is safely berthed, part of the hull will be under the quay line. In such cases, when the vessel is safely moored, the wind pressure acting on the sides of the vessel can be calculated by an approximate formula:

$$\mathbf{P = V^2 / 3} \quad [5]$$

Where:
V = wind speed in m/s
P = Wind pressure (in tonnes)

Remember: This formula is valid and accurate ONLY when the vessel is berthed.

In weather when the wind force does not exceed 15 m/s, the mooring pattern of four headlines, four stern lines, two springs forward, and two springs aft can be applied. However, it should be kept in mind that sudden wind gusts will have a negative effect on the ship and lateral shift off the berth can be expected. In such cases, additional breast lines (as long as possible) should be deployed and storm bollards (if they exist) should be used. Normally, the ports exposed to strong winds or gusts have such storm bollards.

In any case, the Master should be aware of the anticipated weather conditions during the port stay and the weather forecast should play a vital part of the Master's decision for the number of ropes deployed.

If the wind increases more than 15 m/s offshore, the engine and the thrusters should be ready for use and the option of calling for the tugs to push towards the berth should be considered.

Wind speed more than 15 m/s offshore, which is acting perpendicular to the hull, will inevitably create a large lateral shift of the vessel off the berth.

While at Anchor

Anchoring and staying at anchor can be a serious headache for the Master of a PCC. In strong winds, staying at anchor is almost impossible, considering the large windage area of this type of ship. Before staying at anchor, the Master of PCC should consider the following items:

- Suitable anchorage
- Duration of anchor stay
- Critical wind velocity above which the anchor will start dragging
- Preventive measures against dragging

Suitable Anchorage

If the anchorage is a designated one, the Master should select an anchor position that allows sufficient time to deal with dragging anchor situations. As a rule, such anchorage should be more than 3 nautical miles off the 10-meters depth contour line or obstructions on the lee side. As far as possible a suitable anchorage should:

- Be sheltered
- Have sufficient distance between other vessels. Normally the safe distance between a car carrier and other ships should be at least 0.5 Nm (in case of a congested anchorage)
- Have a proper depth
- Have a suitable holding ground allowing a good holding power for the anchor

Duration of Anchor Stay

It is important to carefully monitor the weather conditions. If the ship is to stay at anchor for a longer period, it will be necessary to pay out more shackles in the water. If the expected weather is not fair, but still within the safety margins, there is good reason to pay out more shackles in the water.

How many shackles should be paid out is left at the discretion of the Master, but two empirical standards exist to support the Master in his decision. They are the following:

UK Standard:
$L_C = 27.5 \times 1.5\sqrt{D}$
$N_C = 1.5\sqrt{D}$ [6]

Where:
L_C = length of the anchor chain
N_C = number of shackles
D = depth of the water (m)

Japanese Standard:
Normal anchoring: $L_C = 3 \times D + 90$ (m) [7]
Heavy Weather anchoring: $L_C = 4 \times D + 145$ (m)

Critical Wind Velocity

Calculations for critical wind velocity are necessary to compare the holding power of the anchor with the tension of the chain. The tension varies depending on the wind velocity. If the wind velocity increases and the tension becomes greater than the holding power, the anchor will start dragging. The wind velocity that causes the anchor to start dragging is considered as the critical wind velocity.

The total holding power is the sum of the holding power of the anchor and the holding power of the chain:

$$P = P_A + P_C = \lambda_A \times W_A + \lambda_C \times W_C + L \quad [8]$$

Where:
P = holding power (tonne)
P_A = holding power of the anchor
P_C = holding power of the chain
λ_A = holding power coefficient of the anchor
λ_C = holding power coefficient of the chain
W_A = weight of the anchor (t)
W_C = weight of the chain (t)
L = length of the chain laid on the bottom

From the theory we know that the value of L can be obtained by the following formula:

$$\mathbf{L = L_C - S = L_C - \sqrt{h} \times (h + 2T/W_C)} \quad [9]$$

Where:
$\mathbf{L_C}$ = length of anchor chain veered out (m)
S = length of catenary's curve of anchor chain (m)
h = height of hawse pipe from the bottom (m)
T = external force by the wind (t)
$\mathbf{W_C}$ = weight of anchor chain (t)

As a rule of thumb for Car Carriers, it is accepted that the maximum tension on the chain is five times the wind pressure on the front of the ship:

$$\mathbf{T = 5 \times R} \quad [10]$$

Where:
T = maximum tension of the chain
R = wind pressure on front of the ship (t):

$$\mathbf{R = 0.5 \times \rho \times C_A \times (V \times G) \times A/1000}$$

Where:
$\mathbf{C_A}$ = frontal wind coefficient. For practical calculations, Ca = 0.75
V = wind velocity
G = gust rate, accepted as average as 1.25 (G = 1.25)
A = frontal area of windage (m^2)

The most common anchors used on board car carriers are types: AC-14, JIS Stockless Anchor, and D-Hone. The holding power for specific anchor type can be found in the anchor certificate on board the ship.

The ship may drag her anchor even if the wind speed is less than critical, depending on the water depth, swell, currents, type of ground, etc. The prudent Master will always pay out a proper length of anchor chain based on the meteorological and geographical conditions of the anchorage. The necessary length of anchor chain should be related to the ship's size, anchor conditions, wind force, and the nature of the sea bottom, based on the so-called "risk index" of dragging the anchor. The risk index defines the critical conditions (not only the critical wind force) above which the ship will start dragging her anchor. It consists of a danger zone that indicates when the anchor is expected to start dragging, and a safety zone that indicates the conditions in which the ship will be safely anchored.

Preventive Measures Against Dragging

The anchor will start dragging if the wind exceeds the critical wind velocity obtained earlier. However the dragging can take place even if the wind velocity is less than the critical one when the effect of the swell, currents, etc., is significant. Dragging of the anchor will be caused by the impulse force applied to the ship and subsequent wind stress. When the tension of the cable reaches its maximum due to swinging, the impulse force can be obtained by multiplying the wind force R by the swinging coefficient n, which for car carriers is 5. (See formula 9)

Preventive measures include but are not limited to the following:

- **Keep proper watch while at anchor.**
- **Check the vessel's swinging.** If the vessel is not swinging, but is keeping a constant angle against wind direction it could be indication for anchor dragging
- **Always keep a safe distance from the other vessels:** at least 0.5 Nm in congested anchorage and 1.0 Nm in normal conditions, especially those on the lee side.
- **Drop the anchor at the other side and pay out the cable one-and-a-half times as long as depth of water, thus suppressing vessel's swaying and yawing.** The angle between both anchors should be about 60° to avoid fouling in case of strong wind.
- **Take into account the availability of tugs.**
- **Regularly check the tension of the chain.** If it is tight without slack, it is a sign for anchor dragging
- **Regularly check vessel speed over the ground.**
- **Increase the vessel's draft by filling up the ballast water tanks in order to reduce the lateral projected / windage area.** In this respect, increase the ship's trim by the head in order to shift the center of gravity forward as much as possible and wind pressure center afterwards as much as possible.
- **Use bow thrusters for suppressing swaying and yawing.**
- **The tension on anchor chain can be reduced by using the main engine**
- **Choose the proper method for anchoring.** Riding at a single anchor is suitable when bad weather is expected because the time for heaving up a single anchor will be less. However, the swinging area is comparatively large and holding power is less compared to both anchors being paid out. When the ship is riding at two anchors the holding power is large and the swinging area is small, but the danger of fouling the anchors during swaying and yawing exists. It definitely will take more time to heave two anchors in case of deterioration of weather.
- **Continuously keep an eye on the course recorder.** It will show when the anchor starts dragging. When the course recorder is not recording a regular sine curve, it is an indication of anchor dragging.

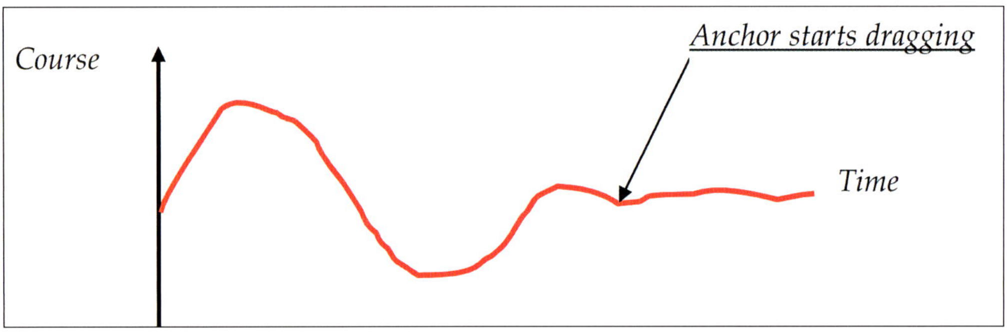

Course recorder graph

- **Consider the possibility of veering the anchor in due time, before the wind reaches critical velocity.** At a later stage, it may not be possible to heave up the anchor at all.
- **Consider the possibility of letting the other anchor (snubber or swing check anchor) go.** The cable of this chain should be about one-and-half times the present depth. In this case, research and experience have shown that swinging of the ship could be reduced by about 50%. However, it should be kept in mind that if the wind exceeds 25 m/s or the depth exceeds 40 meters then the second (swing check anchor) is less effective.
- **Do not forget to monitor the other ships in the area for dragging their anchors.**
- **Continuously keep an eye on the wind velocity.** If the wind starts freshening, the basic preparations for heaving up the anchor should be made, i.e., stand by engine, warming up the windlass if necessary, advising port authorities about the intention to heave up, etc.

The critical wind velocity will be different for different ships and therefore it is very difficult to establish a uniform criterion for when the wind speed will become dangerous. However the following wind speeds should be considered as threshold values:

- **Wind speed is 10 m/s or less:** Normally this wind speed is considered as safe for car carriers. The basic precautions should be taken, such as paying out enough chain, keeping a wide berth of other vessels, etc.
- **Wind speed is 10 to 15 m/s:** In this case, the length of anchor chain is important: in congested anchorage/short period, a minimum 5 shackles is acceptable; in normal situations at least 8 to 10 shackles should be used. The engine should be ready for use, as well as the bow thruster, in order to reduce swing. Vigilant watch should be posted for dragging and to determine when to heave the anchor.
- **Wind speed exceeds 15 m/s:** If the wind exceeds 15 m/s, the most appropriate action is to vacate the anchorage. Attention should be paid to dragging of the anchor by all possible means. The anchor position and the course recorder should be regularly checked.
- **Wind speed exceeds 20 m/s:** This is the limit value of the wind, when the anchor of a PCC with swing check anchor dropped is supposed to start dragging.
- **Wind speed exceeds 25 m/s:** If the ship is still anchored at this wind speed, she should have two anchors down. However, this speed is the critical one for a car carrier anchored at two anchors.

Ro-Ro Ships and Tugs

Beyond question, Ro-Ro ships that are being strongly affected by the wind may require tug assistance during berthing.

For most of the Ro-Ro ships trading in Northern Europe, which are fitted with controllable pitch propeller or twin screw and with bow and stern thrusters, the use of tugs is not necessary because these ships have improved maneuverability.

Car carrier entering the lock in Bremerhaven assisted by a tug

For the largest car carriers, however, this is not the case and they will require tug assistance, in the best case scenario, of at least one tug. In the case of fresh wind, the presence of two or even three tugs is very important.

If the wind force is more than 5 Beaufort, it is highly recommended that car carriers not undertake any berthing operations.

The location of the tugs will vary with the particular vessel, port, and the mooring operation being undertaken. In most Asian ports, the tugs are made fast on port bow and port quarter because the ship will be berthed starboard side alongside to. This is a feature for the most modern car carriers of today.

The use of tugs can be very helpful when the ship is entering the lock as well. For this maneuver, one tug is normally made fast on the aft through a central lead. In this way, the tug can very easily control the smallest deviation of the stern in the wrong direction.

The tugs in European ports, as a rule, are made fast fore and aft through central leads. In this way, they can be used for taking all the way off when necessary, but their influence for bringing the ship alongside is less effective compared to the situation tugs located on port bow and quarters.

The tugs can be divided into two main types: conventional tug and tractor tug. The conventional type has its towing point amidships and can be single- or twin-screw. The tractor type has it towing point ahead of amidships and they can have either Voith propulsion or azimuth drive propulsion.

Whichever type of tug, it can be used either for working on a towing line or for pushing.

Safety Issues Related to Tugs

As it was mentioned above, the use of tugs with large car carrier is very useful. However, there are some safety issues when the tugs are involved in assisting mooring operations and these issues should be taken into account.

Girting

When a tug is working on a towing line, there is a risk, for one reason or another, of being overtaken by the ship. When this happens, the tug will remain aside (abeam of the ship's bow) and the towing line will be under heavy tension. The tug, not being in position to react, could capsize. This danger is higher with conventional tugs. The main cause for girting is the excessive speed of the vessel, so the best solution for avoiding girting is reducing speed.

Securing the Tug at the Stern

When making fast aft, the tugs approach very close to the vessel in order to pass or pick up the stern line. In this maneuver, there is a risk that the tug line will be entangled in the ship's propeller. The best way to avoid such an occurrence is to stop the vessel's engine and propeller, or, in case of controllable pitch propeller, to reduce the pitch to a minimum.

Securing the Tug at the Forward Mooring Station

The problem here is the presence of the bulbous bow. Regardless of the fact that the bulbous bows are properly marked, if the mark is underwater or concealed by a fog, it cannot be seen by the tug master. Therefore, good communication between the Pilot and the tug master is very important in such maneuvering.

The presence of a bow thruster can present another obstacle when making fast the tug line on port or starboard bow. To avoid entangling the line with the thruster's vanes, the thruster should not be used during the process of making fast the tug line.

Effects of Wind and Currents

As has been repeatedly noted, car carriers are very vulnerable to the effects of the wind. Sudden wind gusts can put the tug between the ship and shore or between the vessel being handled and vessels moored nearby, with serious consequences for the tug if it cannot get out in time. This situation is exaggerated if the tug is made fast to the vessel. Therefore, proper assessment of the wind and current is vital in such operations.

Securing and Releasing the Tug

The fairleads of the car carriers and Ro-Ro vessels are at a considerable height above the waterline. When throwing the heaving line, it should not drop into the water but instead it should be lowered onto the tug's deck. The heaving line should be safe for use: metal objects, like bolt or heavy weights, can be very dangerous for the tug's crew.

When releasing the tug, utmost attention should be paid, as this is a very dangerous operation for both crews, the vessel's and the tug's.

If the vessel is speeding up, releasing of towing line can be very risky and very often impossible due to the increased tension in the towing line. Again, the only solution is to reduce speed and maintain good communication between the Pilot and the tug.

BIBLIOGRAPHY

Association of Ship Brokers and Agents (USA) Inc. "Time Charter New York Produce Exchange Form, Code name "NYPE 93." Englewood Cliffs, NJ, 1993. (A later version, NYPE 2015, has been published.).

British Standards Institution. "BS 6349-8:2007, Maritime structures. Code of practice for the design of Ro-Ro ramps, linkspans, and walkways: A guide to procurement, operation and maintenance." London, 2007.

Brown's Nautical Almanac. Brown, Son, & Ferguson Ltd., Glasgow: 2015

The Council of the European Union. "Council Regulation (EC) No.1 / 2005 on the protection of animals during transport and related operations." The Official Journal of the European Union, Web: www.faolex.fao.org/docs/pdf/eur69655.pdf, 2004, accessed March 2016.

Clark, Capt. I .C. *Stability, Trim and Strength for Merchant Ships and Fishing Vessels.*" London: The Nautical Institute of London, 2011.

Code of Federal Regulations (CFR). "Title 46, US Coast Guard, Part 170—Stability Requirements for all Inspected Vessels." US Government Publishing Office, 2008.

_____. "Title 49, Transportation, Part 172.101, Purpose and Use of Hazardous Materials Table." US Government Publishing Office, 2008.

_____. "Title 49, Parts 176, 176.78 & 176.905, Refueling and Battery Charging of Motor Vehicles in the Hold of the Vessel." US Government Publishing Office, 2008.

Dalinga, R. P. "Safe Securing of Trailers and Deck Cargo," *Proceedings of the International Conference and Exhibition on Marine Transaction Using Roll-on/Roll-off Methods.* Rickmansworth, UK: BML Business Meetings Ltd., 1994.

Department for Environment, Food & Rural Affairs. "Protecting the Welfare of Pet Dogs and Cats During Journeys: Advice to Owners." London, 2011.

Deutsches Institut für Normung. "DIN 15020:1-1974-01, Lifting Appliances; Principles

Relating to Rope Drives; Calculation and Construction." Berlin, 1974.

Det Norske Veritas. "Fires on Ro-Ro Decks." Norway, DNV Technical Paper, September, 2005.

"Force of Technology of Lyngby, Denmark." Web: www.forcetechnology.com.

"Hague-Visby Rules." Web: www.lexmercatoria.org, accessed March 2016.

International Association of Classification Societies Ltd. (IACS). "Recommendation 72, Confined Space Safe Practice." London, 2007.

_____."IACS UR Z24: Survey Requirements for Shell and Inner Doors of Ro-Ro Ships." London, 2010.

_____."Requirements concerning strength of ships." London, 2016.

International Chamber of Commerce (ICC). *Incoterms 2009* (International Commercial Terms). 2009.

_____. "Uniform Customs and Practice for Documentary Credits (UCP 600)." 2007.

"International Convention for the Unification of Certain Rules of Law Relating to Bills of Lading ('Hague Rules'), and Protocol of Signature." Brussels, 1924.

International Labour Organisation (ILO). "Register of Lifting Appliances and Items of Loose Gear: Form No. Article 1: Register of Ships' Lifting Appliances and Cargo Handling Gear." Geneva: International Labour Office, Geneva.

_____. "C-152: Occupational Safety and Health (Dock Work) Convention, 1979 (NO. 152). Geneva: International Labour Office, Geneva, 1979.

International Maritime Organization (IMO). *Code of Safe Practice for Cargo Stowage and Securing (CSS code),* 2011 Edition. London: IMO Publishing, 2011.

_____. *Code on Intact Stability for All Types of Ships Covered by IMO Instruments (IS Code)* 2009 Edition. London: IMO Publishing, 2009.

_____. *Code on Noise Levels on board Ships.* London: IMO Publishing, 2014.

_____. *International Code for the Application of Fire Test Procedures (2010 FTP Code).* London: IMO Publishing, 2010.

_____. *International Convention on Load Lines.* London: IMO Publishing, 1966.

_____. *International Life-Saving Appliances Code (LSA Code).* London: IMO Publishing, 2010.

_____. *International Maritime Dangerous Good Code (IMDG Code), 2014 edition.* London: IMO Publishing, 2014.

_____. *International Code of Safety for High-Speed Craft (HSC Code)* 2009 Edition. London: IMO Publishing, 2009.

_____. "International Convention for the Safety of Life at Sea (SOLAS) 2014 Consolidated Edition." London, 2014.

_____. *International Safety Management Code (ISM Code).* London: IMO Publishing, 2015.

_____. "IMO Resolution A.123 (V), Recommendation on Fixed Fire Extinguishing Systems for Special Category Spaces." London, 1967.

_____. "IMO Resolution A.518(14), Guidelines for securing arrangements for the transport of road vehicles on Ro-Ro ships." London, 1985.

_____. "IMO Resolution A.754(18), Recommendation on Fire Resistance Tests for 'A', 'B' and 'C' Class Divisions as Amended by MSC.61(67)." London, 1996.

_____. "IMO Resolution A.800(19), Revised Guidelines for Approval of Sprinkler Systems Equivalent to that Referred to in SOLAS Regulation II-2/12." London, 1995.

_____. "IMO Resolution A.849(20), Code for the Investigation of Marine Casualties and Incidents." London, 1997.

_____. "IMO Resolution A.951(23), Improved Guidelines for Marine Portable Fire Extinguishers." London, 2004.

_____. "IMO Resolution A.952(23), Graphical Symbols for Shipboard Fire Control Plans." London, 2004.

_____. "IMO Resolution A.1050(27), Revised Recommendations for Entering Enclosed Spaces Aboard Ships." London, 2011.

_____. "IMO/ILO Guidelines for Packing Cargo in freight Containers or Vehicles: For Use in Practice and in Training." London, 1990.

International Maritime Organization (IMO), Marine Environment Protection Committee (MEPC). "International Convention for the Prevention of Pollution from Ships (MARPOL) Annex V." London, 2013.

International Maritime Organization (IMO), Maritime Safety Committee. "MSC.98(73) International Code for Fire Safety Systems (FSS Code) 2015 Edition." London, 2015.

_____. "MSC/Circ.729, Design Guidelines and Operational Recommendations for Ventilation Systems in Ro-Ro Cargo Spaces." London, 1996.

_____. "International Safety Management Code (ISM Code), MSC.104(73), amended by MSC.179(79), MSC.195(80), MSC.273(85), and MSC.353(92). London, 2013 .

_____. "IMO Resolution MSC.216 (82)." London, 2006.

_____. "MSC /Circ.506 MSC/Circ.506/Rev.1 of 10 January 1990 "Container packing certificates / vehicle packing declarations." London, 1990.

_____. "MSC/Circ.574, The Calculation Procedure to Assess the Survivability Characteristics of Existing Ro-Ro Passenger Ships when Using a Simplified Method Based upon Resolution A.265(VIII)." London, 1991.

_____. "MSC/Circ.582, Guidelines for the Performance and Testing Criteria and Surveys of Low-expansion Foam Concentrates for Fixed Fire-extinguishing." London, 2001.

_____. "MSC 1/Circ.1272, "Guidelines for the Approval of Alternative Fixed Water-based Fire-fighting Systems for Ro-Ro Spaces and Special Category Spaces." London, 2008.

_____. "MSC 1/Circ.1202, Inspection Programmes for Cargo Transport Unit (CTU) Carrying Dangerous Goods." London, 2006.

_____. "MSC 1/Circ.1206, "Measures to Prevent Accidents with Lifeboats." London, 2006.

_____. "MSC.1/Circ.1318, Guideline for the Maintenance and Inspections of Fixed Carbon Dioxide Fire-extinguishing Systems." London, 2009.

_____. "MSC.1/Circ. 1331, Guidelines for Construction, Installation, Maintenance and Inspection/Survey of Means of Embarkation and Disembarkation." London, 2009.

_____. "MSC.1 / Circ.1432, Revised Guidelines for the Maintenance and Inspection of Fire Protection Systems and Appliances." London, 2012.

International Organization for Standardization (ISO). "ISO 5488:1979, Shipbuilding–Accommodation Ladders." Geneva 1979.

_____. "ISO 7061:1993, Shipbuilding–Aluminum Shore Gangways." Geneva, 1993.

_____. "ISO 9367-1:1989, Lashing and Securing Arrangements on Road Vehicles for Sea Transportation on Ro/Ro ships—Part 1: Commercial Vehicles and Combinations of Vehicles, Semi-trailers excluded. Geneva, 1989.

_____. "ISO 2408:2004, Steel Wire Ropes for General Purposes—Minimum Requirements." Geneva, 2004.

_____. "ISO 2532:1974, Steel Wire Ropes-Vocabulary." Geneva, 1974.

_____. "ISO 3108:1974, Steel Wire Ropes for General Purposes—Determination of Actual Breaking Load." Geneva, 1974.

_____. "ISO 3189:1985, Sockets for Wire Ropes for General Purposes—Parts 1, 2, and 3." Geneva, 1985.

_____. "ISO 4346:1977, Steel Wire Ropes for General Purposes—Lubricants." Geneva, 1977.

_____. "ISO 17893:2004, Steel Wire Ropes-Vocabulary, Designation, and Classification." Geneva, 2004.

International Plant Protection Convention (IPPC). "International Standards for Phytosanitary Measures (ISPM) 15, Guidelines for Regulating Wood Packaging Material in International Trade." Rome, 2009.

Isherwood, R. W. "Wind Resistance of Merchant Ships," *RINA Transactions and Annual Report 1973*, Vol.115. Royal Institute of Naval Architects, 1973.

Kruger, Stefan. "The Energy Efficiency Design Index (EEDI) for Ro-Ro Vessels." Hamburg: The German Society for Maritime Technology, www.ship-efficiency.org/onTEAM/pdf/Krueger.pdf, 2009.

Lloyd's Register. "Rules and Regulations for the Classification of Linkspans." London, 2008.

Maksimavicius, R."Some Elements of Ro-Ro Terminals," Transport: Research Journal of Vilnius Gediminas Technical University and Lithuanian Academy of Sciences, Vol. 19: No 2. Vilnius, Lithuania, 2004.

Maritime and Coastguard Agency. "Roll-on/Roll-off Ships—Stowage and Securing of Vehicles: Code of Practice. London: TSO (The Stationery Office), 2003.

Martin, L. L. "Ship Maneuvering and Control in Wind," *SNAME Transactions*,Vol.88. Society of Naval Architects and Marine Engineers, 1980.

"Operation Manual for the Ramps." TTS Instruction Manual.

NEN. "NEN-EN 12195-1:2010, Load Restraining on Road Vehicles." Delft, the Netherlands, 2010.

Nippon Kaiji Kyokai (ClassNK). "Inspection of Liftable Car Decks of Pure Car Carriers." Web: www.classnk.or.jp/tech_info/tech_img/T484e.pdf, 2002, accessed March, 2016.

Rowe, Capt. R. W., FNI. *The Shiphandler's Guide*. London: The Nautical Institute, 1998.

Standards Australia, Committee ME-025. "AS 2759-2004, Australian Standard™: Steel Wire Rope—Use, Operation and Maintenance." Sydney: Standards Australia International Ltd, 2004.

Stockholm Agreement. "Agreement concerning Shipping Specific Stability Requirements for Ro-Ro Passenger Ships Undertaking Regular Scheduled International Voyages between or to or from Designated Ports in North West Europe and the Baltic Sea." London: The Stationery Office, 1996.

US Department of Labour, Occupational Safety and Health Administration. "Occupational Health Guideline for Carbon Monoxide." Washington, DC, 1978.

_____. "Occupational Health Guideline for Sulfur Dioxide." Washington, DC, 1978.

_____. "Occupational Health Guideline for Carbon Dioxide." Washington, DC, 1978.

Vossnack, E., and H. Boonstra. *Integration of Damage Stability Improvements in the Design of Ro-Ro Vessels*. Delft: Delft University of Technology, 1992.

Websites

www.ecgassociation.eu. Association of European Finished Vehicle Logistics, Brussels.

www.eftco.org. European Federation of Tank Cleaning Organisations, West Yorkshire, UK.

www.aphis.usda.gov. United States Department of Agriculture. "www.aphis.usda.gov/plant_health/plant_pest_info/gypsy_moth/downloads/vessel-certification.pdf".

"Operation Manual for the Ramps." TTS Instruction Manual.

INDEX

D

G

M

R

S

T

U

V

About the Author

Delyan M. Todorov started his seagoing career in 2002 at Stamco Ship Management as a deck cadet. He earned his master's certificate in 2008 and took command of a Ro-Ro ship in 2010. He holds a diploma in marine surveying from Lloyd's Maritime Academy and has a deep interest in shipboard inspections, audits, and surveys. He is also fond of maritime law and marine insurance. He lives in Varna, Bulgaria, with his family.

TRANS FUTUR